CLASS WARFARE

THE ASSAULT ON CANADA'S SCHOOLS

MAUDE BARLOW

A N D

HEATHER-JANE ROBERTSON

KEY PORTER BOOKS

To our children: Caitlin, Mark, Bill, and Charles,
who have been well served by public schools.

Canadian Cataloguing in Publication Data

Barlow, Maude
Class warfare : the assault on Canada's schools

Includes bibliographical references and index.
ISBN 1-55013-559-7

1. Education – Canada. 2. Industry and education – Canada.
3. Politics and education – Canada.
I. Robertson, Heather-jane. II. Title.

LA412.B37 1994   370'.971   C94-931236-3

Key Porter Books Limited
70 The Esplanade
Toronto, Ontario
Canada M5E 1R2

The publisher gratefully acknowledges the support of the Department
of Communication, the Canada Council and the Ontario Arts Council.

Typesetting: MacTrix DTP
Printed and bound in Canada

95 96 97 98 99 6 5 4 3

CONTENTS

PREFACE

CANADIANS ARE ENGAGED IN A STRUGGLE OVER THEIR INSTITUTIONS that is taking on the characteristics of class warfare. On one side stand those who have embraced the free market as the means and purpose of participation in public life. On the other are those who must live with the effects of a system dedicated, by definition, to the acquisition of privilege and profit. This is an ideological conflict.

Disputes among those who disagree on the direction our society should take are not new. What is new, however, is the claim that this struggle is being manufactured by those unable to adapt gracefully to the new rules, by those unable to accept the totalitarianism of the markets. Presented with the threat of global competition, we are told that we no longer have a choice, that the only question worth debating is how best to adapt to the primacy of the markets, not whether to adapt or how much to give up in adapting. The new ideology insists that there are no ideologies, only pragmatics.

The linkage between corporate interests and public policy allows corporations to set the terms of the social contract within national borders, and with the clear intent of erasing these borders. Harmonization requires common policies and similar institutions, but to be assured of success it requires the alignment of the hearts and minds of those who are (however rarely) referred to as citizens.

This book examines one of the venues of harmonization: the classrooms of our publicly funded education system (which includes public and separate schools). Under the guise of "reforming" or even "supporting" schools, there is a great deal of activity in education advancing the interests of the competitive-corporate ideology of the right wing. Some of this activity is transparently self-interested — as when the ultraconservative Business Council on National Issues proposes (with the support of two successive federal governments) to set its own school-leaving exams. Some of it is disguised as good corporate citizenship, as when "partnerships" allow technology corporations to help design schools of the future, which just happen to require one personal computer for every three students. Sometimes it is patently manipulative, as when fast-food giants provide free "nutrition curricula" to classrooms.

While these examples may be offensive, they are benign when compared to the efforts of the Right to reshape whom our schools will serve and what our children will learn. Whether directed to children or policy makers, these efforts have common goals, all of which are self-serving, all of which are designed to increase the "market share" of corporations in the lives of children, in the conduct of public policy and in the shape of our future.

It is not only corporate profiteers who have an interest in school reform; those with little allegiance to any ideology have joined the critical chorus. Schools are vulnerable and in desperate need of renewal. Any institution that has existed for more than a few decades is experiencing the wrenching realities of a transformed social, political and economic context. It is unrealistic to think that public education could have absorbed this loss of stability and continuity effortlessly, particularly as schools were designed to be institutional mirrors of society. As such, when we find fault with our schools, it may be our own reflections that frighten us.

In part, it is this fear that has attracted growing attention to the shortcomings of education, but the direction of school reform is not towards a reconciliation of school and community, or of need and knowledge. As long as schools seemed to be devoted primarily to serving the interests of children and therefore disconnected from political and economic outcomes, they were largely sheltered from close scrutiny. Those involved in the world of schools know that they have always been about the lives of adults as well as those of children, and about the future as well as the present. Education is necessarily based on forecasts and predictions; its proper role can be played only when there is a sense of the world for which students are being prepared, and a sense of the most desirable mix of knowledge, skills and values most appropriate to that world. What has changed is that the school's role is no longer to prepare children to create the future, but to prepare students for an inevitable future over which they will have no control, in which at best they can aspire to adapt to the ruthlessness of the inescapable.

At the same time, it has become the preoccupation of schools and school reformers to devote the classroom to neither preparation for the future nor its creation; rather schools are told they must protect children from the present. Thus, schools have been assigned a host of responsibilities that, taken together, require them to embody and teach values that are increasingly inconsistent with the times: to teach co-operation when competition is the skill with the greatest cachet; to teach love of learning when the utility of applied knowledge is all that is valued; to teach creativity when accomplishment is based on giving a standardized answer to a standardized question. It is increasingly apparent that schools are incapable of swimming against the cultural tide and that their accomplishments, while many, fall far short of the unrealistic expectations of them.

It is this inevitable failure that has encouraged those with no particular investment in the success of the neo-conservative agenda to join in an alliance with corporate interests at the forefront of school reform. It is those who are most anxious about the present and the future, those most attached to the security of their children, those most penalized by the costs of the political choices of recent decades who see in this newest wave of reform a way out, for themselves or for their children. A privatized system, liberated from the "monopoly" of the public sector, promises to serve so many goals: it would generate untold profits for educational entrepreneurs; it would provide parents with the hope of protecting their children from the most "undesirable" elements of the present; it would soothe the anxieties of those concerned that their children are being ill-prepared to be the winners in a future in which defeat is unthinkable. For many with little regard for public education as an institution, the solution is simple. Dismantle the system, let "choice" become the beacon of reform, and abandon those who cannot or will not compete.

This book examines the consequences of proceeding with the right-wing educational reform agenda that is well under way. Because the public has lost much of the sense of the purposes of public education, it will persistently remind readers of what will be lost if we adopt the model of the marketplace as the guiding principle for school reform. It documents the wilful and persistent efforts of business leaders, lobbyists, many governments and the media to destabilize and undermine the schools that we have. The reader will be asked often to consider whether these efforts are misinformed, misdirected or malicious. We make no claim that somewhere a group of powerful people sits around a secret boardroom table plotting to overthrow public schools. We do claim, however, that a harmony of selfish intent and common interests, abetted by an insecure present and frightening future, has presented an opportunity that is being exploited to its fullest extent.

We fear that the potential for the success of this common agenda is heightened by the flawed history of education reform to date. Many opportunities to transform schools have been squandered by mismanaged and politically motivated reforms, by self-serving and short-sighted educational interest groups, enabled by a public determined to see education policy as irrelevant or simply as a black hole of taxation. It is this public that must be alerted to the motives of those driving the school reform debates of today; the public must be made conscious of what it will mean if we take the "public" out of public education, if we turn our schools into pre-employment centres for pre-adults. We believe that a more decent, inclusive and able view of human purposes must succeed over one that views the education of children as an economic activity in the service of privilege and profit.

It is common for arguments such as these to be dismissed because they do not conform to the new language of "blamelessness," to the new spirit of "co-operation" across sectors we are told must characterize Canada's adaptation to the inevitable. It will be said that it is divisive to speak of "warfare": we agree. There are things worth fighting for. We are not prepared to see our schools as one more industry to be deregulated, to see our children simply as human resources to be better managed. If this renders us unfit to take part in the politics of accommodation, so be it.

ACKNOWLEDGEMENTS

IN WRITING THIS BOOK, I REALIZED THAT THERE IS A WHOLE COMMUNITY passionately dedicated to preserving public schools. They gave generously of their time and knowledge and I am most grateful. To Canadians Jim Turk, Leo Broderich, Bob Garthson, Julius Buski, Larry Kuehn and John Calvert; and Americans Gerald Bracey, Robin Templeton, Doug Noble, Robert Peterson, and Andrea Di Lorenzo, thank you.

I am also indebted to the staff of the Council of Canadians whose support made this book possible: Peter Bleyer, Joanne Polsky, Alex Boston, Neil Parekh and Patricia Armstrong. You are the best team anyone could wish for.

Heather-jane joins me in expressing our pleasure in working with our editor Charis Wahl. You set the benchmark in professionalism.

Finally, I wish to thank my wonderful family: my mother and father, Bill and Flora; my husband, Andrew; my sisters, Pat and Christine; and my sons, Charles and Bill.

Maude Barlow

Many colleagues and friends have offered practical assistance in preparing this book: finding obscure references, great articles and useful leads. They embody the spirit of professional collegiality. I am particularly indebted to Marita Moll, Pauline Theoret and other staff members of the Canadian Teachers' Federation and its member organizations across Canada. I also wish to thank those people — teachers, trustees, administrators and faculty — who have enriched my understanding of the fascinating, frustrating world of education. Of all these, I want to recognize Dr. Norman Goble, who taught me that both reason and passion have a place in our work.

My family has been patient and encouraging. Thank you to my mother, the first teacher in the family; to my husband Dwight for never doubting; and to my children Caitlin and Mark for sharing their Mom with the book.

Finally, I am grateful to the directors of the Canadian Teachers' Federation, whose support made the writing of this book possible.

Heather-jane Robertson

INTRODUCTION:
TELL ME WHAT HAPPENED
AT SCHOOL

You start to feel as though your child is a computer into
which the schools are placing a stupidity virus.
PARENT, TO *MACLEAN'S* MARCH 14, 1994

IT CAN BE HEARD IN THEIR VOICES. PARENTS AT PARTIES, IN HOCKEY
arenas, lingering in grocery store aisles, calling in to talk shows,
organizing protest groups. There is a collective sense that things
are not right at school.

While public opinion in support of schools remains higher than
for other public institutions, some observers sense that the passing
grades we give schools are as devalued as those that students are
given for modest accomplishments. Our schools are seen as chronic
underachievers, squandering advantages and opportunities without
reaching their potential, getting by because it is too much trouble to
excel. The public feels unwell about its schools; in the absence of
cogent alternatives for improvement, it is willing to accept the corporate diagnosis: schools are failing because they are monopolies

exempt from competition. The remedy? Force schools to act like businesses and things will turn around.

Within this paradigm of education, nearly everyone is a consumer: students, parents, and especially those who will employ the "finished products." The North American public has been shaped to see itself as a consumer—certainly more thought goes into our needs and interests as consumers than as citizens. Our consumer preferences are to be moulded by those with goods and services to be marketed. Where no need exists, one must be created; where real human needs cannot be met, placebos must be substituted. Consumerism feeds on stimulated dissatisfaction and transitory appetites: what was sufficient yesterday is inadequate today. The credo of consumerism is choice—not only the choices we make, but the very act of choosing. For many North Americans, liberty and democracy are merely the unlimited right to choose.

Perhaps it is because schools have so little in common with consumerism that they are seen as so out of touch with society's needs: schools do not preach competition, they do not cut their losses, exploit their advantages or publicize their strategic plans. Schools do not set out to respond to transitory consumer preferences. Established to meet collective goals and to provide the basis for informed adult lives, schools have little in common with the ruthlessly individualistic premises of consumerism. It is this characteristic that makes schools vulnerable, for today if you are out of the marketplace, you are out of the loop.

LESSONS FROM HISTORY

To understand the current vulnerability of schools requires a little historical context. The principles that provided the framework for early public schools were ambitious in the numbers of students to be taught, but not in the levels of individual attainment. The first schools in Canada were established to imbue the sons of the most privileged citizens with the knowledge necessary to exercise the powers associated with their family's status. "Public schooling" was designed for the masses and had much more practical goals. Literacy and numeracy were seen as useful skills for the working classes; those children disinclined to acquire basic skills could still do the many jobs that did not require book-acquired knowledge. What was to be learned was considered self-evident; there was little discussion about the curriculum, let alone how it should be transmitted. Students fit in, learned, or left.

Learning to read and write might not have been seen as contentious, but from the beginning Canadians recognized that the processes of schooling were associated with beliefs and values. This understanding was reflected when Protestants and Catholics, and later francophones and anglophones were granted the right to create and manage their own schools. Élite private schools, established to reflect values associated with privilege rather than sect, demonstrated that the powerful clearly understood that schools also shape secular belief and knowledge systems.

In Canada, the early structures created to finance and manage schools were left in the hands of local leaders and their communities. Decentralization, however, was not intended as a means of creating schools that reflected local circumstances and priorities, for it was assumed that there were very few weighty matters to be accommodated.

At first, what was to be taught was decided by senior provincial officials. Local school boards selected and dismissed teachers and determined their salaries; it was in the exercise of these powers that community preferences were expressed, often in such an arbitrary way that early in this century, associations of teachers sprang up to deter the abuse of their members.

Teaching was widely seen as a genteel form of missionary service, chosen by default by men with few connections and by women with no other means of support. After the First World War, teachers' organizations were weary of their members' routine exploitation by penny-pinching and capricious school trustees. Teachers began to demand some security and living wages that were paid rather than merely promised. School boards began to cast about for new economies. Whereas teaching had been primarily the calling of men, it became evident that women (unmarried, of course) could provide satisfactory service at a lower salary. Imparting the obvious to docile children was not considered demanding work, and was therefore suitable even for women, who were hired in greater numbers. The status of schoolteacher is still coloured by the fact that those once considered inadequate to vote were thought ideally suited to teaching school.

The expansion, consolidation and rationalization of Canada's schools were primarily due to the ebb and flow of political interests rather than the outcome of debates among competing pedagogical philosophies. Despite a flirtation with the progressive education movement in the 1920s, the idea that schools should emphasize the facilitation of learning rather than didactic instruction did not take hold among policy makers and practitioners until much later.[1] Some early organizational innovations, however, have stayed with us: for example, "grades" were introduced in the late 1870s.

After the Second World War, education reform was preoccupied with administrative efficiencies such as school and district consolidation, and with extending services to isolated and rural communities. As long as schools continued to reflect the somewhat self-satisfied values of their homogeneous communities, there was little to debate. Even such far-off events as battles for school desegregation in the American South only occasionally reminded some people that the nature of our schools had something to do with our political and human values. That residential schools, "educating" aboriginal students, posed a Canadian example of cultural imperialism as well as segregation does not appear to have been widely acknowledged at the time.

A CULTURE OF CHANGE

By the early 1970s, relative prosperity, increased student enrolment, an aura of optimism and a culture of risk taking began to permeate schools. A sense of new possibilities was brought to classrooms by young and enthusiastic teachers, whose services were suddenly in demand. Early members of the post-war baby boom, these new teachers were unlikely to have led campus political protests, but neither were they completely untouched by the prevailing mood of challenge, change and political activism. Few may have been trying to embody *Teaching as a Subversive Activity*, published in 1969,[2] but many young teachers had made its passing acquaintance during teacher training.

Mortified by the success of Sputnik, Americans began to pay more attention to public education, and the effect on schools spilled over into Canada. There was encouragement for schools to become more innovative and more "relevant." Unconventional thinking, however weakly reasoned, was prized. The conviction that how students learned mattered at least as much as which facts they memorized took a firm grip on education's psyche, although few teachers had any concrete idea of how to put process-intensive education into effect. (I recall a graduate-level exam in curriculum methodology I wrote in 1968, consisting of a single probing question about the important matters of the day with respect to curriculum and instruction. I wrote a two-sentence answer. "Only two things are required to teach well. The first is to forget how you were taught; the second is to remember what it was to have been a child." In 1968, this facile response was worth an A+. The course instructor became a dean of education. HJR)

In the crowded schools of the 1970s, there was often considerable confusion and conflict between the old and new guards. Experiments such as open-area schools may have substituted creativity or conviction for good judgement, but above all, these schools were passionate places, committed to the social importance of the work of teaching and learning. Such energy was not surprising; after all, the median age of teachers in 1970 was just thirty; twenty-four years later it is forty-two.[3]

EXPANDING INTO ANTI-CHAOS

During the 1980s, the connection between schools and societal values became more evident.

All socially progressive movements saw education as the key to their goals. Environmentalism took hold, and superficially at least, curricula began to reflect pro-environment values. The movement to desegregate people with disabilities saw the integrated classroom as its most important strategic goal. As less restricted immigration created what seemed to be a tide of new races and cultures, schools were the designated site of socialization for newcomers' children, and often for newcomers themselves. The country's political leadership believed in bilingualism; parents who had made no effort to learn a second language lined up to assign schools the task of creating bilingual students and preserving national unity. Women entered the workforce in increasing numbers; new schools incorporated daycare spaces and after-school programs for latch-key children appeared. Teachers began to attend workshops on how to respond to the unique needs of children from single-parent families. Other social-policy-through-the-classroom objectives followed, from reducing the incidence of drunk driving to preventing the spread of AIDS.

In many of these undertakings, rather than complementing broader community and government initiatives, the activities of schools became the sole public response. Schools became not just part of the solution, but the sole solution to many complex problems. Schools were expected to welcome and fully integrate even those children with the most severe emotional and physical disabilities, without parallel accommodations in the workplace, in the attitudes of communities or, in many cases, in the funding to accomplish this goal. The Young Offenders Act identified schools as important to resocializing and rehabilitating the young offender. The act also identified the need for alternative treatment facilities and community-directed programs. Society judged these latter requirements too dangerous or expensive or unworkable, but the piece of the act that "sentenced kids to school" was immediately implemented.

At some point in the mid-1980s, a shift occurred. Schools were no longer just sites for promoting pro-social values; their purpose became to prevent social collapse. "Anti-racism" replaced "multiculturalism" in schools' vocabulary; media literacy became the means of inuring children to media exploitation rather than fostering critical comprehension. Schools shifted from teaching healthy eating to coping with students who did not have enough to eat; from teaching healthy sexuality to attempting to protect children from sexual predators.

It seemed that schools could also be vehicles for a political agenda while assuaging the public conscience. Inequities of gender, social class, innate or acquired ability, effort and circumstance were to be vanquished; grouping students by aptitude, which was said to reflect social class rather than ability, was eliminated. Schools were to accomplish the impossible by treating everyone as an individual identical to all other individuals. If they only tried hard enough, surely schools could achieve the equity and sanity unachievable elsewhere. The distance between what schools have been told to accomplish and the trend lines of the rest of society comes into clear focus with respect to the problem of violence. The week that high-profile conferences and media specials on school violence were taking place and schools were being exhorted to enforce "zero tolerance" policies, Statistics Canada released its findings on the ubiquity of violence against women, the public clamoured for banned details of the Homolka case, and Mortal Kombat was the top game rental at video stores. Schools are our institutional Sisyphus, endlessly pushing civilized values against the gravitational force of an increasingly uncivilized world.

As schools have become anti-chaos rather than pro-social in their orientation, they are expected to devise ways to counteract social change, even as they are being blamed for society's rising contempt for the values schools have attempted to foster. Are youth racist? Blame the schools. Are playgrounds violent? Do children kill other children? Do disengaged and bitter youth drop out? It is the fault of schools. In a collective attack of anxiety, we have demonized schools for creating social problems and mandated them alone to find the solutions. Our schools' inability to stem the tide of social upheaval single-handedly has been taken as evidence of their failure. Few have questioned whether such a goal might be unattainable, or whether new support and resources for schools might be required, or whether our understanding of the societal problems schools are assigned to solve might be inadequate.

Indeed, the symptoms schools have been told to address restrict them to a very limited analysis of the underlying disease. The problem of youth violence has been reduced to how schools should cope, and perhaps how to provide students faced with assault with "more skilled responses." Teachers have been discouraged from naming sexism and racism as underlying issues, not only with their students but within their profession. Schools must deal with the results without naming the cause.

Problems that cannot be denied can be reframed to be more ideologically acceptable. Child poverty has been officially reduced to child hunger, which is framed as a matter of poor nutrition resulting in "learning impediments." Schools are told to deal with these "learning impediments," perhaps by organizing what is so delicately called a school "feeding" program. There is no acknowledgement that there are poor kids because there are poor adults, and more of them every day. There is no questioning of why the curriculum avoids studying how wealth is generated and protected, whether money might be differently distributed or what causes poverty to be associated with race and replicated in succeeding generations. In the classroom, attention is paid to poor children's self-esteem, not the cycle of poverty. On the contrary, school food programs have been defended on utilitarian grounds: "education officials believe that the pupils will be better able to learn" if they are fed.[4] Presumably, if they could learn while they were hungry, it would be quite acceptable for children to be chronically underfed.

Part of schools' vulnerability, then, comes from the chaos created by doing anti-chaos work under rules that prohibit naming the true problems. While schools have been struggling haphazardly with their new role as social, emotional and intellectual food banks for ever-increasing numbers of damaged children, parents— such as those who described their children as "marketable commodities" before Ontario's Royal Commission on Learning— began to worry.[5] The best educated, most articulate and prosperous parents have come to believe that the academic achievements of their less needy children are being sacrificed to the classroom's non-academic goals. Those who have "struggled to the top" worry that their children's strategic advantages are being eroded. Some blame those "struggling to the bottom": single parents, recent immigrants and those lacking middle-class values.

Parents who have historically expected and received the greatest benefit from education are encouraged to believe that equity and excellence are in competition, and that teachers, vapid and indolent by nature, prefer to teach self-esteem over fractions when left on their own. It is not surprising that such parents are open to critiques of education that appropriate their anxieties; moreover, many parents, too uncomfortable or busy to confront their schools directly, are more than happy to have business and the media do it for them. Parents with little awareness of the education interests of large corporations can be persuaded that business speaks for little Johnny's future as much as for the interests of profit.

The December 1993 issue of *Saturday Night* includes an advertisement for Apple computers. Accompanying a photograph of a schoolgirl of perhaps twelve or thirteen is the text: "Everyone is created equal. Until someone gets a Macintosh." The copy continues, "Life is a road we all travel. We all start at the same place, yet some spring ahead."[6]

The ad is a clever marketing ploy that reduces equal educational opportunity to a matter of students using "personal productivity software" in junior high. Apple's sales campaign was based, undoubtedly, on a very shrewd reading of attitudes towards what impedes or accelerates opportunity. Never particularly rational when it comes to advancing their children's perceived best interests, parents who have already bought the message that the class-·room is as competitive as the workplace can buy an advantage —a computer. Those without a Macintosh are *ipso facto* out of the race.

Yet even those who think they are doing all they can to ensure their children stay at the top are nervous. Some blame other people's children, but more blame what they euphemistically call "the schools," at least in public. The lead from a *Montreal Gazette* article put it succinctly: "Almost half of business leaders in a national survey think schools are failing to turn out adequately trained young people."[7] In their living rooms, and increasingly in their boardrooms, however, their language becomes more direct. After all, schools are simply buildings. If blame is to be laid, it must be laid on people, and this, of course, means those vapid and indolent teachers, protected by hermetically sealed contracts-for-life, enjoying short work days and long vacations, answerable to no one. Indeed, the same article notes that only 8% of the CEOs polled said they believed that the teaching profession attracts Canada's brightest and most dedicated individuals.

How fair is this characterization? Certainly, it is rare to find teachers credited with being smart. A content analysis of the *Globe and Mail* stories during 1991 found that the individuals least likely to be quoted about education were teachers, whose opinions informed only 2% of the articles.[8] The portrayal of teachers as dedicated is perhaps slightly more frequent, although "Mr. Chips" testimonials tend to imply such teachers are exceptions. Moreover, in today's selfish corporate climate, dedication in the service of others is the antithesis of competitive—and therefore smart—behaviour.

Does the perception of teachers as coddled, not too cerebral, out-of-touch with the "real world," insufficiently goal-oriented, and not to be trusted with Important Decisions have a ring of familiarity? Scratch the veneer of political correctness and the same stereotypes emerge about women and their capabilities.

Teaching has always been held to be women's work, whether done by women or men. It has been seen as a natural extension of women's responsibility for children and their willingness to serve others. Men are seen as teaching for other reasons: failure to gain entry to another profession, an inordinate need for security or a lack of imagination or ambition. Although men have had a near-monopoly on decision making beyond the classroom level, schools are seen as places dominated by women or men who think like women. (As one voter said, explaining why he would not vote NDP: "The party has been taken over by women and teachers. I don't have any values in common with those groups.") In the public mind, the way women and teachers see the world is entirely too similar. What is required to get things on track are hierarchy, unquestioning discipline and punitive supervision, as imposed by the masculine world of business. Gender politics, rarely discussed as part of school effectiveness or school reform, nonetheless filters many assumptions about who should define education's problems and their solutions.

DOWNLOADING RESPONSIBILITY

The school's willingness to accept as their responsibility the downloading of social-policy and anti-chaos objectives may relate to women's alleged willingness to be all things to all people. What schools cannot bear responsibility for, however, is the other kind of downloading that is taking place.

The cumulative decline in support to provinces and territories from the federal government, through Established Programs Financing (EPF) and the Canada Assistance Plan (CAP), is predicted to exceed $35 billion by 1995.[9] In addition, every province and territory has been faced with declining revenues from its own tax base. In 1980–81, provincial governments shared, on average, 66.5% of the costs of elementary and secondary education. This had declined to 58.5% by 1992–93.[10] The shortfall has resulted in a greater dependency on property tax, one of the least progressive forms of taxation.

The visibility of local taxes assigned to education has alerted Canadians to the costs of this public service. (Governments do not generally remind taxpayers quite so strenuously how many of their tax dollars are spent on politicians' salaries or international aid.) Whatever the intent, flagging education spending increases its political vulnerability. Downloading the cost of education to the community has encouraged the public to see education as a cost that must be reduced, irrespective of need or benefit.

Downloading has worked so well that some politicians suggest taking it one step farther: the cost of education should be downloaded directly on parents. On January 18, 1993, Alberta Premier Ralph Klein announced education budget cuts that include reducing by half support to kindergarten. Schools are being given a choice: reduce the hours of kindergarten instruction by half or charge parents to maintain the status quo.[11]

Klein's attack on kindergarten sends clear messages about education and political priorities, but also shrewdly reads a society unsure of the value of children and childhood. Proponents of many points of view have sold their political messages by exploiting parental anxieties: the deteriorating environment jeopardizes our children's future, or the deficit is robbing children of their rightful inheritance. At the same time, concern for children as children is in decline: adults are to "invest" in children because they represent "our" future; their current quality of life is of only marginal importance. Family allowance payments were ended, ironically, through a federal program called Brighter Futures. CAP was capped, and the promised national daycare program evaporated because there was insufficient public support for it. Despite an all-party resolution adopted by the House of Commons in 1989 to eliminate child poverty by the year 2000, there were a quarter million more poor children in 1991 than when the resolution was passed.[12]

The public policy and legislative attention that child sexual abuse and neglect had received in the early 1980s dwindled by the 1990s to the prurient attention of the tabloids. Children are portrayed as victimizers as often as victims; adults' distrust of children has brought invented phrases such as "false memory syndrome" into the public's vocabulary. A peculiar entertainment media theme has taken hold: wise or manipulative or supremely capable children (à la *Home Alone*) appear on small and large screens with increasing frequency. Adults have been encouraged to see all children as potentially violent and yet to believe that these very children can be protected from others just like them by teaching them peer mediation. The debate on child pornography is more likely to be framed as an issue of artistic integrity than of damage to children. The public mind has become split regarding the nature, value and quality of childhood.

Similar ambiguities and contradictions turn up in how the public perceives the institutions serving children: quality-of-life rather than quality-of-education has come to shape the public's perception of schools. For the first time, the Canadian Education Association's national public opinion poll has found marked dissatisfaction with schools among those living in the largest urban centres.[13] Current economic conditions appear to shape public perceptions. For example, while respondents living in the Atlantic provinces are more likely than those in other provinces to evaluate their schools and teachers favourably, they are also most willing to fail schools on "preparing students for the workforce," a matter of less concern in areas of lower unemployment. The public knows that it is highly improbable that anything taking place in schools could counteract the multiple economic and employment woes of Atlantic Canada, yet it is easier to blame schools than to analyze the impact of politics and the environment.

Rather than challenging the downloading mentality that holds schools accountable for matters well beyond their reach, provincial governments appear to have welcomed the perception that schools are the problem, as an opportunity to download political heat. Task forces, reviews and royal commissions on education have been established in nearly every province and territory during the last half decade. In its submission to the forty-third session of the International Conference on Education, the Council of Ministers of Education and the Secretary of State reported that these initiatives have been "a major focus for review, reform and renewal in Canada." Moreover, the consequent "diversity of approaches is remarkably appropriate in a country whose educational systems are the responsibility of the individual governments."[14] In fact, however independently rationalized and implemented the studies, there is little diversity among their conclusions. Each makes special efforts to respond to stakeholders, explicitly including both the informal and organized business communities, and each has concluded that measuring and reporting on the performance of schools is a vital component of accountability and future prosperity. Provincial governments understand that to claim educational vision one must gaze to the right.

A WINDOW OF OPPORTUNITY

The provincial reviews gave corporate interests the opportunity to put their own spin on education's problems and solutions. Business effectively used the formal recognition of its new status as partner, claiming the right to shape and even determine fundamental questions about the purposes and means of education. While some saw business's most appropriate participation in schools to be general support, and perhaps co-operation on special projects, a much more influential, integral role for business was sought by corporate leaders. A 1993 Gallup Poll found that 59% of Canadian CEOs believed "the private sector should be actively involved in forming educational policy and shaping curriculum and standards."[15] In other words, it was business's business what students studied in grade three, not just how well they performed. The business-lobby Conference Board of Canada came up with a "vision statement" for education, touting Total Quality Management as a promising model for educational administration.[16] The voice of ultraconservative business, the Business Council on National Issues (BCNI), has proposed that it devise "school-leaving" exams that their members might use in testing entry-level applicants.[17]

Business presence could be felt in the rhetoric of education debate. Downsizing, value-added, productivity, return on investment, total quality and other boardroom terms turned up in education-policy documents written at every level. Mark Holmes, former professor of education at the Ontario Institute for Studies in Education (OISE), launched his pro-corporate proposals for education reform with a discussion of "quality"; schools, he declared, "added some value" to children.[18] Corporate Canada would seem to believe that value can be added without increased investment. Seventy-five per cent of surveyed CEOs agreed "there are many ways to significantly reduce costs without affecting the quality of education."[19]

The various provincial think tanks and roundtables on education provided ample opportunity to get out the message. In every case, provincial governments tabled reports that supported doing more with less, albeit as a tenet of faith rather than the result of rigorous analysis. It is apparent that both the CEOs and the governments they advise have had teacher salaries in mind as the most politically popular way of doing more with less, for teacher unions might well be even more unpopular than politicians. Just ask Premier Clyde Wells of Newfoundland. In abruptly declaring a provincial election on May 3, 1993, Wells singled out the Newfoundland Teachers' Association as the public enemy he would vanquish at the polls. He was elected with an overwhelming majority.

BETWEEN A ROCK AND A HARD PLACE

The backlash against the organized teaching profession was inevitable, for public resistance to groups organized to advance single issues or causes has never been greater, particularly if the groups are perceived as self-interested. Big business has encouraged government and public to see big unions as foot-dragging impediments to economic restructuring and prosperity. However, teachers' unions have also contributed to their own reduced circumstances. For more than a decade, most have been under great internal tension, struggling to fulfil two separate functions: they are responsible for advancing both education and the economic status and employment security of teachers.

During the 1980s, teacher associations began to be visible advocates of "progressive" social policy. This received the grudging support of fee-paying teachers as long as bread-and-butter union issues were proceeding reasonably well. However, as cutbacks created job insecurity, as wage increases were replaced by rollbacks, and as teachers were bashed routinely by the press and politicians, teachers began to have doubts. Some blamed their new vulnerability on their unions' concentration on issues such as global education, violence against women, NAFTA and the constitutional accord. Some teachers saw their union leadership as having escaped the trenches of the classroom to the expense account. When these same union leaders protested that the key decisions affecting teachers and schools were being shaped by forces well beyond negotiations with local school boards, and often beyond ministries of education and provincial governments, it sounded like excuse making to many activist teachers. Unions had taken the credit in good times and shouldn't duck responsibility when things turned sour.

What would constitute doing a good job in the eyes of their members is by no means clear. Some teachers are embarrassed by an unseemly militancy advanced by union leaders; equal numbers believe their unions are too cosy with those who like to be described as partners: trustees, the government and, increasingly, business. The swift and often critical initiatives of these partners have left teacher unions feeling outflanked.

Indeed, teachers' organizations have been out of the loop on a growing number of initiatives. For decades, they had successfully influenced public policy on education. For decades, they have believed themselves to have taken the high ground in defence of public education, Now, faced with reactionary politics and appealingly simplistic analyses of education, teachers' unions have found themselves losing ground with their members and the public. Indeed, the ground is shifting under this key player in determining and articulating education policy.

TRUSTING THE TRUSTEES

While teacher organizations have been reeling from education policy becoming a hot political topic, school boards have been facing their own demons. The forces that had received considerable encouragement and success during the 1970s and 1980s still saw schools as the key agents of pro-social and anti-chaos work. Activists have become more skilled lobbyists and have little difficulty marshalling compelling reasons why schools should respond with greater vigour to a host of community problems, from the apparent alienation of parents who don't speak the language of the schools to the suicide rate among gay youth. Increasing pressure has also come from those who complain of the low "product quality" of graduating students. The most vociferous critics, however, have been ratepayers and their eager champions in the local press. The impact of the 1980s' school board policies are being felt. Capital expenditures for elaborate offices and routine salary increases for rapidly growing bureaucracies have become the focus of televised school board meetings and letters to the editor. Decline in revenues, unfinanced provincial mandates and escalating local needs have put educational philosophy in the shadow of fiscal restraint. Most school trustees campaign without identifying party affiliation, often offering themselves on the basis of a narrow ideological orientation, or in the afterglow of a successful single-issue skirmish. Other candidates present themselves merely as good citizens, claiming no cogent educational philosophy or agenda. Relatively few voters bother to participate in choosing who will spend their education dollars; even fewer voters are aware of their candidate's positions on the many issues that school boards are required to address. Name recognition or a name that appears high on the ballot weighs significantly in favour of election.

Not surprisingly, many trustees have found themselves unprepared to withstand the pressures with which they have been forced to contend. Decisions made one month are frequently reversed the next, often in response to a well-orchestrated public protest. With too few dollars to spend on too many programs, it is essential to fund those programs of the greatest interest to opinion leaders. Typically, these are the most vocal, articulate, motivated and well-educated among the general public. Faced with budget cutbacks, therefore, administrators and boards find it easier to cut services to English-as-a-second-language students than to programs for the gifted.

A SYSTEM UNDER SIEGE

If the demands on schools are contradictory and overwhelming, if unions are paralyzed, school boards are demoralized, and ministries are politicized, does it follow that schools are deficient, mind-numbing and unable to change, as they have been portrayed by their critics?

There is a vast amount of evidence to the contrary, but little agreement on which indicators best reflect the success of our schools. Some would point to the number of Canadians who enter post-secondary education: according to the United Nations, with 64% of Canadians aged twenty to twenty-four still studying, Canada leads all other nations in participation in higher education. Some would say that keeping more than 80% of students in high school until they graduate is a great accomplishment, as fewer than half graduated only a generation ago. Perhaps program diversity demonstrates the capacity of schools to adapt to change: Canada has the highest rate per capita of co-operative–education students in the world. More challenging than program diversity is student diversity, and too few realize that our inclusive system is unique.

Others would say our relative prosperity is owed in part to our education system and the efficiency of our workers. The Japanese Productivity Centre computes Canadian worker productivity as the highest in the world, despite our dismal record on on-the-job training. Some would claim that maintaining a peaceful and progressive democracy speaks more eloquently for the education of its citizenry.[20]

Fewer would point to the smaller, private decisions: library use, which has tripled in Quebec and almost doubled in the rest of Canada in the past two decades; the growing participation of parent volunteers who express their commitment to education not by lobbying school boards but by bridging the gaps resulting from the expansion of need and the erosion of resources. Consistently, it is those closest to schools, because of their own age or that of their children, who are the most satisfied with what goes on in the classroom. Surely their opinions are as valid as those of the provincial auditor or a CEO's speech writer.

Do students know all they need to know to get them through life while seeing to the well-being of others? Of course not. This is, however, due less to the nature of schools than it is to the unpredictable nature of the world. We take it for granted that our schooling could not have prepared us for today's technologically driven society beset with environmental and human problems of such magnitude. We know such predictive capacities are beyond individuals, let alone institutions. Yet we ask that today's schools be judged on "preparing students for the twenty-first century," as if we know exactly what will be required. This expectation renders schools vulnerable to criticisms that cannot be refuted.

When corporations plot a takeover, their target is rarely a company without worth, but one that is valuable and vulnerable. Right-wing leaders have been able to capitalize on a mood of general anxiety, which they have helped to create, and to mould it into an alleged failure of schools. Such a tactic could damage even a strong institution, but the business agenda for school reform has advanced because the traditional gatekeepers who shaped and defended the system had been silenced or sidelined.

Casting schools as the villain and competition as the hero appeals to the human need to keep things simple. Margaret Thatcher is said to have observed that middle-class intellectuals can see everyone else's point of view but have none of their own. She recognized that multiple points of view, however intellectually honourable, are politically suicidal. Popular movements and political leaders prepared to provide chillingly simple solutions to their particular take on a problem will be assured of some following. When they put words to public anxieties, carefully orchestrated and often repeated, myths become facts and followers become believers.

PART ONE:
THE ASSAULT ON SCHOOLS

MYTH #1: OUR SCHOOLS HAVE FAILED US ... AND OUR KIDS

Education is a special problem and may require painful solutions.
Its failure is not narrow and specific but large and general,
a failure of philosophies and intentions.... At every level, business
should be education's most articulate and severe critic.
ROBERT FULFORD, *FINANCIAL TIMES*, APRIL 27, 1992

A FAVOURITE PHRASE OF PROGRESSIVE EDUCATORS IS THAT THE FUTURE is a race between education and disaster. This observation is attributed to H.G. Wells, perhaps apocryphally, and it is usually summoned to argue that education is our only means of protecting ourselves from our self-destructive tendencies. It implies that the product of education is a collective state of mind approaching wisdom and that an educated citizenry can temper its short-sightedness with a long-term view of problems and solutions.

This interpretation of the purposes of education, however, is being transformed by narrow special interests convinced that education is an underutilized commodity, one that can be cleverly exploited to multiply short-term profits. For these corporate interests, public education has the appeal of a virgin forest to clear-cutters: opportunity weakly protected by the muddle-headed and the sentimental.

It is here that not only basic literacy skills acquired at school but also hopes, expectations, values and social understanding take root. Therefore, any group wanting to reshape the future might well start in the classroom.

The essential component of this business strategy is to convince the public, particularly the educational tree-huggers, that education is the cause of disaster, not the best defence against it. As evidence of disaster is not hard to find in current Canadian life, the public's wish to assign the blame for unemployment, racial intolerance, high taxation and even the supposedly growing crime rate hardly needs encouragement. Human curiosity is rarely so engaged as when searching for a scapegoat upon which to heap responsibility for ills, real and imagined. With the enthusiastic assistance of governments, the media and high-profile individuals sniffing out a new item on the populist agenda, it has not been difficult to erode public support for public education. Help has been given inadvertently by inept and sometimes self-interested teachers' unions, school boards, education faculties, well-placed critics and narrowly focused education activists.

No defence of public education that implies it is approaching perfection deserves to be taken seriously. Any observer knows that an institution more than a few decades old is being wrenched by the realities of our transformed social, political and economic context. Schools warrant criticism, but they are being criticized for the wrong shortcomings.

Despite waves of reform washing over schools during the past century—most borrowed from decade-old American initiatives — schools have proven frustratingly resilient, rebounding to familiar shapes, styles and intellectual boundaries as soon as reformers turn their backs. Yet it is the very resilience that frustrates reformers that has also provided schools with remarkable durability. Few social inventions of our design remain so recognizable after a century as the classrooms of the 1890s and the 1990s.

Whether the stability of schools is due to stubbornness or effectiveness is arguable, but it is certainly historically true that our attempts to provide a decent education to most children in Canada have been successful. No nation could achieve our standard of living in the absence of an effective system of bringing large numbers to reasonably high levels of literacy and numeracy. If we accept this to be a historical fact, however, does it necessarily follow that such is the case today? According to education's right-wing critics, our schools are failing. Business should be a prime mover of education reform, for after all, says speech maker John Gardner, CEO of Sun Life, "I doubt you would sit by passively if a key supplier consistently delivered to you inferior and inadequate ingredients, ingredients that were essential to the success of your basic processes."[1]

Tracking criticisms such as these, their sources and their legitimacy is key to understanding the corporate agenda for education. After all, if the public is confident that schools are performing well, it is unlikely to be receptive to the business demands that schools "retool," and the sooner the better. Convincing the public (which was, in Mr. Gardner's case, an audience of Toronto Rotarians) may work, as long as the critics keep pumping out myths and ignoring facts.

THE MYTHS AND THE MYTHMAKERS

Myth: At least 25% of Canadians are illiterate,
and for this we can blame our schools.

The magazine *Western Report* asserts that "three million Canadians are functionally illiterate and innumerate" and that "a million more illiterate young people will be released into an increasingly competitive job market by the year 2000."[2] This statement is deduced from the Economic Council of Canada's "A Lot to Learn"[3] in which the council severely distorted the findings of Statistics Canada's 1989 survey of Canadian literacy skills, on which it claimed to be basing its conclusions.[4]

What the StatsCan survey found was that 62% of Canadians cope easily with everyday reading requirements, 22% can cope but are neither particularly able nor enthusiastic readers, and 16% experience significant difficulties. These findings were twisted by the Economic Council as "proving" that 38% of Canadians could not meet everyday learning demands, a conclusion the study simply does not support.

It is wishful thinking to wonder if the demise of the Economic Council, shortly after the release of its report, was related to concerns about its shoddy research and abuse of the data to advance its agenda. Nonetheless, it was the clear intent of the Economic Council (and *Western Report* and others who quote these high "illiteracy" rates) to blame the schools for graduating non-literates.

Such a conclusion, however, cannot be justified. The Statistics Canada study reports that it is those who are much older, educated in a different time and often in a different place, who made up the bulk of those at the lower end of the literacy scale. Seventy-seven per cent of adults who were born in Canada, whose mother tongue was English and who had completed high school attained the highest level of literacy on the test, and most of the remaining 23% were in the next level. Those "less literate" were likely to be over fifty-five years of age, educated in a different time and often in a different place. Only 7% of those aged twenty-five to thirty-four, and 6% of those aged sixteen to twenty-four had limited reading skills. Moreover, the majorities of both these groups were not Canadian-born, and the time, if any, they spent in Canadian schools isn't known.[5] For an estimated half of immigrant children, the language of the classroom is not their mother tongue but rather a barrier—often unacknowledged—to attaining high levels of literacy.[6]

In 1989, Canadian-born young people in the sixteen to twenty-four age group with literacy problems, according to Statistics Canada, was in the range of 3%. This is a considerable achievement, given that approximately 6% of all youth can be expected to have physical and/or sensory disabilities, and up to 16% have been found to have psychiatric disorders.[7]

Undeterred by such inconvenient facts, the Economic Council proclaimed, "Even the youngest group of those born in Canada showed appallingly high illiteracy rates." Its choice of judgemental and emotionally loaded words is as inappropriate as its conclusion. The StatsCan study conscientiously avoids literacy labels such as "illiterate," "innumerate" or "functional" in describing the literary skills of Canadians. The term "functionally illiterate" is reserved for that stable, small number of Canadians who for reasons of mental or physical disability or other circumstance cannot cope with print material of any kind. Unrepentant, the Economic Council predicts a dire future for fully one-third of our students: "If these figures do not improve, our school system will produce well over one million new functional illiterates in the next ten years."[8]

Given what we know about the relationship between low levels of literacy and disability, illness, poverty, unemployment, family chaos and other such factors outside the control of schools, the council's assumptions about who is responsible for illiteracy as well as its numbers are more than suspect. Yet it is this kind of statement that is seized upon by business-lobby groups such as the Conference Board of Canada, which comprises the one hundred largest corporations doing business in Canada. The Conference Board, in introducing its "vision statement" on education, notes that "the [education] debate is fuelled by statistics that show high rates of illiteracy, even among high school and university graduates...."[9] When the board's use of such a statement was challenged—no survey has found evidence to support such a conclusion, or found so much as one "illiterate" university graduate—Florence Campbell, the officer responsible for the Conference Board's education activities, responded that the Conference Board would stand by its words, not because they were factual, but because "it was what their members believed."[10] The members, of course, are corporations and their CEOs. (The disinformation continues. Mary Anne McLaughlin, Campbell's successor, told a Toronto audience of business executives in November 1993 that "more than a quarter of Canadians are functionally illiterate.")[11]

When the Conference Board keeps spreading false news, it is not surprising that its members come to believe what they are told. What is surprising is that the Conference Board has been prepared to blow its cover as a source of objective, fact-based analysis of economic and social indicators, to be revealed as the lobby group that it is.

Myth: Our drop-out rate is at least 30%; this figure alone proves our schools are failing.

Few Canadians can have escaped the myth that our school drop-out rate is the highest in the industrialized world. A 32% drop-out rate has been quoted in virtually every public statement on education pronounced by politicians or lobby groups. The Conference Board's vision statement draws attention to "high numbers of people who drop out of school, apparently ignoring the tremendous consequent costs to themselves and society."

The 32% drop-out rate is little more than a political construct. In 1991, Employment and Immigration Canada, aware of growing unemployment, asked for a quick reading on the drop-out rate, perhaps intending to shift attention away from its disastrous economic policies. Statistics Canada responded on the basis of the crude figures it had at its disposal. These figures were kept in different ways by each province and territory, but Statistics Canada made a stab at an estimate. As StatsCan made clear when it presented its estimate of 32% for high school leavers, the numbers were obviously inflated, but by an unknown amount.[12]

Employment and Immigration and right-wing education critics quoted the StatsCan numbers widely, but conveniently neglected to advise the public that the statistics were very shaky. Indeed, the $300-million Stay-in-School initiative of Employment and Immigration Canada was established to reframe school leaving as a collective economic liability: the massive problems of the economy were to be blamed on workers not knowing enough rather than on insufficient demand for the skills workers had.

The drop-out myth was eventually exposed. In May 1993, Statistics Canada released revised figures on school leavers. Their original estimates simply counted as a drop-out everyone who did not graduate in the expected year from the same high school in which they had first enrolled. The new study took into account those who transferred, emigrated, or continued as part-time students and those who "dropped back in." It turns out that Canada's drop-out rate in 1991 was 18%. Alberta had the highest retention rate, 86%, and Prince Edward Island the lowest, 75%.[13] In 1971, only 52% of Canadians graduated from high school; in 1956 just 30% of eighteen-year-olds had a high school diploma.[14] So much for "the good old days."

These high student retention rates are a potential embarrassment to education's critics, according to *Maclean's*. "Although few would see the new figures as a vindication of the system, it challenges one major premise of the system's critics. Powerful business-supported groups, such as the Conference Board of Canada and the Corporate-Higher Education Forum, a Montreal-based lobby group, have repeatedly used the 32% figure as proof that the education system is in complete shambles."[15]

The numbers themselves, however, distract the public and critics from looking at underlying issues. Relatively few school leavers drop out for reasons schools can influence. York University professors Paul Grayson and Michael Hall have found that "students who have the greatest probability of being dropouts are those who are disabled; have dependent children; have fathers who have not completed high school; have changed schools a number of times; live with friends or alone rather than with their families; work while attending high school; are male; are married, live common-law or have been separated or divorced; and, have parents and friends who do not consider completing high school to be important."[16] The drop-out rate is thus a better index of youth misfortune than of school effectiveness.

Sensing that basing criticism of schools on drop-out figures was becoming an increasingly shaky strategy, in its story on the revised drop-out figures (which, ironically, it titled "A Measure of Hope"), *Maclean's* simply shifts the grounds of the criticism. "For many critics, keeping students in school is not the main issue. Increasingly, educators, politicians and parents are convinced that Canada's education system is failing even those who graduate."

The extra measures schools employ to encourage, counsel and retain students at risk of dropping out are among the factors driving up the cost of education. That it is easier and cheaper to teach the eager and the fortunate, tends to be conveniently forgotten when the "value for money" discussions begin.

Myth: As Canadians, we spend more on education than [virtually] any country in the world, and we have less to show for it. The money is wasted on huge bureaucracies and overpaid teachers. Whatever our problems may be, they certainly can't be solved with more money.

Equation, the newsletter of the Stay-in-School initiative of the federal government, ran the headline "Advisory Body Finds Huge Diseconomies in Education." The article claimed Canada spends "proportionately more [on education] than almost any country in the world."[17] Perhaps the same source was briefing Prime Minister Mulroney, who, in a speech to the Progressive Conservative Party of Canada in August 1988, claimed that Canadian

30

schools and teachers were wasting "huge amounts" of money.[18]

Four years later, Michael Wilson, international trade minister, proclaimed that Canadians were paying too heavily for schooling. "The problem is not that we are not spending enough on education. The problem is that we are not getting value for it." The *Toronto Star* quoted Wilson as claiming that "studies show that Canada is among the highest spenders on education in the world. Teachers are among the highest paid."[19]

Calculating how much Canadians spend on education is far from an exact science. In part, this is because of the multiple sources of education funding peculiar to Canada, with contributions from municipal, provincial and territorial, and federal sources. But complexity is no excuse for mendacity.

On November 11, 1993, "W5," a CTV public affairs program, presented a program segment that alleged the mismanagement of elementary-secondary education dollars. "Canadians spend more on education than any other country in the world," claimed host Eric Malling. Curious about their source for such a statement, I (HR) contacted the "W5" research department. Barbara Simon, responsible for the background research for this item, claimed her figures were taken from the recently released OECD publication, *Education-at-a-Glance*. What the Organization for Economic Co-operation and Development (OECD), being the kind of research secretariat that it is, considers to be "a glance" would give more modest institutions pause; 24 pages of the 145-page document compared the education expenditures of twenty of the twenty-four OECD member countries.[20]

Among the OECD's findings:

• The share of public expenditure allocated to education from all levels of government averages 12%. Canada's rate, at 14.4%, is the third-highest of the twenty countries compared. These figures, however, include post-secondary as well as elementary and secondary education.

• Public expenditure for education in Canada was 6.4% of gross domestic product (GDP) in 1988. The rate for the United States was 5%; Norway, Denmark and Finland spent between 6.6% and 6.8%. Since GDP varies by country, the same number of dollars is not generated by each shift in a percentage point.

• Canada spends a greater proportion of its education dollars on post-secondary education than any other country, reflecting our tradition of public rather than private universities. However, the proportion spent on elementary and secondary education is the fourth-lowest of the twenty OECD members participating in the study.

• The proportion of Canada's education expenditure allocated to capital (e.g., buildings) was 7.5%, ninth among the nineteen countries reporting.

• The proportion of Canada's education expenditure allocated to teacher salaries was seventh of the twelve countries reporting; compensation for other professional and support staff was fifth.

• In expenditures per student at the elementary and secondary levels, Canada ranks fifth of the twenty countries compared. At the post-secondary levels, it ranks fourth.

• Using the most trusted measure of "national effort," which is the expenditure per student relative to the wealth of each country as measured by GDP, Canada ranks ninth among twenty for spending at elementary and secondary levels, and tenth at the post-secondary level.

And that's it. Only one measure, combined public and private spending at pre-primary, elementary, secondary and post-secondary levels, does Canada rate first. To use figures that reflect Canada's high participation rates of adults in post-secondary training and study to allege fiscal irresponsibility and waste within our elementary and secondary schools is gross dishonesty.

Indeed, given some built-in expenses with which Canadian education systems must cope, our expenditures are quite modest. Certainly, our unique system of decentralization is costly, as duplication is inevitable. Our inhospitable climate and population distribution increase the "cost of doing business" in education, just as they do in other sectors. Desirable features of our system, including large numbers of students being educated in two languages, the widespread practice of integrating students with special (sometimes expensive) needs, and our high retention rates all cost money. The system's obligation to reflect diversity of religion and language is also a costly if appropriate expenditure. As all these features exist as the result of political compromises taken well outside the purview of education, however, it is hardly fair to label them profligate and wasteful spending by schools.

Indeed, a stronger argument can be made for the bargain of Canadian education than the huge diseconomies claimed by education's critics. Politicians are among the least likely to take any responsibility for their share of education's costs. The Liberal *Red Book* promises more of the same: "Despite these high expenditures, there is growing concern among Canadians that our educational system is mediocre and off-target."[21]

Perhaps it is the perceived wastefulness of the system, or perhaps it is parents' growing annoyance that schools cannot be counted on to provide year-round child care, that feeds the myth that in other countries, tax dollars purchase a longer school day and a longer school year.

Myth: Students in all the countries with which Canada competes work harder and longer. Take Japan — Japanese kids go to school at least 243 days a year. Our kids go only half the year.

The popular myth of the 243-day Japanese school year appeared first, it seems, in a 1990 article in *Atlantic Monthly*.[22] The article claims, in addition to Japan's 243 school days, that German students attend up to 240 days, while Canadian students attend a mere 180 to 185 days annually.

Given that *Atlantic Monthly* isn't on every Canadian coffee table, the rapid spread of the longer school year myth required domestic encouragement. Soon it was being quoted by premiers, including Frank McKenna, who made headlines touting the need for school-year reform. Curious about the accuracy of the figures being used in the debate, the Canadian Teachers' Federation contacted the government of Japan to confirm the numbers. The documentation produced some surprising data. According to the Japanese ministry of education, 243 days is the allowable maximum days Japanese schools are permitted to be open. No school, however, comes close to providing this number of teaching days. Indeed, in every province and territory, at every grade level, Canadian students are exposed to more hours of instruction annually than are Japanese students. At the high school level, on average, Canadian students receive 952 hours of instruction compared to 933 in Japan.[23]

Not only is the 243-day figure in error, the official number of school days in Japan includes many non-instructional days used for sports and cultural celebrations, and the school day itself is shorter than the Canadian school day. These facts, however, did not deter Diane Francis from proclaiming in the *Financial Post* in May 1993 that "[Japanese] teachers and students work 240 days a year. Our kids and their teachers get off lightly with around a mere 185 days."[24] (In point of fact, Ms. Francis also misrepresents the Canadian situation. Only one province—New Brunswick—reported fewer than 185 instructional days in 1992; Saskatchewan led with 194.)[25]

Quick to seize upon numbers discrediting our national educational effort, Tom D'Aquino's Business Council on National Issues cites "lengthening the school year" as one of its six priorities for educational reform.[26] It seems ironic that a group with so little respect for what takes place during the school day is so anxious to see the number of days increased. Such contradictions aside, we are told that this is just the start of what we must do if we are to avoid falling "even further behind" our competitors.

Myth: *When our student results are compared*
with those of our international competitors,
we are beaten by nearly everybody.

Everyone knows that every other country's kids know twice as much as our kids at half their age. In 1992, the Economic Council of Canada concluded that "by the end of secondary school, Canada's achievement is weak,"[27] and *Maclean's* special report "What's Wrong at School" reported that on international tests, "Canada's performance is mediocre."[28] Robert Fulford calls our "base standard calamitously low";[29] CEO Norman Kissick says it's a "crisis of mediocrity."[30]

In assessing the accuracy of these judgements, it is important to understand that the data with which we compare Canadian students with those from other countries take into account only students in certain grades and in certain provinces and only in the subject areas of mathematics and sciences.

It is a given of valid research designs that samples must match. If one is setting out to compare the math skills of students in Korea and British Columbia, for example, the only significant difference between the two groups of students should be where they live. All other factors that could influence results—the age of students, the randomness of the sample tested, the method of administering tests and reporting test scores, etc.—must be the same if the results, and therefore the comparisons, are to have any meaning. Particularly important is the "opportunity to learn" factor. Put simply, if one group of students has studied algebra and the second hasn't, student results on algebra tests will always favour those who have had the opportunity to learn algebra.

Those conducting international comparative testing are more than aware of these and others factors that limit the confidence the public should place in bald, unadjusted results. The multi-volume reports that accompany the major studies and the 145-page *Education-at-a-Glance: OECD Indicators* caution against drawing inappropriate conclusions from comparisons of apples, oranges and a few lemons. The education report of the Organization for Economic Co-operation and Development notes that for the factors it presents, those "least satisfactory are the indicators in areas in which national data are often lacking . . . [including] data on the outcomes of schooling."

These limitations are repeatedly, if futilely, called to the attention of policy makers by the analysts. The Economic Council of Canada, which gave schools a failing grade in its report "A Lot to Learn," based its conclusions largely on student achievement on international tests of mathematics and science, despite the warning contained in one of its own key commissioned background papers that "the existence of fundamental differences in the makeup [of the tested populations], and in the content of the curriculum makes comparison of the outcomes attained by students highly problematic."[31]

These fundamental differences included factors that obviously disadvantaged Canadian students. For example, in the Second International Mathematics Study (SIMS), the study most often cited to prove the failure of our schools, the range of Canadian students tested reflected a much wider spectrum of ability and experience than those of any other participating country. Testing expert and professor David Robitaille, writing for the Economic Council, points out that Canada's high retention rate (approaching 82% in the provinces tested) enlarges the pool of potential test takers well beyond the academically able. The Canadian practice of allowing students to choose the subjects in which they enrol creates a very different picture than one would get in countries in which school authorities decided who would—and would not—study a given subject. For example, in British Columbia, 55% of all students in the age group studied were enrolled in the mathematics course from which the sample was drawn. The Japanese students in the group from which the Japanese sample was selected made up just 13% of the age group population.[32] When the achievement of representatives of the top 13% is compared to the achievement of the top 55%, the results will predictably favour the more select group of test takers.

Much has been made of the alleged superior achievement of Asian students in mathematics and sciences. Indeed, education's critics would have us believe that small Asian children rhyme off quadratic equations with the nonchalance our children exhibit when reciting their favourite TV commercials. According to Kazuo Ishizaka, of the National Institute for Educational Research of Japan, much of what we think we know about education in Japan is simply not true.[33]

Speaking to the issue of international tests in May 1993, Mr. Ishizaka pointed out that the Japanese practice of streaming students for ability by school made it easy for officials to shape outcomes by selecting which schools would participate in international testing. Before testing, both staff and students are emotionally "pumped." Exhorted to do their best for the honour of their family, teacher, school and country, students are primed to peak performance levels. Mr. Ishizaka also notes that collating the results is also an issue of honour; schools that face the dishonour of mediocrity simply neglect to pass on their test results to the authorities.

Had Canadian students' scores been dismal, it might be necessary to marshal a lengthier and more complex defence of their results. One could, for example, draw attention to the unique inclusivity of our system: the Canadian practice of integrating children with limited inclination or ability in regular classes is unknown in most countries; similarly, a sizeable percentage of any class being new to the language of instruction is unheard of in more homogeneous societies. That almost one in five Canadian children lives below the poverty line,[34] which means many children come to school hungry—and not just for food—is particularly relevant when comparing the achievement of Canadian students with those in Asian and European countries in which all students participate in school breakfast and/or lunch programs, and in which child welfare is a higher priority.

It is not necessary, however, to dig so deeply into the arsenal of excuses, because there is nothing to excuse.

The following charts, created by the OECD, reveal a rather different conclusion than that of the Conference Board of Canada, cautioning Canadian business to be alert to "a poor showing by our students on international tests." The OECD charts, in fact, demonstrate that when apples are compared to apples, Canadian students meet or exceed the mathematics performance of students from other countries tested.

What is going on? Why do right-wing critics and corporate interests invent bad news about our students and our schools? What does it mean when the press and political leaders discredit the system universally recognized as vital to our current and future well-being? What would we suspect they were up to if the target of disinformation was our public health-care system?

THE POLITICS OF BLAME

There are other myths and other numbers, many of which have taken on a life of their own through repetition, the language of inevitability. That schools are "failing" seems no longer to be contentious enough to require proof or draw rebuttal; it has become a given, a convenient explanation for a host of late-twentieth-century events and anxieties. An editorial blames the failure of the Charlottetown Accord on how schools teach history. In a front-page story about toy-buying trends in the *Globe and Mail*, Alanna Mitchell leads with this claim: "Hounded by fears that the school system is failing . . . Canadian parents are spending more and more money on educational toys for their children."[35] That cash-strapped parents may reject over-priced, over-advertised action figures or that the association of imitative and real violence might affect buying are surely equally plausible as explanations of toy-buying trends; but these are not explored. It's much easier to blame the schools.

CHART A

*Multiple comparisons of overall proficiency in mathematics.
Second International Assessment of Educational Progress, age 13
(1991).*

	Mean	Standard error	Switzerland (15 C.)	France	Italy (E-R)	Canada	Scotland	England	Ireland	Spain (excl. Cat.)	United States	Portugal
Switzerland (1, 2) (15 cantons)	70.8	1.3		▲	▲	▲	▲	▲	▲	▲	▲	▲
France	64.2	0.8	▼		◆	◆	◆	◆	◆	▲	▲	▲
Italy (2) (Emilia–Romagna)	64.0	0.9	▼	◆		◆	◆	◆	◆	▲	▲	▲
Canada	62.0	0.6	▼	◆	◆		◆	◆	◆	▲	▲	▲
Scotland (1)	60.6	0.9	▼	◆	◆	◆		◆	◆	▲	▲	▲
England (1)	60.6	2.2	▼	◆	◆	◆	◆		◆	◆	◆	▲
Ireland	60.5	0.9	▼	◆	◆	◆	◆	◆		▲	▲	▲
Spain (2) (except Catalonia)	55.4	0.8	▼	▼	▼	▼	▼	◆	▼		◆	▲
United States (1)	55.3	1.0	▼	▼	▼	▼	▼	◆	▼	◆		▲
Portugal (1, 2)	48.3	0.8	▼	▼	▼	▼	▼	▼	▼	▼	▼	

(1)   School or student response rate below 85% standard
(2)   90% or less of target population sampled

▼   *Mean significantly lower
     than comparison country*   ◆   *No statistically significant
     difference from comparison
     country*   ▲   *Mean significantly higher
     than comparison country*

OECD, Centre for Educational Research and Innovation, *Education-at-a-Glance: OECD Indicators* (Paris, 1992), p. 119.

CHART B

Multiple comparisons of achievement in arithmetic,
Second International Mathematics Study, age 13 (1982)

	Mean	Standard error	Japan	Netherlands	Canada (BC)	Belgium (Fl)	France	Belgium (Fr)	Canada (Ont)	United States	Scotland	England/Wales	New Zealand	Finland	Luxembourg	Sweden
Japan (3)	60.3	1.5		◆	◆	◆	◆	◆	◆	▲	▲	▲	▲	▲	▲	▲
Netherlands (2, 3)	59.3	1.1	◆		◆	◆	◆	◆	◆	▲	▲	▲	▲	▲	▲	▲
Canada (3) (British Columbia)	58.0	1.3	◆	◆		◆	◆	◆	◆	▲	▲	▲	▲	▲	▲	▲
Belgium (3) (Flemish community)	58.0	1.4	◆	◆	◆		◆	◆	◆	▲	▲	▲	▲	▲	▲	▲
France (3)	57.7	1.3	◆	◆	◆	◆		◆	◆	▲	▲	▲	▲	▲	▲	▲
Belgium (3) (French community)	57.0	1.8	◆	◆	◆	◆	◆		◆	▲	▲	▲	▲	▲	▲	▲
Canada (3) (Ontario)	54.5	1.1	◆	◆	◆	◆	◆	◆		◆	▲	▲	▲	▲	▲	▲
United States (1)	51.4	1.2	▼	▼	▼	▼	▼	◆	◆		◆	◆	◆	◆	▲	▲
Scotland	50.2	0.5	▼	▼	▼	▼	▼	▼	▼	◆		◆	▲	◆	▲	▲
England/Wales (1)	48.2	0.9	▼	▼	▼	▼	▼	▼	▼	◆	◆		◆	◆	◆	▲
New Zealand (3)	45.6	1.2	▼	▼	▼	▼	▼	▼	▼	◆	▼	◆		◆	◆	◆
Finland	45.6	1.3	▼	▼	▼	▼	▼	▼	▼	◆	◆	◆	◆		◆	◆
Luxembourg	45.4	0.4	▼	▼	▼	▼	▼	▼	▼	▼	▼	◆	◆	◆		▲
Sweden	40.6	0.9	▼	▼	▼	▼	▼	▼	▼	▼	▼	▼	◆	◆	▼	

(1) School or student response rate below 85% standard
(2) 90% or less of target population sampled
(3) School or student response rate not available

▼ *Mean significantly lower than comparison country*   ◆ *No statistically significant difference from comparison country*   ▲ *Mean significantly higher than comparison country*

OECD, Centre for Educational Research and Innovation, *Education-at-a-Glance: OECD Indicators* (Paris, 1992), p. 119.

The consequences of trashing schools are apparent. Governments are searching for programs to cut that will draw the least amount of resistance; it is politically advantageous to appear fiscally tough on sectors that "aren't performing." This cosy relationship between education's critics and the governments responsible for schools is incestuous but not uncommon: governments quote the opinions of business lobby groups, business quotes government policy papers developed with the co-operation of education critics, and the media informs the public that unanimity has been achieved. Little by little, public confidence in education is shaken. The payoff for playing the politics of disinformation is new opportunities for those who promise quick fixes.

The arguments that smear schools have been manufactured in the absence or in spite of the evidence. Under these circumstances, what possible explanations are there for what is taking place? One is that we are witnessing a number of coincidental and mutually reinforcing errors, based inadvertently on hastily conducted and misinterpreted research, linked by muddled but well-intentioned reasoning. This model could be called "the collusion of incompetence." The other possibility is that we are watching a consciously orchestrated campaign, a strategy with well-articulated goals, an agenda with a purpose.

THE "PROBLEM" OF PUBLIC CONFIDENCE

It is important to distinguish between the ability of business and right-wing education critics to recognize and capitalize on public disaffection with schools, and conscious efforts to manipulate public opinion against schools. Left to its own momentum, public opinion is unlikely to have driven a school-reform agenda.

Generally speaking, Canadians are and have been quite satisfied with their schools, although they are less likely to talk up the accomplishments of the Canadian education system than they are those of our health-care system, despite comparable differences between Canadian schools and their American counterparts.

Public support for schools persists despite the fact that public satisfaction with familiar institutions is in quite rapid decline. A 1993 Gallup survey measured the lowest levels of public "respect and confidence" yet recorded for eight Canadian institutions, from "political parties" to "the Supreme Court." To the surprise of few, political parties inspired "quite a lot/a great deal of respect" among only 9% of those surveyed, and large corporations edged out large unions by 22% to 19%. Public schools, however, enjoyed 44% support in this category.[36]

Such findings hardly suggest overwhelming confidence in schools, but against the backdrop of general dissatisfaction with "the way things are these days," the levels of support are quite high. The ninth OISE survey on public attitudes towards education confirms relative, if not absolute, public confidence in schools. For example, in 1992, 49% of respondents believed that the quality of education received by high school students over the last ten years has remained the same or improved; this is a 1% increase over the same category tallied in 1969.[37] A public opinion poll commissioned by the Manitoba Teachers' Society in the summer of 1993 found that 63.3% of those surveyed believed that schools were "providing young people today with a better education than their parents received."[38]

As it appears that on matters educational, Canadians are strongly influenced by what happens across the border, it is instructive to note that Americans express similar sentiments towards their schools. The most recent Gallup Poll of U.S. opinion towards public schools invited parents to grade the schools in their communities, and in the United States as a whole.[39] Nationally, 47% gave their local schools an A or B standing, but somewhat perversely, however, only 19% believed that the country's schools overall deserved such good marks. When only those who had a child in school were asked to grade the school their oldest child attended, 72% gave it an A or B. In other words, those with first-hand experience with schools were the most likely to evaluate them positively. Encouraged to believe that somewhere out there, schools attended by other people's children were failing miserably, respondents discounted their own experience and reported what they had been told to believe by successive rounds of education criticism. Years of public-opinion polling by the Canadian Education Association confirms the same finding; the closer adults are to schools, the more likely it is that they will think highly of them.

According to education's corporate critics, such opinions should be seen not as evidence of the public's good judgement, but as an indication of a lack of understanding of the "new realities" of attitudinal and economic restructuring.

Public support for schools has turned out to be a pesky problem. Indeed, the federal Tory government's 1991 consultation paper on education called *Learning Well ... Living Well*[40] had some difficulty credibly reconciling its aim—the need for restructuring education—with the persistent satisfaction of education's "clients." The authors had to concede that "opinion polls confirm that Canadian parents are quite satisfied with the status quo when it comes to their own children." Satisfaction with things as they are, the authors imply, is tantamount to being simple-minded: "Most Canadian parents do not understand that the changing world economy demands a new approach to learning."

We just don't get it.

Perhaps it will be pollsters themselves who will foster our collective attitude adjustment. The tone of a promotional pitch from the Angus Reid Group dated Spring 1993 calls into question the objectivity of their public-opinion research on education. Several assumptions are blatantly built into the preamble aimed at prospective clients wishing to purchase "proprietary questions" to be included in the survey.[41]

According to the Angus Reid preamble, "There are disturbing signs that the country's educational system may no longer be able to fulfil one of its central missions: delivering the highly skilled workforce Canada will require to successfully compete. . . ." The nature of these "signs" is not explored, but in the next paragraph readers are told "there is also a widespread concern that Canadians earnestly reappraise the successes and failures of our educational infrastructure and to forge actionable, perhaps revolutionary, solutions to its problems." This commentary is all the more remarkable for appearing in the marketing preamble, rather than in a discussion of the research findings. (These findings, of course, were not made available to the public whose opinions were sought— only to those for whom the results were worth $7500 per copy.)

In some ways, this story embodies exactly what is going on as we debate the future of our schools. Although it may seem to be a public discussion, there are certain "privileged" players, and their minds are already made up. It is naïve to believe that anything as emotionally charged as education can be freed from the shadow cast by myths. What is new, however, is that the creation and perpetuation of myths about our schools have been incorporated into the agenda of the economic and political Right.

MYTH #2: OUR GRADUATES JUST DON'T HAVE THE SKILLS

Canada is involved in a war. Our universities are the training grounds for our armies to win on the global battlefield.

DAVID VICE, FORMER V.P., NORTHERN TELECOM

DURING THE 1993 FEDERAL ELECTION, MANY POLITICIANS WERE HEARD quoting a disturbing statistic: Canada faces a skilled labour force shortage of 300,000! Our schools and training programs must start producing the high-skilled workers to fill this hole in our nation's economic infrastructure. Otherwise, Canada will not be able to become globally competitive. Progressive Conservative leader Kim Campbell said, "There are simply not the people with the skills to get the job done. . . . It's very distressing . . . a national tragedy." Liberal leader Jean Chrétien added, "There are 300,000 jobs vacant in Canada because our young people lack the relevant skills training. That is unacceptable."

CBC's "Reality Check," a regular election feature of *Prime Time News* designed to verify statements made by politicians, decided to investigate this claim. No one in either the Liberal or the Conservative camp could find its origin, but a little sleuthing by the CBC came up with the answer: the number referred to a study on current job vacancies by the federal government's labour/business think tank, the Canadian Labour Market and Productivity Centre (CLMPC), and was, the centre readily agreed, being misused. There is no way to deduce the shortage of skills from the study, "Reality Check" and the CLMPC concluded. The politicians quietly stopped using the magic number of 300,000 in their speeches.

But the myth has not gone away. Our "failed education system" and "poorly educated labour force" are blamed for the country's economic woes while corporate practices and government policies that favour high unemployment are left unexamined. Proof of a severe skills shortage in Canada would greatly favour an active and critical role for business in the schools; without one, business has a much weakened case for intervention.

The 1991 Chamber of Commerce Report on the Task Force on Education and Training, entitled *Focus 2000*, emphasized the putative shortage of skilled labour in Canada. The Prosperity Initiative of the Mulroney government used the same myth to declare that Canada's learning performance is inadequate and that Canada's whole educational system must be realigned to economic performance.

The Canadian Forum on Learning, established as a result of the Initiative's report, *Learning Well . . . Living Well*, endorsed the skills shortage premise. Paul Gallagher, president of Vancouver Community College, uses the alleged shortage of highly skilled workers as evidence of the need for an increased role for the private sector in education "to supply a great deal of the skills upgrading required in a technologically driven society."

The Business Council on National Issues has called for a "basic employability skills test" on the basis of this myth: "There is a growing consensus that Canada's public education system is failing to encourage or attain superior performance at a time when the economy is becoming more skill-intensive." For good measure, the BCNI also restated the "we're falling behind" myth. "Academic expectations in Canada appear low in relation to those found in many other countries."[1]

The *Globe and Mail's Report on Business* recently devoted most of an edition to the "skills squeeze." "With 1.6 million Canadians out of work, the reskilling of Canada has become a national priority as high-skill jobs go begging. . . . If workers were willing— and education, management and labour able—to solve the skills mismatch, the result would be a healthy drop in the unemployment rate. . . . If you have the right skills, an employer in Canada is eager to hire you. . . . The well-being of the country is harmed because bright young Canadians are not acquiring the skills that our changing economy needs."[2]

The facts just don't bear this out.

THE FACTS

Canadians have more education than ever before. We are staying in school longer. Statistics Canada reports that the increase in those with a post-secondary education far outstripped the population growth over the last decade. Graduates with degrees in engineering and applied sciences account for over 27% of the total occupations listed—by far the largest category. George Mori, senior analyst with Statistics Canada, confirms that our system is producing well. "I don't think our system is failing to produce in terms of the quantity of graduates. Internationally, we compare very favourably."[3]

The World Economic Forum and the International Institute for Management's *World Competitiveness Report*, ranks the world's industrialized countries on competitiveness. It puts Canada in the top five when measuring workers' skills. A UNESCO study on international standards in post-secondary education ranked

Canada first among the G7 countries in annual per-capita science and engineering degrees or diplomas granted. Each year Canada produces nearly three times as many science and engineering graduates per capita as does Germany, and 50% more than Japan.[4]

Yet advocates of the skills shortage myth get away with it because there is no regular tracking of job vacancies by subject done by the government of Canada. At one time, Canada kept fairly advanced statistical records. As well, the Science Council of Canada monitored skills shortages in the sciences on a sectoral basis. These research practices put Canada in the forefront of industrialized countries in the collection and application of such data. However, government record-keeping practices have been cut and, of course, the Science Council was closed down. The only indicator we have now is the Help Wanted Index, a national listing of available jobs, which tells us nothing about how long they have been vacant or why they were vacated. In this, Canada is indeed at a disadvantage: many other industrialized countries are now gathering more sophisticated information.

Dr. Noah M. Meltz, professor of economics and industrial relations and principal of Woodsworth College at the University of Toronto, and chair of the Advisory Committee on Labour Statistics to Statistics Canada, says there is a major gap in our information about skills needs. He and University of Toronto economics professor Frank Reid use other indicators, such as the General Job Vacancy Rates and the Help Wanted Index, to project long-term developments in employment patterns in Canada.

They conclude that structural unemployment—that is, unemployment as a permanent fixture of the economy—has risen substantially in the last twenty years. Asked directly whether he believes that Canada is experiencing a skills shortage, Meltz, a leading authority on the subject, says simply, "Our problem is a lack of jobs, not finding the people to fill them."

A 1994 StatsCan quarterly survey of 5000 manufacturers appears to confirm this view: only 2% of manufacturers complained of a shortage of skilled labour, and less than one-half of 1% said that a shortage of unskilled workers was impeding production.[5]

Within the federal government's Human Resources department is the Canadian Occupational Projection System. By talking to employers, labour unions and governments, researchers can identify likely sectors for job growth, but their estimates are qualitative rather than quantitative. Although it appears that the workers of today need more years of training than those of a decade ago, the statistics do not prove a mismatch between job openings and skilled workers. "Maybe the job is in Tuktoyaktuk and the skills are in Toronto. Maybe the pay is too low for someone who has spent years in school. We just don't know," said one senior government official in Human Resources, who asked not to be identified.

The Canadian Labour Congress examined all the "new economy" sectors: high-tech electrical machinery and equipment; telecommunications equipment; office, store and business machines; aerospace; pharmaceuticals; non-electric machinery. It found that employment in most of these sectors actually fell between 1989 and 1992.

Economist Bruce Campbell, executive director of the Canadian Centre for Policy Alternatives, details job losses from December 1988 to December 1992: transportation equipment, 27,100; rubber and plastics, 21,200; electrical and electronics, 36,300; primary metals, 22,300; machinery industries, 24,700; chemicals, 7000; business services, 9400; advertising, 10,000; communications and electronic equipment, 5700; office and business machines, 1200; electrical industrial equipment, 6700. There were a few modestly bright spots: computer services created 7800 jobs; accounting services, 3900; management consultant services, 13,000; pharmaceuticals, 3300.

Yet, says Campbell, "it is clear that, despite positive signs in a few subsectors, the job-creation numbers are minuscule. There is no sign of an expanding knowledge economy (either in manufacturing or services) to absorb the 434,000 workers displaced from the old and new manufacturing/resource economy, the 111,000 construction workers, and the 104,000 workers displaced from the private sector service economy due to restructuring and recession."

Even that *Report on Business* special skills edition had to admit what Canadians know anecdotally: more than 4,000 civil engineers can't find jobs. "Overall, about 3% of Canada's 135,000 engineers are unemployed, including many recent graduates. As an example, in 1990, 93% of engineering graduates of the University of New Brunswick had jobs within six months of getting their degrees. Last year, only 68% had jobs." A close reading of the argument put forward by the *ROB* suggests that the new skills being touted are, in fact, not those generally thought of when we speak of the new economy, but trades jobs from what one business person quoted in the article refers to as the "old economy."

In fact, says University of Alberta economics professor Harvey Krahn, if there is a skills mismatch, it is not of the high-technology variety touted by education reformers. In an analysis for Statistics Canada called *Quality of Work in the Service Sector*, Krahn challenges government conclusions that Canadians are underqualified and incapable of participating in a high-technology, global economy. He says that many Canadians are working in jobs that underutilize their skills, jobs for which they are overqualified.[6]

Jim Turk, director of education for the Ontario Federation of Labour, denies both that there is a skills shortage and that jobs are demanding more skills. He believes that technology is replacing skilled workers and that hiring tends to favour those with only entry-level job skills. "The distribution of jobs is becoming more pear-shaped. The great bulk of middle-level, middle-skill jobs are being replaced. A minority of them are being up-skilled; the majority are being deskilled." He adds that even within jobs, new technologies are deskilling work. "More and more of the 'skill' is being built into the technology—so that less skilled workers can use the more skilled technologies."[7]

Kevin Hayes, employment analyst for the Canadian Labour Congress, is concerned about the lack of statistical information on jobs available in Canada and the consequent lack of direction for the $3 billion spent on training every year. The government keeps no breakdown on what we are training people to do, does not match need with skill, doesn't have a profile of the unemployed and is not following recent graduates to see if they have found jobs related to their education. "This is the national scandal," says Hayes. "We don't need to fabricate another. With this rate of unemployment it is very hard to believe that we have a skills shortage."

ORIGIN OF THE MYTH

The skills shortage myth in Canada is largely a parroting of U.S. notions and it is to the United States that we must look to find the facts. The most sophisticated job forecasting in North America is done biennially by the U.S. Bureau of Labor Statistics. Their surveys show a consistent pattern: the bulk of new jobs are low-skilled.

The most recent projections list the ten occupations that are going to account for the greatest number of new jobs between 1990 and 2005: only two qualify as highly skilled. The report projects that the largest category of new jobs will be retail salespersons. (Indeed, as we shall see in the next chapter, retail chains created the most jobs in the first thirty months of the U.S. "recovery.") Second will be registered nurses, the first of the highly skilled jobs (but not what most "skills shortage" promoters consider to be high-tech). Third will be cashiers. Fourth will be general-office clerks; fifth, truck drivers; sixth—the second highly skilled job—will be general managers and top executives; seventh will be janitors and cleaners, including domestics; eighth will be nursing aides, orderlies and attendants; ninth will be food-counter, fountain and related workers; tenth will be waiters. Not a scientist or mathematician among them.[8]

Yet the criticism of education in the United States is fuelled by the common notion that America is not producing enough scientists and mathematicians. From the 1983 Department of Education study, *A Nation at Risk*, which blamed the schools' failure to provide skills for America's poor performance in the economic war with Japan and Germany, to present-day school bashing indulged in by corporate heads, the message has been consistent: American business cannot compete because the American workforce lacks the winning skills.

John Akers, then chairman of IBM Corporation and chairman of the Business Roundtable Education Task Force, praised the American "win" in the Gulf War and called for "an equal commitment to rescue our educational system."[9] In a recent best-seller, *Thinking for a Living: Education and the Wealth of Nations*, Ray Marshall, former U.S. Secretary of Labor, and Carnegie Corporation's Marc Tucker warn of a skills crisis "of the same proportions that our defeated foes faced after the war."

George Bush, the "Education" president, issued his famous *America 2000*, which called for a fundamental overhaul of American education based on its alleged failure to prepare young people for the jobs American business was supposedly creating. In a follow-up report, his administration called for a national assessment system to "communicate world-class standards of curriculum content and student performance" and to "certify individual performance and thereby motivate students and their teachers to meet these standards." Performance expectations would be "benchmarked to the highest standard in the world."[10]

President Clinton has endorsed Bush's view and shares his belief that America is suffering a severe skills shortage. Yet studies of the most sophisticated corporations in the United States have consistently failed to find such shortage. Indeed, several key studies have emerged recently that directly refute the shortage theory.

THE REAL PROBLEM

In 1990, the National Center's Commission on Workforce Skills found that 95% of America's employers still use methods of production that require less than an eighth-grade education and minimal training of most workers.[11] The Washington-based Economic Policy Institute (EPI) released a study in May 1993 that examined the wage rates of college graduates to determine whether there was a dearth of skilled workers. (In times of shortage, the few skilled workers command high wage rates. When skilled labour is readily available, the workers' wages tend to be lower.) EPI found that the wages of college graduates fell 3.1% between 1987 and 1991. Highly skilled white-collar workers saw their wages fall more than 3% from 1987 to 1992.[12]

Cornell University economist John Bishop, once a keen advocate of the skills shortage theory, found that, for all their rhetoric about skills, employers have not been willing to pay for them. "The surprising finding is that competence in mathematical reasoning, science and language arts has almost no effect on wage rates during the first eight years after graduating from schools."[13]

A U.S. Labor Department study found that about one-fifth of college graduates were stuck in jobs that were not using the skills and education they attained in college; this points to a shortage not of skills but of jobs.[14] These studies followed a 1991 EPI report that concluded that the slight overall increase in the job skills required would necessitate only .04 years—fewer than 15 days—of extra schooling during the next decade.

In 1992, *Science*, the journal of the American Association for the Advancement of Science, featured the plight of unemployed Ph.D.s in the sciences and outlined alternative career paths. A 1993 *Wall Street Journal* article reported an excess of physical scientists and mathematicians. "Only a few years ago, the idea of a glut of physical scientists was considered absurd," declared the *Journal*. Now, however, scientists face a "black hole" of unemployment.[15]

Arizona State University education professor David Berliner says that the American economy is not able to absorb all the scientists and engineers it produces. "With no increase in the rate of supply of scientists and engineers, we will accumulate a surplus of about 1 million such individuals by the year 2010." He points out that the five most highly skilled occupational groups will make up only about 6% of the job pool by the year 2000. Service jobs, requiring the least technical skill, will constitute about 17% of the job pool by the year 2000.[16]

More important, perhaps, were the findings of a major study commissioned in 1990 by then energy secretary, Adm. James Watkins, to examine all aspects of America's education performance and needs. The study was conducted by the researchers and scientists of the Energy Department's Sandia National Laboratories. If any group of researchers would look for the skills shortage angle, the government reasoned, it would be this one: after all, they worked for the Department of Energy, long responsible for much of the research related to nuclear energy, the military and defence-related sciences and keen on a high-tech future for America.

The researchers of the Sandia Laboratories consulted with all relevant major agencies, including the National Center for Education Statistics, the U.S. Department of Education, the U.S. Department of Labor, the National Science Foundation, the U.S. Bureau of Census and the College Entrance Examination Board. The report, *Perspectives on Education in America*, was completed in the spring of 1991; however, on government instructions, it was not published, but sent for "review" to many of the agencies whom the researchers had consulted.

Professor Daniel Tanner of the Graduate School of Education at Rutgers University, followed the saga of the Sandia study. He found that it was deliberately withheld from the public when officials of the U.S. Department of Education discovered that the findings ran counter to President Bush's national agenda for school reform. Tanner says it was subjected to so much refereeing and criticism and was delayed so long that its potential was neutralized.[17] None of the major agencies consulted by the researchers, including the National Science Foundation and the Department of Education, were able to invalidate the findings because the data had come from their own files. Nevertheless, the study was "effectively suppressed."

An examination of the Sandia study leaves no doubt as to the reason. Among the key findings were:

- Since the late 1970s, every target student group has maintained or improved on the Scholastic Aptitude Tests; performances for the National Assessment of Educational Progress has improved; and high school drop-out rates are declining.
- Despite declines in the college-age population, the number of bachelor's degrees in engineering, computer science and mathematics has increased by more than 75% during the last twenty years; the number of doctorates in engineering and physical science is at or near an all-time high.
- Despite the dramatic increase in the proportion of college graduates in the tested population, thereby creating a larger sample, scores on the Graduated Record Examination have risen significantly since the late 1970s.
- The United States leads the world in the proportion of its population earning bachelor's degrees in all fields, and that lead is widest in science and engineering.

The Sandia study concluded that "the scientific community has done its part in distracting the nation from actual problems in education.... Like the economic competitiveness argument, the 'shortfall' argument portrays the U.S. as losing ground to other countries. As in other areas, our research does not support this." This was not what the Bush administration wanted to hear.

Nor did it want to hear the other findings of the study—that the problems of America's schools are those of inequality, and that priority should be given to improving the education of minority and inner-city children and to the issues of racism and immigration. As well, the study called for better pay and more respect for teachers, a favourite target of education reform. "Much of the blame for problems in education, real or imagined, is dropped at the feet of the local teachers and administrators. This in turn has resulted in low self-esteem and bitterness among many of the educators we interviewed." As to saying that America's schools are to blame for its decline in the global marketplace, "Our research shows that this is simply not true."

A copy of the study found its way into the hands of the *Albuquerque Journal*, which published its findings in September 1991. Energy secretary Watkins issued an immediate repudiation of the study, reiterating his absolute support of the goals of *America 2000*, including the training of more scientists and mathematicians. Professor Tanner points to the sad irony that, while Watkins was calling for more scientists, his own department was operating an alternative teacher-certification program in which unemployed scientists, mathematicians and technicians were being certified as teachers without having to complete a standard teacher-education program.

FALSE SOLUTION

What is the possible explanation? How is it that both Canada and the United States do not accept the discrepancy between the myth of skills shortage and, at the very least, the lack of evidence that such a shortage exists? Why has the Clinton administration shown no interest in the Sandia report and is instead endorsing many of the fundamental principles of *America 2000* in his own education project, *Goals 2000*? Why has the Canadian Council of Ministers of Education placed so much emphasis on school–business "partnerships" when corporate Canada has given back so little to children?

One possible explanation is offered by Tanner: "The negative portrayal of public education has become so ingrained in the culture of social science research and in the media that educators at all levels, from the local school to the U.S. Department of Education, have come to accept this portrayal as reality—to the extent that any really positive research findings are deemed unbelievable." With time, says Tanner, the "facts will kick."

While this theory no doubt helps to explain why so many media commentators, politicians and ordinary people with no particular beef against the education system have bought into the education-reform argument, it does not explain why the argument was put out so forcefully in the first place against all proof.

Jonathan Weisman, who has covered education and business extensively for the Alameda newspaper group in California, holds that big business and its ideological allies haven't the courage to face up to their own problems. Instead, they have indulged in dangerous scapegoating. "What is emerging is a picture of corporate America hiding behind the presumed faults of the education system. The education-reform movement has largely accepted this rhetoric about an inadequate work force and has argued for educational improvement on economic grounds. In so doing, however, reformers have let business off the hook and have gotten themselves hopelessly lost."[18]

Adds Alex Molnar, professor of education at the University of Wisconsin, "Ideologically, it is important for business that public institutions be blamed for the failure of the American economy. It takes the focus off American business and industry for its failure to provide jobs for American workers."[19]

These analysts are just two of a number of critics who say that North American business refuses to redesign production processes to improve productivity through higher skill requirements because it would necessitate paying for them. Instead, business has taken the easy route of downsizing, extracting wage concessions and moving production—skills and all—off-shore. A

1991 survey of American businesses by Louis Harris and Associates found that no more than 25% of the companies studied had made "major changes" to their organizations to adapt to the changed calibre of recent graduates. In spite of their repeated calls for schools to turn out more highly skilled graduates, most corporations are not using even those currently available.

Instead, companies are using marginally skilled workers in North America and outside. Weisman points to a Stanford University study of four successful high-tech companies in California's Silicon Valley. Contrary to the rhetoric of escalating skill requirements, workers were largely isolated from tasks that were deemed too difficult or complex. Perhaps the most striking of their findings was "the low levels of basic skills that are required for successful performance.... We did not observe any skill requirement that could not be achieved with a solid eighth-grade education. Although we have heard stories of how assembly workers need higher-level algebra, sampling, and probability skills to perform adequately on their jobs, we did not observe any requirements approaching this level."[20]

Certainly, thousands of companies are finding it profitable and productive to set up state-of-the-art plants in the free trade zones of Mexico, using few skilled workers. Business guru and university professor Peter Drucker says that it takes three years for a Maquiladora plant to attain the labour productivity of a well-run U.S. or Japanese plant. Dr. Mitsuru Misawa, head of the foreign-investment department of the Industrial Bank of Japan says that labour productivity in the Maquiladoras is higher than that of the United States, as is the quality of the products.

The fact is, it takes a relatively small number of highly skilled engineers and executives to manage a labour force that can be largely unskilled. Therefore, there appears to be little inclination on the part of North American transnationals to slow their transfer of production to developing countries, where the labour force is both unskilled and very young.

Why then do they continue to demand more skilled workers at home? Why, if they seem unwilling or unable to take in the very workforce they have been demanding, are they calling for the overhaul of the education system?

In the United States, deep divisions have long existed in both the economic and educational life of Americans. Demanding reform based on the skills shortage theory takes energy and attention away from the real problems of American schools—those identified by the Sandia study. Asking for more trained scientists and engineers evades the real problems—the profound injustices that divide America along class and race lines—that would require fundamental reform. Demanding a more educated élite serves only to reinforce the economic divisions now present in the American system.

Education writer Stan Karp says the corporate-based American economy "has no real need for universally effective schooling for all. There's no economic need in a profit-driven system for equity claims on educational resources, or for open admission to college, or for reversing the shrinking number of minority teachers, or for empowering teachers and parents in local school governance councils or the many other progressive reform options available. National education policy could be used as a lever for democratic renewal, for increasing the power of ordinary citizens, for expanding the importance of locally-based community institutions, and uniting a diverse population in a much more active, participatory civic life."

Instead, current education demands echo free-market values: "increasing inequality and class polarization, slavish devotion to making government policy serve corporate aims, and retreat from long-standing federal efforts to mitigate, however inadequately, racial and social injustice in favour of privatized social services."[21]

Granted, Canada does not have the degree of class, regional or racial inequities found in the United States, and any analysis must recognize our differences. Canada was founded on a different set of operating principles, and the corporation was never held up as the sole model of appropriate social replication. The concept of equity in education, for students and provinces, was fundamental. As a result, according to the Canadian Teachers' Federation, the Canadian province with the lowest level of spending per pupil for elementary and secondary education spends over two-thirds of that spent by the highest spending province. The lowest spending state, however, spends only one-third of that of the highest spending state. Similarly, the pupil-teacher ratio varies widely in the United States, but very little in Canada.

Historically, Canadian educators have held that our schools should not operate as if they were corporations, because their mandate is to educate all children, not a selective few. Unlike business, schools don't have the luxury of choosing among potential students those they might want to teach. It must take all students in the district, regardless of ability, family problems or income level.

However, Canada's social structure is less different from that of the United States with every passing day. Deficit-fighting governments are cutting deeply into social spending, and Canada is producing an entrenched underclass. The transnationals are blurring or erasing national sovereignty lines, and the rhetoric calling for business to rescue a failing education system is remarkably similar. If it succeeds our education system will inevitably come to mirror that of our southern neighbour.

For big business in both the United States and Canada, creating a false crisis—that the unemployed are at fault for their status because they are not properly trained—has led to a false solution. Blame education for our economic ills, and the social and economic policies that are failing our young can be left intact.

MYTH #3: BIG BUSINESS IS CREATING HIGHLY SKILLED JOBS

We are all swimming in the global labour pool.
RICHARD BARNET

THE COROLLARY OF THE MYTH THAT OUR STUDENTS LACK SKILLS IS another myth: if we just teach the right things in the right way, and turn out the students companies are looking for, business will settle here. Good jobs will come back and new ones will be created in Canada.

While it is easy to find many examples of business criticizing education's "failures," it is much more difficult to find concrete promises of real jobs by the corporate community. In fact, most companies either boast of higher productivity based on permanently "restructured" and "downsized" workforces, or openly acknowledge that, to grow in the new economy, they must concentrate on locations outside Canada. Perhaps this is because, more than any sector, big business knows the truth.

The structure of work and the distribution of jobs have

changed forever with the creation of a global economy. The world is experiencing a watershed economic transformation as great as the industrial and agricultural revolutions. It is characterized by the transfer of economic power from nation-states to giant transnational corporations who operate outside of national law; the creation of huge competitive trade blocs; and an emerging global workforce, in which workers everywhere directly compete with one another.

Transnational corporations now control one-third of the world's private-sector productive assets, conduct over 80% of the world's trade, and control 80% of the world's land cultivated for export-oriented crops.[1] Of the world's hundred leading economies, forty-seven are transnational corporations. Almost three-quarters of the world's nations have smaller economies than do major companies. Ford's economy is bigger than Saudi Arabia's and Norway's. Philip Morris's annual sales exceed New Zealand's gross domestic product.[2] This situation has profound implications for democracy and the future of government as we have understood it.

Transnationals have a head office in one country, but production is scattered in many Third World nations, with tax shelters, administrative offices, and research in still other places. They seek a "world without borders," a euphemism for a tightly controlled corporate system in which they do not have to consider the effect of their actions or decisions on any country, nor are they in any way accountable to its population. Government regulations that benefit the citizenry are a direct threat to transnational growth and independence.

More than 90% of transnationals have their headquarters in the developed world; during the last several years, however, these companies have sharply decreased their investments in the north, transferring job production to the south, to countries that can't afford the labour, environmental or health and safety standards of the developed world.

A GLOBAL LABOUR POOL

In so doing, they are creating a global pool of workers chasing fewer jobs in high-stakes competition. "As the organization of the world's work shifts, more and more of us, from wastebasket emptiers to CEOs of multinational corporations, are waking up to the fact that we are all swimming in the global labour pool," says renowned Washington-based writer Richard Barnet.[3]

According to the International Labour Organization, 30% of the world's labour force is either unemployed or severely underemployed. More than 820 million workers do not earn a subsistence wage. The ranks of human beings not needed or wanted to create the goods or services that the world can afford are growing so fast as to threaten not only global economic growth, but the capitalist system itself.

An estimated 47 million job seekers enter the already overcrowded labour market every year. Within the next twenty years in the underdeveloped world alone, more than 750 million men and women will reach the legal working age and join the unemployed or underemployed. Automation, subcontracting, the increased use of temporary workers, de-unionization and the transfer of production to low-wage locations are creating systemic unemployment in the developed world as well. Between 1979 and 1992, the Fortune 500 companies laid off 4.4 million workers.

Joseph Bower, professor of business administration at Harvard University, says, "Companies are beginning to recognize that they can operate more productively with better work environments for all of their people if they have as many as a third fewer employees. . . . The major political consequence is significant loss of high-paying middle management and technical jobs, as well as a reduction of entry level jobs for young people."[4]

This restructuring is not, as corporate CEOs would have us believe, in order to survive a harsh economic climate. These are deliberate policy and strategic decisions being taken in the corporate boardrooms of the world's transnationals. Companies and their "transformational managers" are rewarded for aggressively and unsentimentally streamlining their workforces, driving workers to produce more with less, shedding national allegiances, evading regulation, forcing countries to drop import restrictions and relocating production where the workers are docile. Jobs are not being "lost" in the First World. They are being shifted to the Third.

The ten largest companies in the United States eliminated 13% of their workers since the recovery began. Procter & Gamble's "Strengthening Global Effectiveness" strategy will shift 10,000 American jobs off-shore. AT&T has cut 25,000 jobs and is threatening to replace 6000 American operators with automated telephone-answering equipment. Bristol-Myers laid off 7200 workers in the last two years to "align its businesses with the changes taking place in the global marketplace and to improve its overall competitiveness." IBM reduced its workforce by over 75,000 from 1986 to 1992.[5] Kodak has moved 20,000 North American jobs off-shore, Philips has cut 40,000 jobs in three years, Exxon has "downsized" by 100,000 since 1990.

American Express, Northern Telecom, Boeing, Xerox, AMR and hundreds more have dramatically met the future with a new face. A recent survey by the American Management Association of 8,000 of its members found that they reduced their staffs in 1991–92 by just under 10%, and in 1992–93, by over 10%.[6] Half of all U.S.-based companies have trimmed their workforces by 10% every year since 1988. Since 1979, the United States has lost 3 million manufacturing jobs.

In some cases, the workforce of a corporation is reduced because the company contracts to outside and/or offshore companies, allowing them to hire non-unionized workers, pay no benefits, assume no pension responsibilities and cut the costs of human resource management. In other cases, the jobs are being directly transferred to the company's plants in low-wage countries. The Big Three North American automakers—General Motors, Ford

Motor and Chrysler Corp.—have cut thousands of jobs in Canada and the United States and expanded in Mexico, where auto production has more than doubled during the past five years. More than 100,000 Mexicans now work in auto parts and assembly plants.[7] Together, the Big Three have sixty parts and vehicle-assembly plants in Mexico and 150 suppliers.

GM derives five times more revenue from Canada, yet it employs 55% more people in Mexico. The reason is simple: the average wages and benefits at a GM–owned facility in Mexico are about 10% of those in the United States, little more than was earned by the first American Ford workers in 1914. In 1987, 68% of the company's 160 automotive components plants were in the United States and Canada, but in 1994, only 48% were located in these countries. J.T. Battenberg, a Ford vice-president, boasts that the change has resulted in dramatic productivity gains and increased annual profits of $1 billion. "We're continuing to move our manufacturing footprint out of the U.S."[8]

Canada's Northern Telecom now has its corporate headquarters in Washington. During the last decade, Northern has shifted thousands of jobs out of Canada, locating production in non-union countries such as Malaysia, Turkey and Brazil or U.S. states, such as Tennessee, North Carolina or Georgia, where worker rights are dramatically inferior to Canada's. Although the company's total global workforce has grown by over 80% in the last decade, unionized jobs have been cut in half.[9]

BLEAK FUTURES

What does this mean for the future of work and workers? It is clear that in the northern countries, millions of young people are being trained for jobs that don't or won't exist where they live. A U.S. Labor Department study released in 1992 reported that 30% of each crop of graduates between now and 2005 will become unemployed. "Training for niches that will not exist is a recipe for replicating the frustration and social tensions that have been commonplace in Third World countries that produce an overabundance of gifted and skilled human beings," writes Barnet.

The myth of free-market economics is that the north will export the dirty, labour-intensive, "bad" jobs and keep the glamorous, high-skilled, high-tech and well-paid jobs; yet the developing countries have just as much talent as we do and are capable of training highly qualified workers, who will work for a fraction of First World wages.

And there is no shortage of these young people. In Mexico alone, 1 million young workers enter the job market every year. In a country with 50% unemployment, it will be a long, long time before they can start to make wage demands on the transnationals who have moved there specifically to take advantage of their situation.

Indeed, "good" North American jobs are being replaced by service-sector jobs paying lower wages. Retail giant Wal-Mart created more U.S. jobs in the first 30 months of the economic "recovery" than any other American company: it pays between $5 and $9 an hour. In 1993, manufacturing shed 255,000 American jobs; the low-wage restaurant industry added 294,000. One study found that of 2,000 workers let go by RJR Nabisco, 72% found new jobs, but at average wages of 47% of their previous pay.

Sixty per cent of American jobs created in the first half of 1993 were part-time; 28% of all jobs created since the recession bottomed out were at temporary help agencies.[10] Millions of the American "working poor" live in states where welfare is almost non-existent and in which citizens work under conditions that would be unacceptable in Canada or Europe.

Ontario labour negotiator Andre Beckerman says North America is allowing its workforce to split: "One part consists of a diminishing employed 'élite' of relatively well-educated and technologically well-trained workers who will continue to enjoy an affluent lifestyle. The other consists of a rapidly growing underclass of less educated, less skilled workers who depend on minimum wage 'McJobs.' This second group is only one small step away from those who have no work at all, nor any prospects of employment."

Writer Walter Russell Mead adds that the new corporate structure is creating an underclass in every country of the First World and an élite class in the Third World. The developed and developing worlds will not so much disappear as mingle, as rich and poor live beside each other everywhere. "There will be more people in Mexico and India who live like Americans of the upper-middle class; on the other hand, there will be more—many more—people in the United States who live like the slum dwellers of Mexico City and Calcutta."[11]

Which helps to explain the growth in the American economy of the "garrison economy" Samuel Bowles, David Gordon and Thomas Weisskopf developed in a study on the rise of security-related employment.[12] They defined and traced two categories of employment they believe to be essential in a society with social unrest and high unemployment—guard labour and threat labour. Guard labour includes the enforcers necessary to maintain order: workplace supervisors, police, judicial and corrections employees, private security personnel, the armed forces, civilian defence employees, and the producers of military and domestic security equipment. Threat labour includes the reserve army of unemployed and discouraged workers whose silent presence helps maintain discipline among those lucky enough to have a job.

The study found that the increase in guard and threat labour accounted for more than 60% of the total increase in employment in the United States during the 1980s. As the country becomes more violent and stability more uncertain, security services are growing apace. During the last twenty years, the rate of unionization of the U.S workforce has fallen by more than half—in the private sector, from 35 to 10%.[13] The jobs that do exist are less stable and few workers now perceive their work to be permanent.

And yet unemployment in the United States, which is slightly more than half our rate, is still manageable. In fact, it is close to the generally accepted definition of full employment.

JOBS IN CANADA

Between 1984 and 1988, 1.3 million jobs were created in Canada; the unemployment rate stood at 7.5%. During the next four and a half years, there was a net job loss of 300,000 jobs. Today, the unemployment rate stands at about 11%—1.6 million Canadians. If we add to these numbers those who have given up looking for work and those who are able to get only part-time work, the rate stands at 20%. Canada has lost one-quarter of its manufacturing jobs—almost four times the rate of manufacturing job loss in the United States.

The news is even bleaker for Canada's young people. Statistics Canada's most recent year-end review reports that they have been frozen out of a shrunken job market and are the biggest losers of the recession. There were 500,000 fewer young persons with jobs in 1994 than before the recession, the agency reported, and young people were not touched by the slight recovery experienced by some other sectors of society.[14]

An analysis of the short- and long-term employment trends in Canada produces some disturbing results: many of the jobs lost in the last five years are permanent losses; high unemployment will be long-term; part-time employment is growing; full-time employment is down; wages are stagnating or dropping; and there is little evidence that Canada is creating the new, high-value, knowledge-intensive jobs that were to be our reward for enduring open markets, free trade, deregulation and privatization.

Let's take these one at a time. The major cause of lost manufacturing jobs in recent years has been plant closures. Canadian subsidiaries are being closed by American companies consolidating production in the United States or Mexico. Canadian companies have moved off-shore to escape taxes, wage laws and regulations. The companies have moved away and are not coming back.

The federal government does not monitor factory relocation, but others do. The *Wall Street Journal* reported that "since the (Canada-U.S.) free trade treaty went into effect, between 400 and 700 Canadian businesses have set up shop in Buffalo." A Conference Board survey of major U.S.- and Canadian-owned manufacturing and resource corporations found that most have been shutting down some production in Canada and are concentrating investment in the United States.[15] A 1992 survey by the American Management Association of 200 of its U.S.-owned member companies with affiliates in Canada and Mexico found that they plan to expand employment in their Mexican operations by 13.7% during the next three years, 3.3% in the United States and only 0.7% in Canada. Corporations with Canadian subsidiaries employing more than one hundred workers actually plan to reduce their Canadian workforce by 2%.

When the recession of the early 1980s ended, the factories reopened and the jobs came back. The result of the current recession, however, is permanent job loss. The government of Ontario has documented 580 closures of major production facilities between January 1989 and August 1993: 481 were permanent. Permanent closures accounted for 65% of all layoffs during this period, compared to less than one-quarter during the 1981–82 recession.

The myth that big business is creating highly skilled jobs is not backed up anywhere. No forecasts by any major think tank or research institute, including those ideologically sympathetic to business, predict any improvement in the employment figures for the next decade. A 1993 study by Statistics Canada found that more Canadians are facing long-term unemployment than ever before. Since the beginning of the recession, the number of workers unemployed for more than a year but still looking for work has more than tripled. More than one in four unemployed workers have been out of work for more than six months.

This is worse than at the peak of the 1981–82 recession, the study confirmed.[16] Our "jobless recovery" is turning into a "jobless economy."

Almost one-third of all workers now hold temporary or part-time jobs. Nearly 60% of the jobs created in 1993 were part-time. At present, almost 1 million people, mainly women, are working part-time because they cannot find full-time jobs. If present trends continue, by the year 2000, half of Canadians will be "contingency" workers. As full-time jobs disappear, Canada is creating its own working poor.

According to both Statistics Canada and the Canadian Labour Congress, even workers who have remained steadily employed have seen virtually no increase in their real wage.[17] The average weekly increase in earnings hit a record low in 1993; average family incomes fell. A study of displaced workers by the Ontario Ministry of Labour found that three years after they were permanently laid off in 1988, 22% were still unemployed. Those who found a job experienced an average pay cut of more than · $2500.

So much for the cheerful predictions of new, high-tech jobs just around the corner. So much for the emergence of a new economy that is competing on the basis of innovation, high productivity and a highly skilled workforce. So much for another myth.

Certainly, there is a need to create high value-added restructuring. Canada, all seem to agree, must shift job emphasis from resource-based and manufacturing to "knowledge intensive" industries. Canada must move out of the sectors vulnerable to low wage competition and develop new industries better suited to a highly advanced workforce.

The trouble is, this is not happening. Workers are not moving from lower to higher skill and wage jobs. Indeed, there is every indication of the opposite. Says the Canadian Labour Congress in a study of jobs available and expected: "The major conclusion is that there are very few signs of widespread 'positive restructuring' in Canadian manufacturing, and that the widely heralded 'new economy' is more myth than reality."[18]

Moreover, Canadians cannot rely on a strong public sector to fuel the economy and provide jobs as we have done through past recessions. Indeed, the current unemployment figure in Canada would be worse if the public sector had not continued to hire during the past several years. Between 1988 and 1992, educational services created 67,100 jobs; health and social services, 49,000; government administration added 32,400. But Canada's public sector entered a formal recession in the spring of 1993, contracting by 0.8%.[19] Provinces have slashed their public services in 1993–94 in unprecedented ways, and the federal government has placed a hiring freeze on the public service and is downsizing all social spending.

CORPORATE COP-OUT

These disturbing statistics present some crucial questions that educators should ask the business community when it charges that Canada's education system is failing: How do you respond to these numbers and predictions on jobs, and the forecasts for high unemployment, particularly for young people? What are you doing to create good jobs for students when they finish school? Why are you so deeply concerned about the education of young people, yet unconcerned that their employment prospects—whatever their education—are bleak? Why are you not as preoccupied with their future as their current training?

In fact, why does Canada's business community not consider high unemployment to be a negative thing? No corporate voices objected when the former Conservative government refused to implement an adjustment program for workers displaced by the Canada-U.S. Free Trade Agreement or when the current Liberal government refused to implement one for workers displaced by

NAFTA. A 1993 leaked "heavily censored" internal Bank of Canada memo endorsed high unemployment, declaring that reducing Canada's unemployment rate would "take us well below the natural rate" of joblessness.[20]

The reality is that high unemployment keeps up competition for jobs, thus keeping wage demands and inflation down, which is good for business. This helps explain why business leaders are optimistic about the future in Canada when most Canadians are not. A 1993 Conference Board of Canada study found that consumer confidence had plummeted to a three-year low, while business confidence was at a four-year high.

That's easy to explain, says a study by Wood Gundy. The very fears that haunt workers—job insecurity and wage restraint—are fuelling business optimism. "Corporate Canada is brimming with optimism, buoyed by explosive earnings and booming exports. At the same time, household Canada is despondent, brooding over painful tax increases and a jobless recovery. . . . Soaring productivity has breathed new life into corporate profits and exports, but it's also meant that household employment has enjoyed little of the benefit of an expanding economy."[21]

Thus, the Organization for Economic Co-operation and Development (OECD) predicts that Canada's economic growth will lead the world in 1994–95, but the jobless figures won't change. "The growth will reflect the reform of Canada's social programs, the reduction of farm subsidies and the overhaul of our health-care system."[22] In other words, the growth will be corporate and export-led, fuelled by lower labour and social costs for business as life becomes harsher for most Canadians.

But Canada is less and less on corporate minds; they are looking to the U.S. market, not the domestic market, for sales. Production planning is bypassing Canada. Not surprisingly, then, the Canadian Manufacturers' Association recently reported that manufacturing for domestic consumption in Canada had fallen by more than 26% between 1989 and 1994. And manufacturers in

Canada invest less in machinery, equipment, worker training, research and development than any other country in the OECD.

It is against this backdrop that business demands for structural change in how and what we teach young people must be considered. Simply put, if we knowingly train young workers for jobs that don't exist, i.e., if we train a glut of young people for the jobs available, knowing that the resulting competition will drive down wages and create conditions that may be good for business, but not for anyone else, we are sowing the seeds of great social unrest.

Economic policies of the last decade in Canada have unlinked the interests of big business from the interests of other Canadians. To be sure, there are conscientious business leaders who are good corporate citizens of Canada, but they have been placed at a disadvantage by the new rules that favour those most ruthless.

Companies can no longer discriminate by buying from Canadian suppliers. They can no longer be forced to employ Canadians to sell or produce their products here. American corporations operating in Canada no longer have to keep an office or plant here. They don't have to keep their technology here, even if it was developed in Canada at public expense. They are free to make production-location and research-and-development decisions based strictly on profits, without regard for the social fallout of their choices on their Canadian workers or the Canadian taxpayer, who is left to pay for it.

With rare exceptions, these business interests are the same powers who are dictating to the nation's educators. How have they come by this right? A business community with the right to influence education would be a business community that had proven itself to be a social partner in Canadian life. It would be one deeply concerned about projected high unemployment among the young. It would be developing a full-employment strategy, not seeking every available vehicle to cut costs, slash employment and move work away from the country. It would be working to protect social programs and would be deeply concerned about the effects of automation instead of replacing workers with robots as fast as it can.

Such a business community would know that workers making better pay put money back into and stabilize the economy; it would therefore work hand in hand with organized labour, not moving its production to non-unionized foreign sites. A business community with the right to influence our schools would be working through the United Nations and other international agencies to form an international code of conduct for transnational corporations, not allowing the law of the jungle to regulate people.

Finally, a business community that had earned the right to profoundly influence the future of our young would not be training them to fit into a system of dog-eat-dog competitiveness that will work against their own interests and those of their families and communities.

PART TWO:
THE ARMIES OF THE RIGHT

WHAT DOES BUSINESS
REALLY WANT?

His first day job is in kindergarten.

ADVERTISEMENT FOR MODERN TALKING PICTURES SERVICE,

MADISON AVENUE "EDUCATIONAL SERVICE" COMPANY

A GRADE NINE STUDENT IN A CALIFORNIA HIGH SCHOOL FLICKS OFF the light. NBC *Newshour* music fills the room. Award-winning former NBC anchor Jim Hartz appears: "We've made hasty conclusions about what is good for the environment," Hartz intones, sitting in what appears to be a newsroom. "We're here to explore the facts." The "facts" he gives the students are that plastics are ecologically "ideal material"—to produce, recycle, burn or toss in landfills. "The experts all agree that polystyrene plastics [Styrofoam] rate well on environmental criteria." Students get the point and, in interviews after watching the video, praise its "caring" nature. But most students miss the minuscule copyright notice. *Polystyrene, Plastics and the Environment* is owned, produced and distributed free of charge to schools by Mobil Corporation, one of the world's largest manufacturers of plastics.[1]

What does big business want with our schools? Undoubtedly many believers in the business ideology entered this controversy to deflect blame for corporate North America's shortcomings and mistakes, or from a desire not to allow the questions of equality and social justice to dominate the debate on education. But such apologists and social conservatives do not account for the sustained growing interest in our young. Why is business preoccupied with education, after neglecting it so long? What's in it for them?

Some corporate leaders may have a personal sense of philanthropy to the community or the less privileged, but the business of business is to make money. It is not in a business leader's interest to challenge a system under which so few can earn so much and give back so little.

Hints of what business wants with schools can be found in *Partners in Education*, describing the mutual benefits of school-business partnerships. It is published by the Coquitlam, British Columbia, school district and suggests schools "decorate company offices for the holidays.... Invite media to events to recognize partners.... Have students or teachers help employees brush up on skills.... Help at business seminars passing out information and brochures.... Conduct a Business Appreciation Day.... Conduct a research project for the partner.... Assist with activities for children at a company Christmas/Easter party.... Publish articles on the partner in the school newsletter.... Invite a CEO to be 'principal for a day'."

In return, business can "help to write grants to fund school projects.... Offer marketing, public relations, computer or other consulting to school board or school.... Conduct mock job interviews.... Teach Junior Achievement classes.... Provide speakers for graduation assemblies.... Conduct classes at the community partner's site, addressing such topics as the importance of entrepreneurial skills and labour market trends.... Provide summer jobs for teachers."

In other words, business gets access to free student labour, free local advertising and public relations from the school, the opportunity to influence curriculum and student attitudes and the chance to bid on school contracts and give a teacher a "real job." Not bad.

North America's corporations have three fundamental goals for their preoccupation with and investment in North America's schools. The first is to secure the ideological allegiance of young people to a free-market world view on issues of the environment, corporate rights and the role of government. The second is to gain market access to the hearts and minds of young consumers and to lucrative contracts in the education industry. The third is to transform schools into training centres producing a workforce suited to the needs of transnational corporations.

GOAL ONE: IDEOLOGICAL ALLEGIANCE

As government debt and unemployment have grown over the last decade, so too has the debate on solutions and the role of governments. Competing economic models, often characterized simplistically as "job creation" versus "deficit reduction," are now part of our national debate, as they are all over the world. The position of the schools in this debate is to expose students to an array of economic models and present them with the critical faculties to assess different solutions and competing ideological positions.

However, the system's ability to remain impartial and open-minded has been compromised as cash-starved schools all over North America have accepted corporate donations in money and materials. From fast-food to energy to health, corporations are peddling their perspectives and viewpoints through "resource" materials in the schools. What is, in effect, a special-interest perspective is presented as fact, and when it is taught in the classroom, it has the added weight of the system to give it legitimacy. Other perspectives on the economy—or the environment, consumers' rights and other issues—do not have the same access. Non-profit groups cannot compete financially with big business. Offered as objective analysis, this ideologically biased teaching is compromising teacher, school and system.

Educator Alex Molnar says, "Business provides speakers and materials to explain how our market economy works, implicitly or explicitly representing free enterprise theory as some sort of natural law of economics. This is desirable from a corporate point of view because it helps to ensure that public discussions of economic policy and business practices will stay within narrow technical boundaries. But it undermines the school's ability to help students learn to think critically about economic issues and smacks of the kind of indoctrination we so rightly criticize in totalitarian states."

When a corporation sponsors a lunch program, provides educational materials or backs literacy classes, it becomes very difficult for the school to avoid complementary business-oriented economics curricula. When an oil company sponsors a school conference on the environment, the likelihood of any serious dialogue on the oil sector's role in energy depletion or oil spills is reduced. If this oil company then provides the school with a set of state-of-the-art texts and videos on the environment—supplies most schools could never acquire with public money—the material becomes a core teaching resource of that school.

What are the educators of the Toronto Board of Education likely to teach their students about the nutrition value of Pepsi, or the corporation's increasingly controversial international reputation regarding the marketing of its product to Third World children, now that Pepsi has been given exclusive rights to its vending business? Toronto teacher Gord Ekelund asks, "Will a clothing manufacturer with factories in Guatemala be willing to sponsor a fashion design program in a high school where members of the history department have put together a unit of studies dealing with the obscene environmental and labour practices in the Maquila zones of Mexico and Central America?" [2]

The problem grows when a board of education becomes dependent on corporate sponsorship for a significant portion of its budget, "bartering ethics for donations for jobs." It grows again when the companies want to sponsor their version of current issues in the schools. Nowhere is this more evident than in the private sponsorship of environmental "education." Corporations are keenly aware that this generation of young people is more focused on pollution and wildlife devastation, and corporate polluters are flooding schools with materials that minimize environmental damage.

A Dow Chemical-sponsored video, *Traces of Today*, created in conjunction with an education marketing company, Modern Talking Pictures Service, claims "scientific studies and practical experience around the world has shown that incinerators are an environmentally safe method for disposing combustible material, including plastics." Modern, which claims to reach more than 35 million students a year, also markets other corporate videos: Procter & Gamble's *Planet Patrol*, Johnson Wax on the ozone layer, the American Coal Foundation, on—you guessed it—coal and the environment, and many others. Exxon has designed an elaborate package of lab experiments, tests and videos to teach children how to "make responsible energy choices." Of 370 pages of lessons and information, only 15 deal with the environment and these "prove" that big business is dealing responsibly with the problem.

A Fairfield, Connecticut company, Lifetime Learning Systems (LLS), specializes in the creation and marketing of corporate-sponsored "educational programs"; their materials have reached more than 2 million teachers. LLS created a school program for a state utilities company, whose objective was to "re-educate consumers to the realities of the energy crisis and increase public support for nuclear power development." LLS boasts that the company surveyed participants after the project was completed and was pleased to report that opinions shifted an average of 20% in favour of the utilities' position.

These companies are doing more than single-issue propaganda, however. With rare exceptions, they hold a free-market world view and want the next generation to share it. They want students to buy into the culture of competitiveness: nations must liberalize their trading systems; sell off public assets; deregulate their markets, including telecommunications, energy and transportation; and generally eliminate the barriers to the free movement of capital.

In such a system, nation-states, institutions and social structures become virtually obsolete; social programs are an inhibitor of the entrepreneurial spirit and natural creativity. Preaching the culture of competitiveness in the schools promotes this version of capitalism and sets out to undermine, without being too blatant, values of co-operation, equality and collective rights.

Teaching students to compete prepares them for the dog-eat-dog environment of the global economy, in which they will compete against one another for scarce jobs. Teaching them to respond to the external motivation of testing equips them to respond to the external motivation of a corporate mission and management structure. Teaching children one world view of the economy trains them to accept that corporate world without question. Teaching the values of individual free enterprise prepares the students to adopt corporate loyalty—mission, uniform, company song, corporate culture and all—over loyalty to group, class, country or union.

In such an environment a student learns that when the boy seated next to her drops out of school, he is solely responsible for the decision. In the words of the Conference Board of Canada, he has "apparently ignor[ed] the tremendous cost to himself and society."[3] What happens to him is of no concern to her. She is learning to blame the unemployed for their condition from the safety of a job. Her lack of concern is echoed by economists who describe the problems of an "overemployed economy," in their justification of a high rate of unemployment. She will believe, as she walks past the food banks, that "those people," like the boy in her class, simply made the wrong choices.

GOAL TWO: GAINING ACCESS TO NEW MARKETS

Schoolchildren are the largest untapped consumer market in our society; the public-education system is the largest public enterprise still to be privatized.

The recent interest in children age twelve and under as a market has followed an explosion in spending on and by them in recent years. Family patterns and lifestyles are changing: purchasing decisions once made by parents alone are increasingly made by families together or children alone. In the United States, the direct income of children is $9 billion a year, and children age twelve and under now annually influence $132 billion in purchases. As a result, advertising to children has taken a dramatic leap.[4]

Commercials are entering our classrooms—sometimes blatantly, on "education" videos; sometimes subtly, on logos that accompany a project or free samples of a product. Children's television was deregulated in the early 1980s to allow product advertising to accompany programs aimed at children. A member of the Federal Communications Commission responsible for the decision said, "Now the marketplace will take care of children." Sure enough, over 85% of children's television programming is now produced by toy companies. Saturday morning cartoons are one long commercial; children as young as two are conscious of brand identification, which they learn from television. Those whose consumer-allegiance is still up for grabs are being targeted; and now, they will not even get away from it at school, where they are particularly vulnerable to manipulative marketing.

Peggy Charren, president of a California-based children's

advocacy group, says, "Kids are getting pitched walking down the hallways, kids are getting pitched eating lunch, kids are getting pitched sitting in the classroom."

"THEY'RE READY TO SPEND AND WE REACH THEM!!" shouts a LLS industry advertisement. "Kids spend 40% of each day in the classroom where traditional advertising can't reach them. Now YOU CAN ENTER THE CLASSROOM through custom-made learning materials created with your specific marketing objectives in mind." Consumer Kids, a two-day workshop in Toronto, offered corporate executives segments titled "Marketing in the School System" and "How to Grow Your Customers from Childhood."

Modern Talking Pictures says, "We can help you deliver a message to his classroom that he'll carry into young adulthood. If he's in your target market, call us. . . . Modern product sampling can help you develop brand loyalty even before she becomes a serious shopper. To put your product in her hands, call us. . . ."[5]

The goals of brand identification and product loyalty are particularly offensive—and convincing—when the companies cloak their promotion in some form of educational good. McDonald's sponsors a school program on nutrition in which the Big Mac represents all four food groups (the vegetable component being the exposed lettuce leaf).

Often, the corporate invasion takes the guise of rescuing an impoverished school system no longer able to buy supplies or technical equipment. The company gets to advertise its product to the students in exchange for providing video equipment to the school. It also gets to create and sell other technical equipment, testing programs or curriculum materials to the system. It is not coincidental that the leaders in this business "bail out" of education tend to be major high-tech companies, such as IBM, Xerox, AT&T, Northern Telecom, Kodak, Boeing and General Electric.

The Ontario Federation of Labour's Jim Turk says, "Think for a moment about education more narrowly focused on performance standards, using explicitly competency-based models, stressing national examinations and standardized tests, with intensified math and science emphasis and organizational restructuring for accountability and enhanced productivity. Such an educational system is ripe for a significant increase in the newest technologies and services being peddled by these companies."

Indeed, the education industry in Canada is larger than the mining, forestry, food, beverage, rubber, plastics and clothing industries combined. It employs one in ten Canadians and will grow dramatically as communities see the presence of high-quality educational facilities as a powerful advantage for economic development. [6]

The New American Schools Development Corporation initiative, set up under former president George Bush, earmarked $1 million in start-up grants for private schools in each congressional district. Executives from America's largest corporations were named to head the agency overseeing the project, which was freed from public governance.

The commercialization of the classroom and the corporate intrusion into the education system are working very well. They are producing a generation of children who, as Ralph Nader describes them, are "growing up corporate." They are treated— and often see themselves—as consumers-in-training, pre-workers, future entrepreneurs. Such children ask few questions and do not challenge the culture of competitiveness.

GOAL THREE: RAISING THE FUTURE WORKFORCE

Education psychologist Gerald Bracey commits cultural heresy. He says that North America has too many educated people; that the mantra that "all children can learn" is both meaningless and unrealistic. It is also dangerous, because unrealistic expectations are breeding great social unrest. The real problem is the overproduction of qualified young people for a dramatically shrinking workforce. There is a critical discrepancy between the educational levels that jobs require and the educational level students are acquiring. Using statistics published in *Education Week*, Bracey points out that "over the last fifteen years, the probability of landing in a poor paying job has increased for all levels of education, albeit more steeply for high school dropouts than for those with some college."[7]

However, an overqualified workforce in a shrinking job market gives a great advantage to employers. Jim Turk believes that education has reverted to one of its traditional functions in our society—a way of sorting people. Education is being forced on workers because it is one of the key bases on which employers decide who gets the opportunity to work.

"Whether the job is deskilled or not, the employer can demand qualifications that have little or no correspondence to the requirements of the job. Education, for employers, is a useful means to sort people at a time when there are far more workers than jobs. Any worker who objects to the demand for more and more credentials on the grounds that she can do the work is cast aside in favour of five who comply with the employers' demands." And it is a worker's compliance, more than his education, that is important to employers.

The pressure on employees is great. Not only are fewer expected to produce more, but the competition to win and keep the few precious jobs is intense, particularly as technology replaces workers.

Fast-food giants McDonald's and Burger King are prime examples of the new workplace. Both used to function as labour-intensive, low-tech businesses that employed both high- and low-skilled workers. The bulk of their costs were wages. Both, however, have introduced sophisticated technologies that reorganize work patterns; both are now high-tech workplaces that do not need skilled workers. The companies can hire the least demanding available employees, from teenagers to senior citizens, give them shift- and part-time work, provide minimum training, pay low wages and still produce a consistent product anywhere in the world.

Willard Daggett, head of the New York-based International Center for Leadership and Education, explains that, in an automated hamburger restaurant, you can press buttons to order a hamburger, to specify how you want it done and what you want on it, and get it thirteen seconds later. The laser cookers and information systems that make this possible will eliminate 80% of fast-food jobs in North America in the next five years. The skilled people still employed will be those who know how to run and maintain the new equipment. What happens to the others? That's someone else's problem.

In theory, these few highly skilled workers will receive high wages; however, with such competition, employers can keep wages down even among highly educated workers. As more people become better educated, employers will have a deeper pool from which to choose workers to fill the dwindling number of jobs.

Motorola has instituted academic and technical tests of employees, largely non-essential assessments or training unrelated to the job itself. The company uses the tests to determine pay rates, including downgrading the jobs of seasoned, highly skilled workers. These non–performance-related tests are used as a weapon against the employees and to maintain a sense of insecurity in the workplace that is beneficial to management.

Corporate North America is pressing for a more highly educated workforce in order to effect a workerless economy. Douglas Noble, a highly respected New York-based education activist and writer, says that the celebration of education and skill can go hand-in-hand with the deterioration of work for the vast majority so long as a visible minority reaps the rewards, and the rest strive to be among them.

He points out that this is precisely the situation in Japan, which has been held up as a model by many education reformers. In that country, "lifetime employment" applies to a dwindling core of workers; the peripheral workforce, which makes up about 75% of Japan's labour force, is considered secondary. Says Turk,

"More education without a change in the range and nature of jobs does not create any wealth. It merely shuffles the deck. If everyone in Canada had a Ph.D., we would still have a million and a half unemployed, a million underemployed, and many millions doing boring, mindless, poorly paid jobs. More education for some allows them to displace others, but it does not create new jobs nor increase the overall opportunities for the population as a whole."

Workers and students buy into this model of necessity. They know they face high unemployment, high job insecurity and increased competition for secure jobs; education is a potential competitive advantage. They are encouraged to see education not as part of a whole life, but as an edge in the job search. Our schools are preparing students for this reality by teaching them the values and skills compatible with this perspective.

What are these values and skills? They are best exemplified in the concept known as Total Quality Management, but which goes by many other names, including Quality Circles, Team Skills Program, Workplace Participation, Employee Involvement Team and Japanese Production System. The promise is more worker participation and decision making, enriched job content, replacement of union-management conflict with workplace co-operation to improve service, search for excellence, and create devotion to the company. The goals of TQM, however, are not nearly so worker friendly, although workers are being asked to buy into them.

Trudy Richardson of the United Nurses of Alberta has studied what TQM has done to her province's hospitals, findings that are replicated in studies of similar programs on production lines.[8] The goals include speeded-up production, as both individual workers and work teams become highly competitive; just-in-time production, which demands peak performance at all times, again established through competition; management by stress, which forces workers to produce above capacity; job "restructuring," which means job loss; deskilling, in which professional and skilled jobs are analyzed and broken down into minute tasks, the less skilled of which are given to less skilled workers, thereby reducing the number of skilled jobs; multi-skilling, whereby workers learn one another's tasks, which enables the company to reduce job classifications and lower wages; and the downloading of management tasks with no extra compensation.

As well, TQM seeks to establish a corporate culture that stresses individual responsibility, reduced wages and benefits, increased competition, the acceptance of contracting out and privatization, corporate loyalty, above all, and the erosion of collective bargaining. Canadian Auto Workers' research representative David Robertson describes the General Motors training programs, which even the company calls "cultural training." Interpersonal skills and "employer identification"—unquestioning loyalty to the employer—are given more weight than is technical training at GM and at Northern Telecom, which describes its training program as building "a strong corporate culture which encourages the workforce to accept the company's goals as its own."

Schools are being pressured to train students into this corporate culture, indoctrinating them in individual competitiveness and loyalty to company policy. Many are applying the TQM model to the school. Says Doug Noble: "Above all, high-tech corporate interest in education reform expects a school system that will utilize sophisticated performance measures and standards to sort students and to provide a reliable supply of such adaptable, flexible, loyal, mindful, expendable, 'trainable' workers for the twenty-first century. This, at bottom, underlies the corporate drive to retool education and retool human capital."

THE DISINFORMATION HIGHWAY

To reach young people, as consumers, as future workers, as the social architects of tomorrow, business is looking to the powerful medium-of-choice for kids, high technology. Information is increasingly delivered not by books and teacher lectures but by computers and telecommunications (which are less easily regulated to reflect the consensus standards set by boards, parents and governments). Technology is becoming the way to bypass the system and go directly to students with a message. While this is as true for environmentalists, labour groups and others trying to persuade young people to their view, no other sector will have as much financial access as corporations to ride the highway into the schools.

The now-famous information highway is the current centre of great corporate interest; ownership stakes are very high as speculated profits are astronomical. In Canada, the estimate runs to $100 billion in the next thirty years; in Japan, $500 billion; in the United States, $1 trillion.

There has been a furious merger mania in recent years, uniting telephone, television, computer, video and retail companies in preparation for the explosion of sales opportunities in the next step of the technological revolution. Theoretically, the information highway will give anyone who can afford it access to all information ever produced.

The largest media merger in history recently took place between Bell Atlantic and the cable company TCI. Their combined service is almost half the American market for cable and phone service. MTV, VHI and Nickelodeon are forming an alliance to get into the home-shopping market. They are all owned by Viacom, which owns networks, cable systems, broadcast systems and 800 movie theatres; it has recently taken over Paramount Communications, which owns a movie studio, a major publishing empire and Madison Square Garden.

In Canada, a Quebec company, UBI, formed by the giant Vidéotron cable company and backed by the National Bank of Canada, Hydro-Québec, Loto-Canada, Hearst Corporation, and Canada Post, is planning to wire Quebec. With its takeover of Maclean Hunter, Rogers has become "Canada's undisputed multimedia mogul, controlling a corporate octopus with tentacles that reach into nearly every communications field," says the *Toronto Star*. It will control up to 70% of some cable markets.

Says Mark Silver, CEO of Chatham-based STN, "Nobody is resting. We have a very young and aggressive group here that knows we're in a war and knows that at the end of the day, we had better be the winners."[9]

Stentor is an alliance of our major telephone companies formed to pressure the federal government into deregulating the industry and allowing phone companies access to cable. Only deregulated competition can finance this modern miracle, the company argues, and Stentor wants the public interest, in the form of government control, out of the way. Federal industry minister John Manley has hand-picked an advisory committee, which will advise him in private. Community-television worker Mark Surman wonders why the public will have no say in this process. "Although it may be inevitable that future information systems will take on a commercial bias, this does not mean that our government should invite the big information providers behind closed doors for a 'let's divide up the turf' party."[10]

The phone and cable companies are urgently lobbying governments all over North America to allow private corporations to build the system, and their PR firms are working overtime to convince the media and educators of its glories. But there are urgent questions of control. What will happen to Canadian culture and public broadcasting if private corporations control a deregulated broadcast medium? Toronto writer and filmmaker Fred Bacher says, "When you consider the income needed to turn a profit from the size of the highway's investment, you must conclude that whoever wins control of it must pave its surface with absolute cynicism: the most streamlined and cheapest of commercial programs will be its asphalt."[11] U.S. TV mogul Barry Diller is enthusiastic: "I have seen the future, and it is retail."

For educators, there will be additional pressure to open up the education system to the "products" of the information highway. Furthermore, the exclusive nature of this vision of high technology will widen the gap between those who can afford these educational opportunities and those who can't. Despite our society using technology to deskill workers and put people out of work, many school boards are racing to establish partnerships with the very corporations who will not be hiring their students. These include the phone and computer companies behind the information highway, such as IBM, Bell and UNITEL.

Working with Stentor and UNITEL, the Canadian School Boards Association, Canadian Home and School and Parent-Teacher Federation, the Canadian Association of School Administrators and the Canadian Teachers' Federation are urging the federal government to use funds from the national infrastructure program —a fund to create jobs for the unemployed—to link Canada's schools to the information highway. Their ad says: "Access to electronic networks will give our kids a strategic advantage in a competitive information-based economy."[12] George Bush couldn't have said it better.

A *Globe and Mail* supplement on the information highway contains a warning to teachers, who are too "slow" to embrace technology in the classroom. "One of the most important elements that is needed in order to prepare the Canadian education system for the Information Highway is a major mind shift. Everyone within the education system has to be made to realize the importance of both the Highway and of his own individual role in preparing his students for the future.

"According to [general manager of the Information Highway Division of Canada for Anderson Consulting] Tom Nealey, in order to be truly effective, this direction has to come from the top down. 'Someone has to take a look at how to manage that $55.5 billion [the amount Canadians are spending on education every year], to find out what kind of stake Canada is willing to drive into the ground in order to set the goal for integrating this technology into education,' he says. 'We're a little fuzzy at the top level, the level of the prime minister and his ministers. We need to take a stand and give guidance from the top down. It's not enough for one school board to team up with IBM.'"[13]

The issue is one of control. Technology is a neutral tool. It will serve the interests of those who design and command it.

The pressure for our schools to join the highway is coming from the very corporations who are also lobbying to remove it from the public domain and to turn it into a giant electronic retail service. Once the technology is privatized, it will be next to impossible to force accountability of content. Those who would profit from children will be one step closer to their goal.

Hijacking a Culture

Unless we make a clear choice to change our course, we may find ourselves drifting to where we don't want to go.

LINDA MCQUAIG

BIG BUSINESS INTEREST IN OUR SCHOOLS IS SYMBOLIC OF THE AMERIcanization of Canadian education, which in turn is part of a major current transformation of Canadian economic, social and cultural life. It comes as no surprise to anyone who has witnessed the transformation of the workplace and the street. Canada is experiencing an unprecedented corporate-led assault on the sense of collective responsibility upon which the country was founded.

All institutions are under intense pressure to operate as if they were a business. The corporate model, based on head-to-head competition and survival of the fittest, is the prototype for all government and, more recently, educational institutions. As our countries merge, Canada finds itself adopting American-style individualism, unabashed entrepreneurialism and a culture of competitiveness.

CONTINENTAL DRIFT

During the last decade, Canada has fundamentally realigned its orientation from east-west to north-south, in essence becoming part of a new borderless North American economy. The resulting harmonization can be seen everywhere. To stay alive, Canadian business must export, and most companies are massively restructuring to serve a North American, not a Canadian, market. Thousands are moving production and jobs to the United States to be nearer the large centres of population and to cash in on low wages and anti-union states.

Virtually all control over foreign investment in Canada has been removed, and thousands of Canadian enterprises have been taken over by American and other transnationals, who often shut down production and convert the Canadian arm to a warehouse or marketing division. Canada is now seen by North American corporations, whether Canadian-based or not, as another "state," about the market size of California.

The world's largest retailer, and America's third largest corporation, Wal-Mart, has invaded the Canadian market with a vengeance, swallowing Woolco stores in one gulp. Deregulation in the telecommunications industry has opened the door to the same invasion of U.S. firms; as many as eighty companies, including AT&T, and all the major American competitors, have set up shop to lease phone circuits at deep discounts, bringing to Canada the same cutthroat competition, consumer confusion and industry layoffs that characterize the system in the United States that was deregulated a decade ago.

Our tax structure is being adapted to the reality of a continental, indeed global, economy in which capital can move across borders as if they don't exist. The federal government is contracting out many operations formerly handled by the public service, and competition for these contracts must now be open to American companies. One of the last acts of the Mulroney government was to award the contract to computerize the entire delivery system of Family Allowance, Canada Pension and Old Age Pension cheques to a Texas-based transnational formerly owned by Ross Perot.

The federal government is no longer using a Canadian computer reservation system nor a Canadian credit system for travel. When our public servants and politicians travel, they use the American Airlines system to make their plans and pay for it with American Express. Canadian Airlines has been "rescued" by American Airlines. Canadian National is now CN North American. Canadian Pacific's new logo merges Canadian and American flags.

Canadian culture takes up less air and screen time than ever. Protections have been eliminated steadily—postal rates for Canadian magazines, promised film distribution regulation, tax credits for Canadian films, legislation to keep Canadian book publishing companies in Canadian control. The Liberal government disgracefully permitted the sale of educational textbook publisher Ginn to Paramount (Viacom) after slamming the former Mulroney government for doing the same thing with Prentice-Hall years earlier. Only 25% of publishers of educational books in Canada are now Canadian.

Canada no longer has an energy policy to protect our supplies of natural gas and oil. Water is a "tradeable commodity" under the terms of NAFTA, setting the stage for massive water-diversion projects to the thirsty U.S. midwest, California and Mexico. An acre of Canadian forest is being clearcut every twelve seconds (Brazil cuts one acre every nine seconds), mostly by foreign-based transnationals.

Our constitutionally mandated transfer payments to less advantaged regions are being wound down, assuring a future of great regional disparity resembling that of our southern neighbours. Universality in all social programs, except health care, is history. Our system of unemployment insurance is being fundamentally reorganized to conform to the system in the United States where few citizens are entitled to it. Even health care is under severe strain, and some provinces are openly setting the stage for a user-fee system.

Most provinces have broken collective bargaining agreements, even those whose governments have traditional ties to labour. Canada is developing an entrenched underclass and our middle class is under assault. Increasingly, we are adopting the American definition of welfare as charity for those unable to make it in a system that goes largely unquestioned, and moving away from our traditional view of welfare as a protection for the community as a whole. We are becoming a harder people, less compassionate about the unemployed, less responsible to one another.

FREE TRADE IN EDUCATION

Given these sweeping changes to Canada's structures and values, and the unprecedented continentalization that has occurred in so short a time, it is not reasonable to suppose that Canadian education can escape the pressures to harmonize with the U.S. system of education. The corporate push to influence education will be uniform across the continent, to establish common standards for educating the future workers of North America.

In this crusade, its greatest allies are the Canada-U.S. Free Trade Agreement and its successor, the North American Free Trade Agreement.[1] These trade deals have incorrectly been sold to the Canadian people as mere processes to liberalize trade and establish mechanisms to solve cross-border disputes. In fact, they establish a whole new framework of social and economic policy for the Americas and create an alternative non-elected continental governing structure.

John Calvert, of the Canadian Union of Public Employees, and Larry Kuehn, of the British Columbia Teachers' Federation, have written *Pandora's Box*, a study of NAFTA, corporate power and education. They warn: "NAFTA, like the Canada-U.S. Free Trade Agreement before it, treats many of our social institutions, including education, as service commodities that must be opened up to the competitive pressures of the marketplace. The assumption that educational services can—indeed should—be treated as economic commodities constitutes a fundamental break with our Canadian traditions and presents a clear and present danger to the educational programs that we cherish."[2]

Here's how NAFTA poses this danger. First, the deal opens up Canada's services, including many public sector and educational services, to U.S. companies for competition in our market and for government contracts.[3] Although it technically allows governments to run public education systems, they must do so within the rules set out in the sections dealing with services. This is the catch. NAFTA gives U.S. companies what is called "national treatment rights." This means that Canadian governments must treat them as if they are Canadian and cannot give preference to a domestic company. The rule applies to provincial governments and contracts, as well. In other words, governments cannot favour Canadian companies, even if they believe that in culture, broadcasting and educational services, a Canadian perspective is crucial to the product.

Second, Canadian governments can no longer require that companies bidding on Canadian contracts maintain a presence in the country.[4] As Kuehn and Calvert point out, U.S. companies can carry out work or services in Canada without having any investment in the country, without providing any employment, and without even having an office in Canada. This means that public licensing and regulation of educational-service providers would have to be carried out in a manner that does not favour Canadian firms. What will that mean to Canadian standards and content?

Third, NAFTA extends what are called "procurement rights" to American companies, enabling them to bid on public and government contracts.[5] It establishes an implementation timetable for the different levels of government, starting with the federal government (U.S. companies can bid as equals, with no preference given to Canadian companies for government service contracts over $50,000 and government construction contracts over $6.5 million) and Crown corporations. Under this provision, for example, the federal Liberal government could not reverse the contracting out of the delivery of Canada's social security cheques to an American transnational on the grounds that this work should go to Canadians.

For provincial, state and local governments, procurement rights do not begin right away, but the process for establishing them does.[6] The provision for negotiation of procurement rights is clearly stated in NAFTA, and the intention of opening up other levels of government to transnational bids is quite explicit.

NAFTA negotiators argued that these concerns, raised by educators and others, were exaggerated because the agreement allows for some exemptions to the above rights if a province wants to exclude certain current public practices from a NAFTA challenge.[7] But there are so many qualifications to this exemption that they are almost meaningless. Definitions of exemptionable categories are to be negotiated by trade committees sometime in the future. As well, it must be proved that the service in question is intended to be maintained as a public service. A province cannot bring in a public daycare program, for instance, without paying huge compensation to private U.S. firms for loss of potential future business. Nor could a former public service that had been privatized be returned to the public jurisdiction.

Most important, however, is the NAFTA requirement that each province must list the services it wants exempted from a NAFTA challenge, then negotiate them with other provinces, then with the federal government and finally with the United States and Mexico. At all three levels, the process will pressure provinces to drop exempted practices.

Several provincial governments are currently privatizing many educational and other public services and functions and could use the NAFTA exemption negotiation process to eliminate programs and services by leaving them off the list. The Klein government in Alberta is perhaps the most radical in its privatization drive. Should Alberta come in with a very sparse list of public services it wants to keep, under NAFTA, future Alberta governments, of whatever political persuasion, could never get back these now-privatized public services.

The federal government is trying to download social responsibilities, as it is "unable" to retain its commitment to regional transfer payments. It could use the process to encourage the elimination of public programs at all levels of government, which would let it off the hook for delivery, especially as NAFTA also requires the federal government to take "all necessary measures" to make the provinces comply with the terms and spirit of the agreement. Finally, both the United States and Mexico are undergoing massive privatization of their educational systems and would likely use the process to encourage Canada to do the same.

Moreover, the process is ongoing: all governments must continue for years to negotiate the practices, laws and public programs they want listed for exemption. Nothing that might be given exemption status will be considered permanently exempt. Such "non-conforming practices" are at odds with the goals and market principles of the trade deal; it is therefore desirable that they be done away with.

NORTH AMERICAN EDUCATION, INC.

The economic harmonization of the continent will forever change the nature of education in Canada. It will become more privatized, much closer to the American system, and will operate on a more commercial basis, allowing business, big and small, to move into this once restricted sector. As jobs become more scarce and the competition for them more fierce, and as education comes to be viewed as a competitive advantage, education as a business is attracting more corporations and entrepreneurs. As privatization proceeds, they will have a growing market for their goods.

Under NAFTA transnationals can now develop educational products for a pan-North American market. American firms, because of their size, will have a market advantage and will be able, under NAFTA, to operate their data processing in low-wage Mexico. Like other U.S.-based corporations, they now view Canada as part of a single North American market and will be impatient to erase any inconsistencies in the systems.

With high-tech telecommunications, one might operate a college, trade or language school from Florida, say, for all of North America without employing a single Canadian or Mexican and not all that many Americans. The information highway will make it possible for teaching to be done electronically. Thus, a private American corporation could win and fulfil a provincial contract to provide teaching materials or advise on cost-cutting without leaving head office. Several provinces have already hired U.S. management consultants to advise on cutting health-care costs.

As long as educational services are performed by the public sector, they can be kept in Canada, but once a service is privatized, it must be governed by NAFTA rules of "national treatment" and cannot be returned to the public sphere without financial compensation to private interests that were making money in that area or might one day. Calvert and Kuehn say, "Consequently, as a larger share of Canada's overall education spending is channelled through the private sector, as U.S. firms exercise their rights under NAFTA, more and more of Canada's educational system will become 'Americanized'."

For instance, the government of British Columbia decided several years ago to contract out the preparation of grade twelve provincial examinations. When the contract with the local firm expires, it will have to be opened to competing firms from all over the continent. The Department of Education will have a difficult time arguing that cultural concerns should keep the contract in British Columbia. Under NAFTA, such action could be challenged as a false barrier to free trade.

In 1992, the Ottawa Separate School Board hired Texas-based Energy Education Ltd. to advise it on energy conservation, at a cost of $17,000 a month, and design a curriculum for the students on how to implement the project. The board also hired a $50,000-a-year "energy educator." After several trips to the company's Texas headquarters in the president's private jet, the chairperson of the school board put the proposal to the trustees without sending the contract to tender. Angry school trustees charged that the company was being paid to "turn off lightbulbs" and rightly pointed out that Canadian companies, including Ontario provincial government consultants, could do the job a lot cheaper. It was a disgrace, they argued, to allow private American consultants to design student curriculum when the board was laying off teachers. Should their concerns result in a resolution to hire a Canadian company when the contract comes up for renewal, however, the board would be in violation of NAFTA.

At present, such contracting extends to support services such as cleaning, food services, school-bus transportation, building maintenance, computer services and consulting. Eventually, U.S. firms will be able to bid on government educational purchases of computers, supplies and teaching aids. American fast-food chains, such as Wendy's and Pizza Hut, have already obtained contracts to provide cafeteria services to many U.S. schools and universities and now have the right to bid in Canada.

ServiceMASTER is a large U.S. school maintenance, housekeeping and food-service management company that is aggressively moving into Ontario schools. The Ontario Secondary School Teachers' Federation has documented cases of employee harassment, the use of inferior cleaning materials and chemicals resulting in health and safety violations, and reduced standards of school cleanliness. Yet, under NAFTA, there is no way to curtail the growth of ServiceMASTER (whose corporate name, short for "Service to the Master," reflects its fundamentalist Christian origins) in Canada.

The current debate in Canadian schools about YNN, the for-profit youth education and news network, will seem a mere skirmish when its American competitors expand into Canada. NAFTA and the GATT establish an international framework to protect the private investments of telecommunications firms, while opening public systems to privatization.

Calvert and Kuehn say, "Telecommunications is treated simply as a profit-making industry which should be largely freed of any government regulation or interference. In the process, all other approaches to telecommunications are displaced. The fact that a communications system is the vehicle through which a nation speaks to itself, or that a telecommunications system has cultural and other non-economic functions, is simply ignored."

When the deregulated information highway becomes a reality, dominated by transnational phone, cable and retail giants, and when non-Canadian companies are guaranteed national treatment in Canada, there will be no way to prevent the mass marketing of American for-profit "educational services" once the precedent has been set by YNN. And there will be no way to force the services to offer Canadian content—after all, the companies will not even have to have an office in Canada.

Another crucial set of corporate rights contained in both NAFTA and the GATT that have wide implications for education is called intellectual property rights. For years, large transnationals, which hold the vast majority of the world's patents, have been attempting to enshrine ownership and control of technology and knowledge in international law. Who owns the fruits of learning has long been an ethical and legal question of complexity. In Canada, a compromise position of public and private rights has characterized our approach and legal framework. Knowledge was viewed as common heritage to be used for the public good, but public access had to be balanced with the rights of the inventor or creator.

The new system, however, skews the balance away from the public interest. The intellectual property provisions of NAFTA and the GATT treat knowledge as a commodity and the exclusive property of the company that takes out a patent on it. That this knowledge may be the consolidation of years, maybe hundreds of years, of collective research, by many individuals or even communities, is irrelevant. He whose lawyers seal it in a patent owns it. The large pharmaceutical, publishing, telecommunications, computer, agribusiness and other corporations specializing in leading-edge technologies stand to gain world-wide monopoly rights.

This has enormous potential ramifications for Third World countries, whose massive genetic wealth, in the form of seeds, herbs and natural medicines, is being appropriated by transnationals and then sold back to them at punitive prices. It has enormous implications for the health of the world's poor, for whom newly restricted generic drugs determine life or death. But it also has serious implications for education and who will have access to the technology that carries it. The trade agreements cover interactive computer and audio-visual learning devices, out-of-country cable and satellite transmission of educational programs, and learning aids. These rights will give transnational educational service companies the power to extract royalties from our public-education system that will go to private interests outside of Canada.

UNIVERSITIES FIRST

To speculate on what this might mean to our schools, we should examine our universities, which are already moving down this road. Canada's universities and colleges, like our schools, have a different history than their American counterparts. They have been created as public institutions accountable to the public through government. The United States favours private institutions financed by foundation and corporate wealth as well as by governments. Even the public system set up to serve less affluent students has now been forced to chase private sources, and the distinction between public and private has blurred.

In Canada, cash-strapped universities are also turning to business for sponsorship, as governments cut back on funding. This is creating serious ethical questions about who owns the results of research done on their premises—and what research gets done. Universities have the researchers and scientists; corporations have the money.

Journalist John Harris says, "Knowledge that was free, open and for the benefit of society is now proprietary, confidential and for the benefit of business. Educators who once jealously guarded their autonomy now negotiate curriculum planning with corporate sponsors. . . . Professors who once taught are now on company payrolls churning out marketable research in the campus lab, while universities pay the cut-rate fee for replacement teaching assistants. . . . University presidents, once the intellectual leaders of their institutions, are now accomplished bagmen."[8]

In exchange for free merchandise, universities offer exclusive access to students for corporate sponsors. A professor's ability to attract private investment is now often more important than academic qualifications or teaching ability. Provincial and federal funding to post-secondary institutions is also increasingly tied to commercial considerations. The federal government is giving research grants to individual faculty members whose projects have commercial viability while cutting general transfer payments. That this grant money should directly benefit business is stated clearly in funding-agency mandates.

Universities now have CEOs, business-liaison officers and corporate advisers. Fund-raising campaigns are increasingly, of necessity, the priority of the administration, board of governors and faculty; and in more and more universities, the arts and humanities, considered "soft," largely because they do not attract corporate sponsorship, are being phased out. Companies footing the bill for the departments that survive increasingly consider the results of research to be their own.

A department will often consider the number of patents it has registered to be more important than the number or quality of its faculty members' publications. Some are establishing their own foundations and companies to license their research for patents in co-operation with the private sector. Many universities now have an intellectual-property office that seeks private enterprise partners. The University-Industry Liaison Program of the University of British Columbia advertises that its intellectual-property office issues approximately one commercial licence a month for technologies originating in its labs. In its pitch to industry, it offers to match business projects with the right faculty and the university's reserved seat on the government granting committee.

A convergence of academic and corporate heavyweights has formalized these interlocking interests in the Corporate-Higher Education Forum, a national coalition of university presidents and corporate CEOs designed to merge goals and activities. Modelled on the American Business Higher Education Forum, the Canadian group promotes corporate-education interaction by placing members on one another's governing bodies. Like its American counterpart, the forum campaigns against government regulation of post-secondary education and for closer business-education ties. It actually advocates maintaining government underfunding policies to allow free-market forces to replace the public interest by making universities more dependent on corporate funding. The forum advocates that "activist corporations" set up their own development offices to negotiate deals with universities as part of their business strategy.

A guide published by the Corporate-Higher Education Forum on university-business contracts called *Spending Smarter* is very clear on who should reap the benefits. "The question of who has the right to so called 'Intellectual Property' in a research endeavour is a very complex one. . . . It is obviously important for both the corporation and the university to limit disclosure to the project at hand. One should also anticipate that the work may trigger ideas or open up paths of investigation for the researchers. Instead of trying to capture some of these rather ephemeral aspects of the transaction, Option 1 is structured in such a way that the 'Deliverables' and other Intellectual Property, belong to the company."[9]

Harris describes a discovery in chemical-pollution control in a lab at the University of Waterloo. There are no cheers, no rush to make the discovery public or share it with colleagues. The business interest that funded the project keeps it quiet until patents are secured. Next to be determined are royalty shares for faculty, jobs for grad students, and marketing plans. Thus, a discovery with significant potential for the environment is now in the hands of a private transnational, out of Canadian control, safe from being used for the public good.

CONTINENTAL EDUCATION SUPERSTRUCTURE

As post-secondary education in Canada becomes more like that of the United States, the next logical step is the creation of North American educational institutions to harmonize standards, training and certification for education professionals. It is, of course, highly desirable to establish models of educational co-operation across the continent and globally, but it is essential to examine the motivation behind the projects now underway and the form they are taking.

To see what the future of continental education would look like, we must examine the make-up and history of the U.S. Business Higher Education Forum (BHEF) and the Canadian Corporate Higher Education Forum (CHEF), the corporate lobby groups behind the project. The BHEF links representatives of the corporate Who's Who—Ford, AT&T, Pfizer, Eastman Kodak, Johnson & Johnson, Rockwell, Heinz, General Electric, and others—with university presidents in a sustained campaign against government regulations, environmental protection, health-and-safety laws and equitable income distribution. York University professor David Noble, formerly with MIT, explains the origins of this group: "Created at the initiative of industrial executives and the leaders of major research universities, the BHEF has been housed by the American Council on Education, a higher education trade association which has been promoting corporate and military agendas in universities since its founding during World War I."[10]

It includes many of the same corporate players appointed to former president Bush's New American Schools Development Corporation, established to funnel corporate funds into for-profit elementary schools, which is spearheading the movement to privatize American schools.

The Canadian CHEF, like the BHEF, is made up of the CEOs of many major corporations, including Imperial Oil, Spar Aerospace, Xerox, IBM, Alcan and Du Pont, all sponsors of free trade agreements. It has close ties to the Business Council on National Issues, which is calling for higher university and college tuition fees, the replacement of provincial transfer payments with direct grants to students to enable them to choose public or private institutions, and government cutbacks to post-secondary education. The BCNI was the most influential lobby group behind the Mulroney government's economic and social policies—privatization, the destruction of universality of social programs, massive deregulation, and disciplining the workforce through unemployment and competition for jobs. Key players in these groups are represented at the conferences and meetings being held across the continent.

A series of tri-national conferences—in Racine, Wisconsin; Guadalajara, Mexico; and Vancouver, British Columbia (at UBC) —have brought together senior North American educational officials and university administrators to facilitate the creation of an "academic common market in North America." Notably absent among the delegates were teachers' organizations, faculty associations and unions, who might have questioned the group's corporate-sounding mission statements.

The United States Information Agency describes the purpose of the conferences to "promote a North American approach to the development of higher education programs and projects."The Vancouver meeting, in September 1993, was called the International Symposium on Higher Education and Strategic Partnerships: The Challenge of Global Competitiveness from a North American Perspective. It called for a North American distance education and research network; a trilateral electronic information highway "to be easily accessible by the academic community, business, and government foundations"; a North American corporate higher education council, comprising senior representatives of the corporate and higher-education communities of the three countries "to act as advocates . . . for further partnering in the realization of mutually agreed objectives"; and a consortium of North American business for trilateral research, development and training to "secure private sector funding, through the membership of individual corporate citizens of the three countries, to be used to implement research and training initiatives of value to both the corporate and higher education communities."

Canada's participation in the group is co-ordinated by the Department of Foreign Affairs, signalling that a convergence of purpose is being sought between higher education and the free-market model of continental trade and economic development. In other words, the government is collaborating in turning over the future of higher education in North America to the corporate forces behind NAFTA, and to their aim of commercialization and privatization of our universities.

Recently, the governments of Mexico and the United States have been meeting to discuss ways to co-ordinate their primary- and secondary-education programs. They are focusing on shared curriculum reforms, teacher exchanges and redesigning teacher education. These meetings signal negotiations under another provision of NAFTA that is of concern. The agreement establishes a process for the harmonization of professional standards of teachers across the continent. It calls for the "development of mutually acceptable professional standards and criteria" including "conduct and ethics, professional development and re-certification and scope of practice."[11] The Canadian institutions responsible for teacher standards must provide recommendations to a commission set up under the agreement; it will review these recommendations and those from the other countries, and develop for adoption common standards "within a mutually agreed period."

The intention to override Canadian authority in education isn't even being denied. Trade minister Michael Wilson responded to teachers' concerns over certification in May 1993: "Professional services rank as one of the most important components of cross-border trade in services. . . . There is every logic to seeing that trade agreements covering cross-border services address matters of licensing and accreditation."

This notion of education and educators as tradeable commodities is particularly troubling in light of how far some institutions have gone in planning a North American system of education. The School of Education of the University of Southern California prepared a document on common certification in which it called for an enforceable system of common education programs, certification and standards: "A tri-national commission should consider how the three North American countries will determine fitness to work or provide services. The establishment of a common set of education standards could be formally enforced through a certification system acceptable to all three partners."[12]

Standards for educators vary widely on the continent and reflect the cultural and societal values of each country. Their harmonization, particularly if driven by an economic agenda, would

seriously invade the countries' political and educational sovereignty, as the new process, which Canada is legally obliged to
enter, will ultimately give a tri-national commission more power
over professional standards than the federal government has been
given in our Constitution.

The harmonization of the continent along a corporate model
is well underway. The process will give Canadians an opportunity
to confront the ideological nature of the attack on public schools
and to understand the crucial role of education in the political life
of a nation. For many who rarely question the purpose or nature
of our schools, the conscious recognition of their part in the transformation of Canada may provoke the question: How will a Canadian public system, serving our needs and teaching our culture and
social commitment survive? For to remodel a society, it is essential
to influence the hearts and minds of the young. At its most basic,
the assault on Canada's education system is an attack on the
history, culture and values of the nation itself.

THE RIGHT-WING ALLIANCE
AND THE POLITICS
OF EDUCATION

Education is becoming the public policy issue of the decade.
MACLEAN'S MARCH 14, 1994

A school is not simply a building, or an organizational convenience.
It is not simply a place where teachers come to teach. It teaches in
its own right, and very powerfully. We cannot afford to ignore its
political content, for the reality is that the whole school is a
vehicle of political education.

KEN OSBORNE, PROFESSOR OF EDUCATION, UNIVERSITY OF MANITOBA

BY DEFINITION, EDUCATION IS POLITICAL. LITERACY AND KNOWLEDGE
enable citizens to make choices concerning their future and to
acquire beliefs about people, systems and priorities. Education is
power; power is political.

The recognition of this evident connection has shaped our tradition of maintaining education as a public institution, guided by
democratically determined public policies—at least in theory. The
temptation for special interests to exploit the political potency of
education is too great for it to be left in the hands of those with
only their own opportunities to consider. Thus public education
has not been intended to serve the particular priorities of parents,
teachers or future employers—or even those of the government of
the day. Public education is intended to balance the interests of all

citizens, since we all stand to profit—or lose—from the skills, knowledge and attitudes acquired by children at school.

Education cannot be depoliticized. Indeed, its political nature should be made more evident, so that the public can more readily identify the intent and impact of education reforms. Why are changes being made? Whose interests are being served, and at what price?

These questions are answered too often by those with their own political stakes in the public's perception of education. As education rises as a public expense and as a policy issue of substantial political risk, governments and opposition parties have looked to education reform as a way of boosting their standings in public opinion. When governments abandon the half-completed reforms of their predecessors or announce new initiatives, they are more often courting short-term political gains than supporting the complexities of much-needed changes in schools.

As the tide of the Right rises, the majority of current education reforms predictably reflect neo-conservative assumptions. Some, however, are of the type usually associated with the Left, brought in by governments elected on "progressive" platforms. While these governments have largely abandoned their left-leaning policies on managing the economy and redistributing income, they have used school reform to convince their electors—or perhaps themselves— that some of their progressive principles are still intact.

Whether originating from the Left or the Right, reforms directed at short-term political ends are almost always harmful to the classroom and impede the implementation of real, sustainable change. As Michael Fullan, Canada's internationally renowned school-change expert, notes, politically motivated reforms produce "overload, unrealistic timelines, unco-ordinated demands, simplistic solutions, misdirected efforts, inconsistencies, and underestimation of what it takes to bring about reform."[1] Furthermore, to get maximum political mileage out of an initiative, it is necessary to exaggerate the need for it; in education, this means that the problems in the existing system and the benefits of the innovation both must be overstated. Mindful of the conservatism of the public when it comes to education, politicians usually promise that things will simultaneously stay the same and yet be different, that nothing will be lost and everything will be gained as soon as the changes are made.

Once the political mileage has been wrung out of a reform, its implementation—and its contradictions—are left to teachers and school board officials. This is especially true when the public begins to question the wisdom of the reform. For example, one might have expected B.C.'s education minister, Anita Hagen, to have defended—or at least mentioned—her government's sweeping education reforms in her education budget speech. But public enthusiasm for the Year 2000 reforms her government had mandated was low, and so she avoided the controversial subject altogether, instead devoting much of her speech to praising "alliances between schools, business and the community."[2]

It is expedient for the politician generals to redirect criticism of floundering school reforms to the front lines whenever possible. But the front lines find it hard to defend chaos. Speaking for many others caught in similar circumstances, one teacher struggling in Year 2000 limbo writes about her unsuccessful, year-long efforts to simply get a copy of the curriculum guide and equipment necessary to teach her newly mandated grade twelve math course:

> I heartily resent being unable to do the job I wish to do, that I am
> apparently being asked to do.... I heartily resent the criticism
> that I expect will be levelled at me, my professional group, the whole
> public school system for the inadequacy of the apparent product.
> And this resentment does drive me to tears of frustration.... It is not
> that we do not want to implement [the new programs]; it is that we
> are physically incapable of doing so.[3]

Having so often been hung out to dry and left to defend reforms without the means to make them workable, teachers are increasingly reluctant to support change of any kind. They are also frustrated because of the inability—or unwillingness—of policy makers to understand that the complexities of educational change go far beyond ordering new textbooks.

Although it is relatively easy to introduce small, incremental changes to individual schools and classrooms, undoing current practices, such as streaming or grading, need detailed—even inspired—implementation plans if they are to succeed. During the last decade, systems experts have claimed that every institution, from family to government, is essentially organic: if you change one part of the system, all parts of the system change to accommodate the innovation. Nowhere is this truer than in schools. This does not justify the status quo, but it does demand that we become more adept at anticipating the unintended as well as the intended outcomes of the reforms we urge.

Education policy analyst Doug McCall has identified twenty-three formal processes through which any educational innovation must pass before it is adopted within a school system.[4] Although such figures may suggest bureaucracy gone mad, the multiple decision points indicate historical nervousness about leaving schools vulnerable to innovations or reforms created for political reasons. Schools rarely change quickly precisely because they were designed not to shift according to each gust of any prevailing political wind. Such ponderous conservatism is out of step with today's hunger for "just-in-time" institutions, but pretending that the fine-tuning represented by these twenty-three processes does not exist is not the same as eliminating those that may be unnecessary.

Leaders, particularly those determined to do things differently, need to understand the culture of education and how things work if they are to be successful in making things change. Ministry officials, once typically drawn from the senior ranks of the education sector, are now more likely to have political than professional credentials. In Ontario, Bernard Shapiro, an internationally recognized educator and former head of the Ontario Institute for Studies in Education (OISE) served as deputy minister of education in the Liberal administration. Under the NDP, Shapiro's successor was Bob Mitton, "a career bureaucrat well known, among other things, for his work for the Social Credit government in B.C. where he had helped privatize highway maintenance."[5]

It seems that all opinions on education are equally valid. Ironically, while education policy is becoming more critical to political fortunes, ministers of education and their ministries no longer wield the influence they once did. Education decisions are made at least as often by treasury boards with an eye on expenditure as by officials with more direct accountability for the impact of those decisions on schools. And while it may be a familiar politician's face announcing a decision affecting education, the political intent is likely coming from interests growing more powerful than governments.

TESTING THE SYSTEM

Politically motivated reforms nearly always flow from simplistic analyses and justifications that ignore systemic ramifications. Educators have been unsuccessful in communicating how the characteristics of schools are interrelated, and how the most well-meaning reforms can set off a chain of unintended and almost irreversible consequences.

The School Achievement Indicators Project (SAIP) of the Council of Ministers of Education, Canada (CMEC) provides an excellent case study. Kathryn Chang Barker traces what she calls "accountabilism" and its association with nation-wide testing back to Richard Nixon.[6] President Bush took up the call; his "America 2000" education policy statement announced plans for "a national framework for what students should know and be able to do; creating a set of exams based directly on the framework; and setting grading criteria for the exams."[7] Not surprising us, Prime Minister Mulroney joined in responding to business demands for "product-testing" students.

National testing and "standards" had been called for, directly or indirectly, by the Business Council on National Issues (BCNI), the Conference Board of Canada, the Canadian Manufacturers' Association and the Canadian Chamber of Commerce.[8] On this issue, the Liberal government is prepared to take the political risk of threatening the provinces' jealous territoriality on matters of education by encouraging the public to view the prospect of national testing as the solution to the complex problems of schools. Provincial and territorial governments, eager to be seen as "doing something," have bought in.

As predicted, Lloyd Axworthy announced to the Council of Ministers of Education that "the federal government will assist the provinces in further development of 'national education tests'." This would have come as no surprise to anyone familiar with the Liberal's *Red Book*, which warned that "Canadian children are not only competing with children at the next desk; they are competing with children in other countries whose education systems are giving them a better start in life." The need to develop "an agenda and approach," the Liberals believe, will require co-operation between business and education. The government's role, in addition to funding an expanded version of the "National Indicators Test," will be to back the BCNI's proposal for a "voluntary" National Achievement Test, which they present as an opportunity for students and their parents to "track the progress of our educational systems in meeting the goal of higher achievement."

As more than one critic has observed, if testing created excellence, American students, the "most-tested" students in the world, should be winning the education sweepstakes—an inconvenient observation, not raised in media and voter scrutiny of the *Red*

Book. The public may not yet be convinced that more testing results in better education; but surely, Canadians will eventually get the message if they are given a little encouragement.

A Decima poll taken just months before the announcement of the SAIP tests found no evidence of a groundswell of public demand for standardized testing or widespread concern about accountability. This led the pollsters to remark, with evident frustration, "We must also question the efficacy of the efforts of some corporations, and in some instances, governments, to convince Canadians, such as those in this poll, that we indeed do have problems that could affect our productivity and world economic position in the future. . . . If there is a problem, and the authors believe there is, then other methods of mobilizing the Canadian public to be concerned about this matter need to be considered."[9]

As an "other" method of getting the public's attention, standardized testing fulfils the most political criteria. There has been no decline in the public's naïve faith in the objectivity of numbers and no increase in the sophistication (or, perhaps, willingness) of the press to interpret statistics with an eye to their reliability. Interjurisdictional comparisons fit into short soundbites, and testing doesn't require complex implementation plans or teacher training. Testing doesn't even require evaluation! Those things that are easiest to test, of course, happen to coincide with the priorities of the business community: computers can score a math exam much more cheaply than markers can wade through a creative writing assignment.

Testing is politically attractive precisely because of its association with "objectivity"; as a result resistance to testing appears to be the stance that is politically motivated. To much of the public, widescale testing of mathematics or any other subject appears to be as neutral—and exact—as measuring room temperature. Yet it is neither. Mass testing—or, more precisely, the fallout from mass testing—is a powerful force for curriculum reform and for shaping the goals of education. What has been and will be tested becomes a priority, not just in the public mind or ministry policy, but in time and attention in the classroom. Other instructional priorities recede, thus shifting curriculum balance effortlessly and without debate.

Current balance, such as it is, attempts to recognize the multiple goals of schooling. If human beings are more than their cognitive capacities, then schools must respond to more than cognition. The development of curiosity, judgement, empathy, aesthetic appreciation and skill, respect for difference, and so forth have time and again been validated by the public as capacities schools should encourage. How to approach these goals and how much emphasis each should receive have been the stuff of decades of curriculum debate. Measuring students' progress towards these goals is much more difficult than measuring their success in spelling or computing, but surely that complexity is precisely what makes those goals so important to teach.

Standardized testing can measure only what students already know (or, perhaps, correctly guess); such test results measure only the frequency with which students give the same answer as other students to questions posed by someone else, questions for which the answer has already been predetermined. Such assessment has its place, but few of us believe that education should be devoted exclusively to teaching other people's answers to true-or-false questions, or that our future will be secured by more people thinking in exactly the same way. As highly publicized, comparative, ubiquitous standardized testing becomes the method of choice for ceding ground to education's most conservative critics, standardized learning according to a standardized curriculum and from a standardized text must follow.

It is ironic that many of those who call for increased standardized testing also talk about the need for students to acquire the skills of working with others and to solve problems creatively, apparently unaware of the contradictions inherent in their demands. There is little motivation for students to develop the skills of group problem-solving, or to hone their abilities to think critically, if their success is to be measured exclusively by the extent of their personal possession of easily measured facts and competencies. In a test-driven system, if it doesn't count it doesn't matter. Nor is there much motivation to teach anything beyond facts and techniques, when teachers are told that it is only test results that count.

This narrowing of content means that the skills teachers have acquired over decades are becoming redundant or even undesirable. The large textbook publishers (who also design and market the major standardized exams) proudly proclaim that their materials are "teacher-proof": just follow the text and scores will improve. Setting goals, selecting new content, designing instructional strategies, evaluating achievement, modifying lessons so that they have meaning for increasingly non-standardized students—these roles become vestigial in a system with no purpose other than sorting the high scorers from the low scorers.

More testing, it is said, will stimulate improvement through competition, but standardized testing cannot inspire creative change. Testing frenzy tends to freeze existing problems in place, reinforcing a mentality that promotes doing more of the same, only with greater intensity. It becomes too risky to be innovative, too dangerous to deviate from the curriculum-as-tested. There is little magic involved in raising test scores on two or three subjects. It can be done by neglecting other, harder-to-measure goals and subjects, or by making the system more élitist, freezing out those students likely to drag down the class average. And one can always teach to the test—it all depends what we are willing to sacrifice to the politics of bar graphs.

Any scheme of student evaluation that is politically motivated will only hurt the system it claims to be improving: this is a poor substitute for genuine accountability. The consequences of standardized testing are already being felt in changing curriculum priorities, the narrowing of teaching and learning, the lowered enthusiasm of students, the decreasing attention we give to at-risk students and almost every other school activity. These outcomes need not be intentional for them to be real, and they will not disappear simply by being denied.

REFORMING FROM THE RIGHT

Political ideologies are assumed to be independent of educational philosophies, but what one believes to be in the best interests of society (or of a particular slice of society) shapes one's beliefs about what should go on in schools. Michael Apple, well-known critic of American education, refers to the ascendency of a powerful conservative alliance that is shaping public thought about not only what schools do, but also what schools are for. He says,

> In essence, this new alliance has integrated education into a wider set of ideological commitments. Its objectives in education are derived from the same principles that guide its economic and social welfare goals. These include the expansion of the free market, the drastic reduction of government responsibility for social needs, the reinforcement of an intensely competitive structure of limited mobility, the lowering of people's expectations for economic security, and the popularization of what is clearly a form of Social Darwinism.[10]

Survival of the fittest is the message, but for public consumption, right-wing education reform must be couched in the language of excellence and achievement. This strategy promises to be just as effective as the efforts of the conservative alliance to manipulate our political consciousness and economic policies. Business has worked hard to convince Canadians that their interests are our interests; business invested a great deal in having the public see the deficit as the only issue of economic importance, and to convince the public of the inexhaustible opportunities presented by the Free

Trade Agreement and NAFTA. And while many Canadians are distrustful of, if not hostile to these political motives of business, we seem unprepared to regard their sudden interest in the reform of schools with similar scepticism.

The conservative alliance has had on its side public anxiety about a harsh economic climate (largely of its own making, but for which it takes no responsibility). The legitimate fears of parents about their children's economic and social prospects, and even for their safety, have been appropriated by the conservative alliance to move arguments about education onto their own ground. An article ostensibly about violence in schools is headlined "Smothered By Its Own Weight: Total Privatization May Be the Only Way to Fix the Crumbling Public School System."[11] To adults without children, exaggerated claims about the cost of education can always be exploited. The legitimacy of the non-competitive goals of education, such as the development of critical understanding, cultural literacy or reflective personal development, can simply be dismissed as too expensive or associated with child-centred education and, thus, moral decay.

The message that schools are doing the wrong things, and doing them badly, directly challenges the competency—and often the integrity—of the teaching profession. The politically inspired reforms of the last decade have not only de-skilled teachers, but demoralized them. In addition to the "change-overload" of program and curriculum reforms, many teachers resent the downloading of social responsibility on schools, demands for which many feel unsuited or unprepared, particularly when how well teachers play the roles of substitute parents or social workers is considered irrelevant to their evaluation by the public. Heavy-handed management styles once familiar only in the most autocratic of businesses have become common in schools, with predictable consequences and confrontations.

Surrounded by evidence that many parts of the system aren't

working, some teachers have eagerly joined "reform from the right" advocates. Viewed superficially, conservative reforms hold out the hope of simplifying and making manageable the tasks of schools and teachers, even if the price is to amputate some of the basic purposes of education. While some teachers have supported the resistance of their unions to politically inspired reforms, perhaps more have simply tried not to be drawn into either side of the debate, either because they fear reprisal or because they have chosen to be disinterested. As one newspaper editor mused, not unsympathetically, many teachers are too busy teaching to be worried about education.

The conservative alliance, then, faces little threat from the profession vested with the responsibility of "advancing the cause of education." Assumptions about creating counter-alliances drawn from "the community sector," as it is sometimes called, have turned out to be shaky: labour, women's groups, nationalists, and activists within other causes in the public interest have many faults to find with the education system as they see it, and many battles of their own to fight against the Right. Many do not see education as a political cause, but unless the political agenda is recognized, it cannot be effectively challenged.

THE CURRICULUM AS POLITICAL TEXT

I think if I had my way, we would only teach six core subjects in high school. I realize that my list is selfish to my industry's needs, but it is nonetheless what we need. 1) English; 2) Mathematics; 3) Physics; 4) Chemistry; 5) The importance of showing up for work; 6) How to get along with others. With only half my tongue in my cheek, I think we get all the geography, law, ethics, and probably more than enough biology from TV.

Gary Johncox, Vice-president, MacMillan Bloedel

The primary means of influencing what schools do and whom they serve is to control what is taught. Curriculum guidelines attempt to answer the difficult question "What is worth knowing?" This question is political because of the other questions that determine how it is answered. Who decides what is worth knowing? How? Why?

Most readers will recall being taught that "in fourteen-hundred and ninety-two Columbus sailed the ocean blue" and the tale of the "discovery" of America that went with the rhyme. For most of us, only the protest of aboriginal peoples raised in conjunction with the 1992 commemoration of this event made us aware that America was not "lost" at the time it was "found," and that only through perpetuating a shameless degree of Eurocentrism could it be considered to have been "discovered." Yet this story contributed to our view of history, "savages," heroism and, perhaps, even the validity of land claims.

What is more interesting, perhaps, is how the curriculum possibilities expand in light of new understandings about what is worth knowing. A teacher encountering 1492 has several choices. Should she omit the contentious event, given its unpleasant associations? Should it be taught as an example of cultural and political imperialism? Should she promote what Columbus accomplished but soft-pedal the conquest theme? Is this an appropriate context in which to discuss current land claims and their validity, or to explore the quality of life of aboriginal peoples? Should aboriginal students be asked to present their views on the story, or would this approach reinforce already existing tensions?

Each of these strategies raises questions about power and how it is distributed, and whether such questions should be avoided, recognized or challenged as part of students' education. While in theory the curriculum allows for the application of professional judgement in selecting an approach, teachers have found it prudent to let the curriculum guide answer the question of what is worth knowing, or to select an approved "curriculum resource," prepackaged and uncontroversial. In a system under such close scrutiny, it becomes important to anticipate which questions and which kinds of content are least likely to stir up parents, administration and trustees—a classic case of the self-censorship that flourishes under political pressure.

A similar analysis can be brought to bear in considering the content of every discipline. Curriculum that implies (or promises) that science is objective, that nature is for harvesting or that welfare is for people who can't look after themselves is sending messages that are deeply political. Curriculum directly validates particular points of view and teaches assumptions about privilege and power through the topics it evades as well as those it addresses.

Moreover, the curriculum is not limited to transmitting selected knowledge. It also explicitly attempts to develop attitudes and both human and technical skills that illustrate how schools reproduce or challenge the distribution of power. The old model of "girls take home ec, boys take shop" or the newer notion that musicianship or trigonometry or foreign languages are optional raises questions: who decides which skills are necessary or desirable for which students? What assumptions are being made about the place of the individual in an economically and socially stratified society?

While much of the public may assume the attitudinal component of the curriculum is dictated in some curriculum document or another, the reality is quite different. Certainly, there are formal lessons taught about "respecting diversity," but subtext is much more powerful than text. If the school turns a blind eye to racial or sexual harassment, posters extolling "no means no" or "together we're better" have little effect other than to alert students to adults' hypocrisy. The strongest political message is sent each time a student learns that to challenge authority, no matter how arbitrarily it is exercised, is to get into trouble. Students then learn that the right to participate in decision-making is rationed and carefully guarded from those who are most affected by the decisions by those who hold the most power. This is a lasting political lesson.

INSTRUCTION AS POLITICAL REINFORCEMENT

Instruction is as political as the curriculum it teaches. Instructional choices send messages to students about whether knowledge and understanding are generated or merely received. If instruction is text-centred, or consists of answering other people's questions in ways that are expected, or if learning is primarily an individual pursuit, students reach predictable conclusions about knowledge and power and competition. Instruction that claims to teach critical thinking but narrows the range of what students may think about mocks its own purpose. Instruction that is limited to teaching what will be tested and that encourages acquiring credentials or marks rather than knowledge teaches that what really matters is not what you know, but what other people think you know.

Instruction may seem to be merely methodology, but choices about how to teach are nonetheless shaped by unconscious assumptions about which students deserve the greatest share of instructional attention. There is no indicator of school graduation and success stronger than socio-economic level, which in turn is tied to the variables of race and gender. Who studies for how long and to what level of success is intensely political; although influences beyond the classroom shape these patterns, they can be reinforced in schools.

The scarcest—and potentially the most valuable—resource in the classroom is teacher time and attention. The most thorough examination of how this resource is distributed has been undertaken by those concerned with gender and schooling. Why do girls come to school "ahead" of boys, but typically leave behind them on every objective measure? The answer turns out to be time and attention.

White middle-class boys receive a disproportionate amount of teacher time, more encouraging feedback, questions of greater difficulty, and greater tolerance for poor behaviour. They are over-identified as candidates for "enriched" programs, and when they need extra help or remediation, they are referred for special services at an earlier age and for less acute problems than are girls. Girls are more often rewarded for interpersonal competence than for task competence, but tend to be ignored. Boys who are not white and those who are not middle-class tend to be treated like girls.[12] Most of these dynamics occur outside the conscious awareness of teachers, but many teachers who have attempted to become more self-conscious about their distribution of time and attention have experienced backlash from students, parents and, often, their colleagues as well.

The suggestion that schools contribute, even unconsciously, to the perpetuation of inequality based on gender, race or class is often furiously denied. The role of schools in pre-sorting and slotting the adults of the future is disguised whenever students appear to be choosing their own futures. Curriculum options provide the illusion of student choice, a choice free of the expectations of others or the effects of political forces. That the choices of the students who are secure and well-to-do are as predictable as those of students living on the margins does not seem to shake our faith in free will or in the political neutrality of schools. Most teachers want to believe that inequity persists despite, not because of, children's educational experiences. Many parents of children who profit from the skewing of educational opportunities are swift to react when their entitlements seem to be threatened in the name of equity; even if others make poor choices of their own free will, why should those who don't be penalized?

Certain patterns of student choice receive a great deal of political attention. Girls' long-standing disinclination to study the sciences has been identified as a threat to our collective economic well-being. (Evidently, choice matters only as an issue of competitiveness.) The federally financed Canadian Committee on Women and Engineering warned, "In this period of global competition and rapid technological developments, employers cannot be satisfied with anything less than the best engineers available, regardless of their gender."[13]

In response to this peril, education ministries across Canada put girls-math-and-science at the top of their agendas with a vigour that other equity topics rarely enjoy. This was because the issue was framed as an employer-and-profit problem rather than as a matter of equity. It is surely ironic that impetus was given to the formation of the committee, struck presumably to determine why young women found engineering unfriendly, by the murder of fourteen female engineering students.

There are patterns of program choice considerably more "gendered" than the sciences, but they do not receive comparable attention. For example, while between 25% and 45% of senior high school Physics students are female, a far smaller proportion of women can be found in similar post-secondary courses. High school enrolment in subjects such as Advanced Politics (65% male) and Child Development (95% female) show stronger enrolment patterns by gender than Chemistry;[14] however, as attention to these "choices" might draw attention to the distribution of power, they are among the "choices" routinely ignored.

Nowhere are the political dynamics of student choice more evident than in streaming the academically able from those assumed to have more limited expectations and abilities. Streaming is the practice of creating different clusters of subjects at differing levels of difficulty for various groups of students. In theory, aptitude determines choice, but socio-economic class turns out to be the variable that makes the difference. While streaming exists formally as education policy only in some provinces, it thrives in most schools and at every grade level even when no such policy is on the books. In Ontario, the longstanding practice of dividing students at grade nine into one of three streams is being phased out, but not without controversy. The authors of "Stacking the Deck: The Streaming of Working-Class Kids in Ontario Schools" report that children whose parents had unskilled occupations were about ten times as likely as those from professional families to end up in basic level programs, the "lowest" of the three streams. They also found that other programs streamed children in similar ways: "Children from dominant-class backgrounds are disproportionately represented in the growing number of elementary-level enrichment and second-language immersion programs, while lower-class children predominate in the expanding slow-learner, behavioral and learning disabilities classes."[15]

The Ontario government's decision to end streaming was promoted as an effort to put an end to the schools' replication and reinforcement of class-based injustices. Life, however, is not that simple. Whether class-induced or not, real—and considerable—differences among students will not vanish simply because labels are removed. Teachers who protested that eliminating streams was a poor substitute for a societal commitment to equity were silenced as reactionaries. Those who supported the changes but asked when they might expect the training, textbooks, curriculum guides and student evaluation policies they would need were silenced as closet reactionaries. Those who asked how greater ability differences would be accommodated in light of the performance pressure of "excellence" and standardized testing were silenced as being opposed to accountability. Although destreaming will profoundly change every high school class in Ontario, most teachers have received only a few hours' orientation, and few school boards have received additional resources. This feeble political response to the very difficult questions of educational equity invites backlash; when destreaming fails to transform the expectations and life "choices" of students, schools will be blamed again.

What is at the root of the predictable choices of class, gender and race runs much deeper than the classroom, and so do the solutions. The effects of our political choices show up in the classroom as "capacity to learn."

POLITICS AND THE CAPACITY TO LEARN

The characteristics of children as learners and their capacity to learn is political. It is what children are encouraged or able to contribute to their education that receives the least sustained attention, despite alarmist headlines. Those outside schools tend to consider school reform in terms of changing teaching and the curriculum; yet instructional pyrotechnics and computer simulations are inadequate antidotes to hunger or anger or despair. Students with a low capacity to learn are those who have little to offer to the transaction between them and the instruction to which they are exposed. Without this transaction, teaching may take place, but learning cannot.

During the hearings that were part of the process undertaken by Ontario's Royal Commission on Learning, co-chair Gerald Caplan referred continuously to the "40% factor," the estimated 40% cent of all Ontario students who come to school with one or more problems so severe that ordinary assumptions about their ability to progress make no sense.

Globe and Mail columnist Michael Valpy accompanied Gerry Caplan on his tour of Ottawa-area schools. What he saw led him to wonder "whether Canadians may be drawing very wrong conclusions from what they read and hear about their schools— whether they may be linking their dissatisfaction to problems with pedagogy rather than to the state of their children."[16]

Valpy said, "Our schools, in every community and to an unprecedented degree, are being expected to cope with physically and emotionally unhealthy children, neglected children, children whose parents lack the time and energy to be with them, substance-abusing children, children with minimal social skills, children from a vast range of bruised, stressed and fragile families." Somehow this reality doesn't get through to education's critics full of facile advice about standards and accountability.

Valpy concluded that schools have not succeeded in telling

their communities how much time they spend on socialization skills: "good manners, physical hygiene and grooming, moral values, self-respect and respect for others, how to handle anger, why not to destroy school property, what and how to eat properly—all things that might have been assumed to be the prime didactic province of the family."

These are not curriculum choices, they are curriculum necessities, because without these skills and values learning cannot take place, not only among those who are short of food or skills, but also among the others, who can become the direct or indirect victims of classroom anarchy.

At one Ottawa high school Valpy and Caplan visited, 43% of the students were living either on their own or in single-parent families. If they are typical of Ontario's youth, research suggests almost 20% of students have at least one psychiatric disorder. Dr. Paul Steinhauer, senior psychiatrist at Toronto's Hospital for Sick Children, says, "Child neglect has become endemic in our society. Everywhere we look in Canada, children are failing to flourish. Rich kids, middle class kids, poor kids . . . all are dealing with risk and neglect unimagined and unimaginable in previous generations."[17]

In another high school, the visitors talked to two teachers assigned to develop a "school-to-work" transition program to serve "at-risk students and lower-level academic achievers." The teachers explained that they spend an "inordinate amount of time and effort" ensuring that the students simply turn up at their placement on time, and teaching them how to eat civilly in a workplace lunchroom, how to groom themselves and how to be presentable for their initial interviews with employers.

It is not surprising that those with the most intimate contact with "the 40%" react with anger and despair when they open their newspapers to see their efforts trashed again. Columnist Andrew Nikiforuk describes a highly public battle taking place in London, Ontario, which started with a school board member using access-to-information provisions to obtain school-by-school test results. To the surprise of few, there appeared to be a growing gap between schools in affluent areas and those in poorer areas. Yet the explanation, according to the trustee, could only lie with teachers, since "there shouldn't be a correlation between income and class unless educators entertain self-fulfilling prophecies about certain neighbourhoods." Nikiforuk concluded, "Commitment counts for more than social class in schooling."[18]

Nikiforuk is wrong. True, some experiments of great imagination, backed by their communities and endowed with gifted teachers (and often charitable dollars) have been able to transcend, for the short term, the chronically limited success of at-risk students. Nonetheless, our teachers don't lack commitment; it is not teachers who decide whether early intervention programs for high-risk students or showplace high schools have funding priority. What is lacking is a commitment by policy makers and opinion leaders to those with little to offer by way of political support or economic advantage. In families without hope or prospects are children without hope or prospects. No amount of teacher "commitment" can make up for the absence of enough adults with enough time to provide a loving, stimulating and respectful environment, for the absence of reading materials in the home, or for negative attitudes towards learning. Education is no substitute for breakfast and no solution to abuse.

Ironically, it has been the condition of these most marginalized and needy students and the schools' attempts to respond that have attracted the attention of one part of the conservative alliance and opened an opportunity for its political agenda.

SATAN IN THE CLASSROOM

While the public has been generally unaware of the political context of education, a vocal minority has become obsessed with the classroom as the vehicle of ideology. Many Christian fundamentalists believe the contemporary classroom to be the tool of Satan. This view is gaining influence within the conservative alliance and is succeeding in chilling progressive reforms and in shaping education policy.

The Christian Right has its eye on everything from the school library to science texts, from the goals of education to outcomes-based education. Well-organized and utterly committed, the religious Right has been particularly visible when reform proposals are put out for public consideration.

One of the targets of some Christian fundamentalists has been any restatement of curriculum objectives that implies an "inculcation of universalism." Arnold Burron, education professor and Christian-education spokesperson, explains that fundamentalists evaluate all school practices on their relationship to "supersessionism," the doctrine of the exclusivity of Christianity and the belief in Jesus as the sole route to eternal salvation. "Universalism" is incompatible with supersessionism, and universalism is read into anything that smacks of humanism.[19]

It is the failure of schools to appreciate the intensity of this conviction that has got them into difficulty, Burron says. He uses as an example Maine's document on core curriculum. The typical, seemingly uncontroversial statement reads, "Students with a common core of knowledge work cooperatively and actively in group decision-making, whether in small groups or in the larger society; are able to listen, share opinions, negotiate, compromise, and help the group reach consensus."

Burron points out that "traditional Christians challenge this objective because it seems to promote relativism as a desirable goal. They object to fostering the abilities to 'compromise' and 'reach consensus' when such practices could lead in certain situations to capitulation to group pressure or to approval of behaviours that a Traditionalist interpretation of Christian Scriptures prohibits, such as homosexuality." Moral absolutes, he explains, are incompatible with the encouragement of tolerance or other secular virtues.

The religious Right also takes exception to contemporary ways of thinking about learning. Larry Kuehn reports that a fundamentalist group headquartered in Terrace, B.C., offers workshops around that province "proving" that the Year 2000 reforms are part of a Satanist plot.

> The heart of the right-wing and religious fundamentalist complaint is centred in the constructivist idea that meaning is created by the student. They believe in revealed truth, rather than constructed meaning, and see education as a hierarchical delivery of that truth, with the teacher to fill the student's mind with information ...[20]

Granted, some of the claims of fundamentalist critics seem too absurd to gain much general support. It is unlikely that a significant constituency would agree with evangelist Pat Robertson's assertion that schools are mere fronts for New Age cultists: "apparently there's nothing wrong with having gurus come in to lecture or having seances and meditation. These practices are going on right now in many schools ... [m]any of these same occult practices have been used in public schools to 'retrain' our sons and daughters and to indoctrinate children into the New Age."[21]

To Robertson and his followers, schools are the last ditch from which to repel the insidious progress of the bogeyman called "the New Age," a movement of astonishing reach propelled, they claim, by adherents that include the United Nations and Yale University.[22] The potential of ultra-fundamentalists for influencing widespread reform has until recently been disregarded, given the extremism of their worldview: however, the operational side of this segment of the right-wing alliance for school reform has been highly successful, usually because their agenda has been strategically presented as "educational" rather than "religious."

Robert L. Simonds, president of the National Association for Christian Educators and Citizens for Excellence in Education, publicly refers to his organization as "Citizens for Excellence in

Education"—dropping the reference to "Christian"—when advancing his movement's ideas. In an article appearing in *Education Leadership*, the widest-circulation education magazine published in North America, Simonds claims groundswell support for his movement to end "child abuse in the classroom."[23] CEE claims 1200 chapters and 3500 school board members; it fights against AIDS education and increased funding to public schools with equal vigour. CEE's agenda, he claims, threatens only "those with a personal agenda to turn schools into institutions of psychological manipulation and to produce robotic students on political correctness." He claims that this manipulation takes the form of teaching "atheistic socialism" through "hypnotism, the occult, necromancy and Eastern religious practices."

Again, most would assume such statements from the fringe could be safely disregarded; however, CEE has been enormously successful in creating anxiety about particular classroom and curricular practices. CEE targets devoting time to "self-esteem," "critical thinking," "sex education," "multiculturalism," "global education," and "safe sex." CEE argues that these are peripheral to academic excellence, but it is clear that they are under attack because they are "anti-Christian."

Many Canadians who have been exposed to the criticism that schools are negligently devoted to "whole language" instruction and "child-centred" learning would be amazed to discover these criticisms originate with the American ultra-fundamentalist religious Right: the literature of the various Quality Education Networks and Associations for Quality Education springing up across Canada is not explicit about their religious roots.

The religious Right claims to "have become a force to reckon with nationally" and in this matter, at least, they are not exaggerating. In Canada, groups like Albertans for Quality Education have had an enormous influence on education reform. In the United States, they have been particularly successful in influencing the content of textbooks in states such as Texas, which have adopted mandatory prescribed texts and readers. (Teachers are said to be subject to fifty-dollar fines each time they are caught not teaching from the text.) These large states represent an enormously lucrative market to publishers; not surprisingly, therefore, they attempt to satisfy the tastes of the activist far-Right lobby, with textbooks increasingly reflecting the most narrow and uncontroversial restating of America's "basic values." These are the same publishers that produce Canadian textbooks.

This can take curriculum far beyond cautious conservatism. The fundamentalist school board of Lake County, Florida, has decreed that teachers "can only discuss other countries if they make clear America is 'the best of the best.'"[24] The trustees believe that this is necessary, for if students "felt our land was inferior or equal to others, [they] would have no motive to go to war and defend our country." Ultra-nationalism, it appears, fits nicely with the other "strong family values" the board wishes to promote. Even before this faction took electoral control of the board, it had successfully lobbied for policies supporting reduced sex education, the teaching of "creationist" science, and the rejection of programs for disadvantaged children.

The religious Right has announced new items on its agenda for educational reform. At the top of the list is local parent control of education, and a rejection of centrally-mandated curricula. As a political strategy, this is a shrewd choice. Given that community awareness of the political context of education is so limited, and questions of educational philosophy so remote from the activities of most parent groups, the community school is the equivalent of a sitting duck to a well-organized special-interest lobby. Yet it is not just the debate on education that the far Right seeks to influence through lobbying, it is explicitly after political control. Potential candidates have at their disposal CEE's handbook, *How to Elect Christians to Public Office*. They claim electoral success beyond their fondest hopes.

AN ALIGNMENT OF PURPOSE

The "conservative alliance" has always comprised strange bedfellows, whose pragmatic interests coincide more often than their world views. It is unlikely that most members of the religious Right have any particular sympathy for maximizing the profits of transnationals, nor would business lobbyists be likely to list New Age necromancy as the predominant classroom evil. Yet the religious Right claims to receive not only moral but financial support from big business. As you will see, both have a vested interest in destabilizing public schools and their hold on the education of children.

For different reasons, the conservative alliance has come together on an agenda for school reform that would dramatically restructure and reconfigure public education. The alliance agrees on a cluster of structural and political reforms that suit its different purposes: it advances them by exaggeration, and by capitalizing on the vulnerability of schools. It succeeds not so much by peddling its ideologies, but rather by appealing to public and parental anxieties. Some parts of the conservative alliance no doubt have little sympathy for some of the extreme opinions of its more unusual members, but it is naïve to underestimate the alignment of purpose that drives the reform agenda. Intended or not, the multiple effects of reforming from the Right have weakened the system to the point of near-collapse, at least in the minds of some of the concerned public. The greatest asset of the conservative alliance may be that so few of us realize what is going on, and why.

PART THREE:
REMODELLING EDUCATION

RESTRUCTURING FROM
THE RIGHT

*In education, the term "restructuring" is used with the
connotation that "Perestroika" had in the former Soviet Union."*[1]
PENELOPE GURNEY AND BERNARD W. ANDREWS

NO TERM IS MORE POPULAR IN CURRENT EDUCATIONAL DISCUSSION
than "restructuring." It appears as a noun, adjective, verb and
adverb in thousands of documents. Its popularity would suggest
praiseworthy consensus, but in fact it has been appropriated and
redefined by the ideology and idioms of the marketplace.

Within professional discourse, the term restructuring represents an important concept. For several years it has been argued
that schools have been weakened by incremental reforms intended
to enhance function, such as the implementation of a new math
curriculum, or exposing teachers to workshops on how to build
student self-esteem. Such disconnected function-oriented reforms
tend to validate tinkering rather than systematic reform. For a
variety of reasons, these functional reforms rarely have their
intended impact, often because the structures into which these are

inserted leave constraints intact. For example, reforms that encourage cross-disciplinary studies flounder on the subject-specific department structure of secondary schools. Encouraging meaningful collaboration by teachers working in atmospheres of exaggerated autonomy and professional jealousies may be futile. Thus reforms have been thwarted not only by scepticism and poor planning, but also by the political and concrete structures that reinforce the status quo.

Thus the good ideas (and, certainly, some poor ones) of reformers have been sabotaged by the apparent intractability of the structures of education—the rhythms, patterns, assumptions and common experience of schools—as well as by the more tangible conditions of the school curriculum, building and governance. Unless we can get at the structures, it has been argued, there is no point tinkering. We have reached the limits of the changes possible through incrementalism; transformational change is required. Specifics (and priorities) may vary, but it is this quite radical position that is encoded in the term restructuring.

Innumerable symposia, conferences and professional articles pursuing the promises of restructuring have sprouted, usually featuring opinions that describe the need for change far better than they spell what a restructured school would look like or how new structures would improve function. This is not surprising, as consensus regarding the need to change is much greater than the consensus on what a restructured school should be like. Public consultations on education reform reflect this confusion: the common thread is that there is no common thread among those who care enough about public education to express an opinion.

Some opinions, however, speak louder than others. Well-publicized, well-financed opinions crafted to trigger positive public responses to key words such as "choice," "democracy" and "accountability" also exploit public anxiety and parental concern. These opinion shapers offer limited educational choices in the face of an "inevitable" future. The premise that education is about creating alternative futures has been discarded: instead, we are to teach students to cope with an unavoidable future of known, frightening characteristics.

It is in this context, then, that the concept of school restructuring has itself been restructured, appropriated from the debate on better schools to a debate on how to use schools, and therefore children, to further the interests of those who believe they own the future.

Tellingly, the argument for educational reform is no longer based on the needs of students, but on the needs of the workplace, a euphemism for employers. Thus, Gurney and Andrews begin "Studying the Roots of Restructuring" with the following:

> The workplace today emphasizes flexibility, fast response to change, and continuous innovation. Hence schools and universities are questioned as they deliver programs that are often in conflict with society's needs and expectations.[2]

Here the euphemism "workplace" in the first sentence is replaced by "society" in the second, providing rather chilly confirmation of Neil Postman's observation that we are no longer a culture, but an economy. The authors continue: "Restructuring requires rethinking and a shift in paradigm." Indeed it does.

This new paradigm applies to both society and education; it requires convincing the public that their prompt, harmonious alignment with the interests of the great money changers is their best hope. The easiest way to obtain consensus is to convince the dubious that there is no choice, that opposition is merely negativity left over from the old, unenlightened paradigm.

Creating a "strategic convergence" of the inevitable begins with convincing the public to think of schools as businesses, and to expect from schools what they would from any goods-and-services–providing enterprise. When the practices of schools contravene the practices of the marketplace, they demand alignment. To accomplish this goal, import the language of business, which holds considerably more cachet than the jargon of education. Thus clients rather than students, missions rather than goals, investment and outcomes rather than teaching and learning have become the language of education debate. Lost in this translation is the meaningful distinction between the purposes of education and the purposes of business.

Schools are not businesses. They are not factories. They do not exist to generate profits; they were not created to exploit a market niche or to create consumer demand. Students do not sit overnight half-completed on an assembly line; these "inputs" have their own experiences, wills and characteristics. They go home—or elsewhere—at night. Children participate in the "service-delivery" of education.

The only model of education that has a parallel to industry is the most offensive, in which the learner is a passive, empty vessel into which easily digested material is poured. The process that pours most efficiently, spills the least, and costs the least, is the best. Vessels that are damaged are rejected; pouring devices of greatest endurance are prized.

Obviously, such a paradigm is deeply flawed. The proponents of education-as-a-business would have us believe that we can appropriate some characteristics of the marketplace while avoiding the less pleasant ones. This is a false promise. The process of the marketplace is to sort the winners from the losers as efficiently as possible. Can we focus on "excellence" stimulated by competition, and avoid the educational equivalents of "just in time" manufacturing, capital-risk management, sunset clauses and acceptable levels of toxic waste? For when business enters education, it sells something more than brand names. It sells a way of looking at oneself and society. As Jonathan Kozol says, schools shape the soul of the future adult population.[3]

Yet supporters of the business paradigm repeatedly insist that skills matter more than soul. Randall Denley, education columnist for the *Ottawa Citizen*, writes:

The first and perhaps most fundamental thing our boards of education must do is shift their attitudes toward the people they serve; parents and their children. The key words are customer service, competition and choice.[4]

Denley seems to have cut his list short. The key words of today's business climate are downsizing, contract-stripping, globalization and social dumping. Perhaps he believes that we can purchase half a loaf of market mores, as does Meir Porat, who has just launched Akademia Enterprises, Inc., which trades on the Alberta Stock Exchange. Porat intends to offer an international baccalaureate program to students at a chain of private schools to be set up in major Canadian centres.[5] This challenging academic program comes at a rather challenging price: $9000 per year for tuition, $3000 for supplies and an additional $9000 if room and board are required. Porat believes he will be "finding the balance between education and profit-making." Surely Porat's schools would not likely have to contend with the more distracting issues faced by the average community school—hunger, poverty and apathy. This is the appeal of educational "sorting," whether streaming students within a school or into schools with different "value systems," such as charter or private schools. The "choice" may be framed as one of religion or values, curriculum or codes of conduct, but what it comes down to is the structural maintenance of inequity: good schools for the best, what's left over for the rest. This is competition for cultural capital at its best.

Formulations of the school as marketplace do not come under the auspices of the Reform Party or the Fraser Institute. The myth that education is apolitical encourages listeners to the debate about schools to identify contrasting positions, but not the ideologies on which these positions are based.

If politics is about the application of values, as well as about the distribution of power, education can never be separated from ideology, and ideology begets principles. The principles of the marketplace, described in the slogans of business—"total quality," "front-line decision making" and "entrepreneurial leadership"— are being applied to school management. The curriculum is being weeded of non-essential "learnings"—production is being stream-lined. Technology is replacing human labour and ensuring standard-ization in classrooms. The focus on outputs has led to zero-defect objectives; several post-secondary institutions plan to warranty that graduating students will be free from "defects."

Jim Downey, president of the University of New Brunswick, is typical of those eager to buy stock in the culture of competitive-ness. In 1990 he said:

> Encouraged by a strong political consensus that education reform
> is essential to prosperity, business leaders have been among the
> most radical and active reformers. Much of this reform involves
> transferring to schools the organizational, management and free-
> market strategies that have proved so successful in business.[6]

"Successful" is a relative term. From the perspective of manage-ment and shareholders, closing plants and reducing the workforce is an unequivocal success. From the perspective of employees, the same events look quite different.

And so it is with education. The free-market strategies to which Downey refers are not simply hypothetical musings. They are part of the life of schools, not just a matter of educational debate. Some would say the debate is nearly over, that the school of the future is here.

TECHNOPOLY IN THE CLASSROOM

In British Columbia, the new fibre-optics network merging into the information highway is known as Ubiquity. It is everywhere, inevitable; the future will be what advances in technology make it.

The information highway is well under construction, but travellers are not encouraged to concern themselves with where the highway is leading.

Perhaps it is to a holy place. My (HR) eleven-year-old daughter took part in a school field trip to one of the shrines of high tech: Telesat Canada. Along with the standard field-trip permission form came a caveat: no jeans allowed. No jeans, children were told, because they would be entering a business environment. Respect had to be shown in word and deed. Jeans had been considered appropriate attire for visiting every one of Ottawa's museums, the Houses of Parliament and the Governor General's residence. Eleven-year-olds know that the only place you don't wear jeans is church. Perhaps the satellite dishes atop the roof of the Telesat building symbolize our collective redemption.

Of course, such value-laden language is rarely applied to technology. The rapid, frequently unplanned and expensive introduction of computers to classrooms has been justified on the ground of vocational and practical utility. Number alone is considered evidence of progress, despite their low utilization in many classrooms. The goal of computer literacy was added to the curricular agenda of schools during the 1980s although, as Ivor F. Goodson and J. Marshall Mangan point out, a precise definition of this term has never existed.[7] Computer literacy seems to refer to students "becoming comfortable with" computers rather than acquiring particular technical skills. Such conditioning to the ubiquity of computer technology and its place in the future of every child has often been acquired at the price of textbooks and library acquisitions and staff. Computers have been key in shifting the public's perception of schools as a vocational rather than developmental arena, with rarely a nod to the ideological implications of technology; it has been accepted as "a value-neutral, technological necessity of modern life."[8]

Stephen Lewis has warned that a preoccupation with computers is forcing more traditional and more enriching forms of literacy off the agenda. David Suzuki has said that the "cry for computer literacy has been ... one of the biggest cons ever foisted on the school system."[9] Yet there is no evidence that these voices have been heard in the debate on the role of technology in schools—or even that "debate" properly describes schools' response to the possibilities offered by technology. The critical discourse, such as it is, tends to cast schools (i.e., teachers) as modern Luddites, out of touch with "ubiquity."

Columnist Randall Denley complains that local schools have missed the boat on technology, despite the public's "extremely modest" expectations. He laments that the computer has not yet seized its place as "a primary method of learning."[10] Sometimes ubiquity takes a while.

Authors Jennifer Lewington and Graham Orpwood are still hopeful. "The networking of computers, now commonplace in offices, is likely to transform schools as we know them within the next two decades."[11] How alarming that today's classrooms do not resemble offices! In cautioning "technology will never be the complete answer to the problems of teaching and learning," they nonetheless imply, without detailed exploration, that the "problems" of education are highly susceptible to the intelligent application of technology. It would appear that more use of technology is synonymous with better use. Perhaps the mere purchase and display of technology is an adequate substitute for the development of skilled usage.

We have seen the future of schools—and we can even take a tour.

A visit to British Columbia's Burnaby South High School is a chilling event to anyone familiar with the arguments persuasively crafted by Neil Postman in his 1992 book, *Technopoly*.[12] Postman sees schools as one of our primary means of socializing the young into technopoly, a culture that subjugates people to the interests of technology, elevates the pursuit of quantity of information over meaning, and divorces the population from belief systems, as information management has no moral core. He traces human interaction with technology as our negotiation with its powers; implicit in this struggle has been the recognition that technology solves some problems, but creates others.

For Postman, among others, negotiations have failed. The problem of information technology has been reduced to how we can obtain more information faster. He traces the development in the West of "a unity of improbable hope" in technological salvation and marks the points at which technological progress first became synonymous with, and then a substitute for, human progress.

Originally, schools were designed to select and order print information, quite intentionally excluding what was considered distracting, of poor quality or unrelated to student development: children need fundamental concepts to give meaning to new ideas and experiences that they integrate. Schools functioned as information filters in much the same way that families protected children from premature access to "adult" topics and experiences. One wonders, however, how schools can create meaning among children bombarded with meaningless bits of information not attached to any organizing principle beyond devotion to more and better access to yet more information.

Burnaby South provides visitors with an information kit reminiscent of those touting the promise of time-share investments. The introductory pamphlet explains that "in 1987, the Burnaby School Board initiated a district-wide program to restructure its secondary schools. This restructuring involved . . . an aggressive move into the application of modern computers and communications technology."[13] The "partners" in this $34.5-million venture include IBM Canada, BCTel, Dynacom, Creative Learning Systems, B.C. Hydro and half a dozen others. The 1500-student school features 500 networked IBM computers (with soon-obsolete DOS operating systems), 185 networked video monitors and a remote-control distribution system linking classrooms to a media centre (also known as the "head-room") through a fibre-optics system.

The school's promotional folder notes that "for IBM, it's an example of partnership at its best," representing "one of the most advanced networking solutions anywhere in North America. . . . That means users will have instant access to and retrieval of information on an unprecedented scale — up to 75 video channels, including satellite feeds." No doubt Postman would find this solution yet more evidence of the problem of information glut among the users, conventionally known as students. According to this promotional material, education is enhanced because learning can be individualized; each teacher becomes the "facilitator — not the purveyor — of knowledge." The substitution of "knowledge" for "information" is a prime example of the elevation of all data to the same status of meaning. There is no discussion of how patterns, meaning and human purpose and judgement are to be derived from information. Perhaps this problem has been solved by another technological innovation: students at Burnaby South can access the American Press wire service; AP even supplies instantaneous lesson plans with their feature articles. If Paramount can write curriculum, why not AP?

This may be the kind of innovation that Burnaby superintendent Elmer Froese has in mind when he talks enthusiastically about the success of this joint venture: "In some cases it's been a surprise to see how technology that was originally designed for corporate use can be so valuable for students in the classroom."

Other articles in the kit quiver with anthropomorphized excess: "The nervous system runs on a fibre optics spine." The British Columbia School Trustees Association claims that "all data required for education [and] learning is carried on this spine."[14] Clearly "data" have replaced the inclination, experience and capacity of teachers and learners.

Some believe people can be replaced, too. Artificial intelligence expert Roger Shanks — whose Institute for Learning Sciences is financed by IBM — thinks we should "replace teachers with computers since most teachers are intellectually ill-equipped to deal with schoolchildren . . . but they could still serve as teaching assistants to computers."[15]

The Burnaby South materials explain that instead of having biology students performing dissections, technology-serving teachers could simply call up a laser disk, and students could watch an expert dissection. That these two experiences are not interchangeable from the students' perspective is ignored. The promotion next laments the insipidness of "old" low-tech schools, in which students passively watched a teacher in front of a blackboard. Presumably, passively watching a video is qualitatively superior; that technology automatically adds value is a tenet of faith in technopoly.

Everyone associated with Burnaby South takes care to forestall criticism that the school is a heartless showplace for technology; the building is referred to as an educational village; officials points with pride to the inclusion of a school within a school of deaf students, for whom technology has increased access to hearing culture. Yet it is not the theatre or the indoor track that thousands of international visitors come to see, but the technological innovations that are touted as the blueprint for the school of the future, "brimming with innovation and vision." The vision is not limited to what superintendent Froese refers to as a "rollout of robust multimedia," but to a partnership with corporate interests. He describes IBM as "equal partners in terms of intellectual capital and professional contribution. We've discovered the reciprocal benefits of mutual objectives."[16]

It is the fallacy of mutual objectives, of course, that is at the heart of this matter. Froese's objectives, and those of the board he represents, ought to be those of his students and their long-term interest as members of a society drowned in information and starved for purpose. The objectives of IBM are limited to profit. For IBM to exploit educational opportunities requires stimulating an exaggerated demand for IBM's goods and services but it also requires a strategic reformulation of the purposes and practices of education in ways that will increase demand for IBM's products.

Thus high-tech companies have been among the most vocal of those wishing to see schools restructured to produce, as Postman puts it, "a technocrat's ideal: a person with no commitment and no point of view but with plenty of marketable skills."

It would be wrong to suggest that such reductionistic thinking drives every advocate of the integration of technology into the classroom. Many passionately champion the potential of new technologies for democratizing the classroom, enhancing the creative and critical faculties of children and responding to those who have difficulty learning in more conventional ways. Their arguments will not be repeated here; they have ample opportunities, many audiences and no shortage of partners to advance their claims. To discuss technological solutions for education's problems as if they were mutually exclusive, however, does nothing to illuminate how they are enmeshed. To claim technology is merely a tool unattended by ideology and limitations is disingenuous: for technology is not just tool, it is teacher. This is what Marshall McLuhan foresaw when he said that the medium is the message; it is what Plato meant when he said, "The discoverer of an art is not the best judge of the good or harm which will accrue to those who practise it."[17] All in all, not a bad premise to carry into restructuring negotiations with our corporate partners.

GETTING LEAN AND MEAN

The Ottawa Board of Education endures widespread criticism when it is alleged that the board had out-muscled Big Brothers at a local booth selling Nevada tickets. The sympathy is with Big Brothers. No one asks when education became a needy charity.

Ottawa Citizen, March 2, 1994

No serious discussion of school restructuring is complete without a reference to the costs of education. While, as noted in earlier chapters, the relative costs of elementary and secondary education in Canada have been routinely exaggerated, and the unavoidable costs associated with our geography and legislative decisions routinely overlooked, education is still a substantial public expenditure. The pattern of downloading the tax burden from federal to provincial to municipal levels has ensured that as the population ages and the number of children per family decreases, fewer taxpayers have the kind of direct association with schools that they have with garbage collection or congested traffic.

As taxpayers hear that schools have failed, they are understandably cynical about trustees' dilemmas of funding priorities. Education is a labour-intensive activity, so personnel costs have been under pressure. During the last few years, education budgets have been directly subsidized by teachers' salaries. As politicians sensed that unionized professionals would be a safe or even popular target, they have ripped up teachers' collective agreements and imposed salary cuts, breaking the basic rule of collective bargaining. The relative decline in teacher salaries compared to the average industrial wage began in 1987 and has continued. It is unlikely, however, that these cuts will satisfy either budgetary or political requirements.

The targeting of social spending, which includes health and education, to counter a national economic crisis has been extensively documented. As Michael Apple puts it, the public has been trained to view their shiny new cars as good but the taxes for the roads that enable them to drive as evil.[18] Encouraged to see taxes as equally burdensome to everyone and any progressive redistribution an excuse for the wealth-producers to abandon the country, governments are faced with few political alternatives to reducing expenditures, or so we have been told.

Education is not the only sector to feel the economic pinch, of course. However, unlike hospitals, which close beds to achieve economies, schools cannot shut down desks. Unlike public libraries, schools cannot close every second Thursday. Unlike motor vehicles offices, they cannot treat graduates like new drivers and simply increase graduates' waiting period. Although the public may support education funding (fewer than 14% of respondents to CEA's poll believed Canadians receive poor value for their education dollars),[19] ratepayers rarely seize the microphone at school board budget meetings to insist that more tax dollars must be spent on schools. Vocal taxpayers usually argue that cuts to other school budget items fund their pet projects.

The debate on funding takes place in the context of the myth that expenditures have no bearing on the quality of education. Certainly, where and how money is spent is important, and all education dollars are not directed efficiently and to their best purposes; but money spent is directly related to benefits.

This is not a popular position, in a climate of threatened tax revolt, hostility to bureaucracies and contempt for the value of anything associated with the public domain. Public expectations have not contracted with budgets. As one parent recently put it at a budget meeting, "I know you are facing a very difficult time, but I paid taxes for eighteen years before I had a child in your school system."[20] Such parents demand a return on their investment, hard times or not.

Certainly, these are hard times, and when you're hungry, even a Big Mac looks appetizing.

PARTNERS LEARN TO DANCE

The visibility of corporations, their philosophies and their products in Canada's classrooms is in large part the result of relentless downward pressure on budgets. While some may see corporate involvement in the lives of children as an evil necessity, others, from classroom teachers to ministers of education, see corporate involvement as benign or even beneficial.

No doubt this is because these relationships are framed as

partnerships rather than sponsorships, let alone advertising or marketing opportunities. Cash or in-kind contributions are widely viewed as making possible desirable ends otherwise beyond available budgets.

The videogame giant, Sega, through the Youth Foundation, along with Tetra Pak Inc. (of the juice boxes), Office Depot Inc., IBM/EduQuest and thirty other principal sponsors are behind the Computer Learning Foundation (CLF), endorsed by forty-nine states and the ministries of education of British Columbia, Quebec, Manitoba and Ontario.[21] The foundation produces and markets software and courseware to parents, teachers and school systems; it features an elaborate program of sweepstakes events that reward program participation. CLF materials proclaim that the foundation's "basic philosophy is one of partnership." One might expect an educational venture to have a basic philosophy that pertained to students and learning, but CLF merely argues that "our schools desperately need more funding to acquire new technology products." CLF's solution is a "multiple corporate-partner label-collection program," sure to reap rewards "if local business and community members partner with their local schools." Children are to bring labels and proofs of purchase of sponsors' products to the school; sponsors refund up to 1% of the revenue these labels represent.

In order for this to happen, the CLF proposal must appear on a staff meeting agenda, someone must send away for a registration kit, teachers must duplicate promotional materials (on school paper), children must be urged to participate and the advertising materials are sent home. Children then nag their parents, purchases are made, someone cuts off the sticky top of an unrecyclable juice box, fills out the form, attaches the box top and stuffs it in a backpack. A teacher collects it, fills out another form and mails it. For this the school nets approximately 0.3 cents towards the purchase of the reward the literature describes as free. Assuming a $3000 computer system is the reward the school chooses, it would require just under 1 million juice box labels to claim it. Anyone assessing this cost-benefit equation as being one of partnership is unlikely to be in business for very long, yet the foundation claims the project "has been designed for the benefit of schools, rather than purely for the benefit of corporations or retailers."

The number and forms of similar partnerships are increasing at such a rate that virtually no school in Canada is free of a corporate logo. But these efforts are small-time compared with what is taking place south of the border, where companies such as Coca-Cola have become part of the "adopt-a-school" movement, in which the company provides the needy school with "management and technical assistance, equipment and building renovations, teacher training, student employment, and curriculum materials."[22]

Perhaps we'll catch on. The Conference Board of Canada sponsors National Awards for Excellence in Business-Education Partnerships and holds annual conferences promoting partnerships as "helping to improve Canada's competitiveness and quality of life."[23] To be eligible for an award, such partnerships should demonstrate "mutually beneficial collaboration."

The award-winners are featured at the Conference Board's annual national conference. Recent conferences have continued the corporate strategy of running schools down and then modestly proposing themselves as the solution. Gedas Sakus, then president of Northern Telecom, once advised conference participants that "education could adopt and adapt a business approach to competitiveness, seeking out new pedagogical solutions in the same way business pursues ... strategic alliances [and] joint ventures." At the same conference, Jim Downey, president of the University of New Brunswick, explained that market-like reforms will be good for teachers, whom he described as "dispirited" members of a profession "which lacks the cachet and funding to compete with other professions."[24]

How association with business will enhance teachers' status is a mystery, given that it is the business voice that openly or quietly complains about the burden of taxation and teachers' collective contribution to this problem. Reacting to a public letter from a local business association supporting a lock-out of teachers (resulting, the Saskatoon board proudly claimed, in a "savings" of $1 million), Saskatchewan Teachers' Federation representative Fred Herron was unprepared for betrayal by the schools' "partners," describing the businesses' position as "very surprising and disappointing." He was, however, "not the least bit interested in jeopardizing the business relationships that teachers have established with many of [these] firms."[25]

PLUGGED INTO PROFITS

YNN's service will be valuable to advertisers because they can't get their messages across at all to students who zap away from advertisers at home. So now advertisers will have that opportunity.[26]
Rod MacDonald, President, YNN

In 1992, the Youth News Network (YNN) began pitching a worn but clever proposal to ministries of education and school boards. The bait was $50,000 worth of "free" equipment—a satellite transmission receiving system, two VCRs, one portable video camera and television sets for each participating school. These could be had in exchange for just twelve minutes of the school day. Nine and one-half minutes would be devoted to a television news broadcast aimed at students, the rest to market-targeted advertising. YNN's prospectus offered but did not commit itself to future improvements, consisting of an educator's channel carrying profession-relevant programs, and a classroom channel for student programming.

Modestly, the proposal claimed that "YNN is not media literacy in and of itself" but rather "a tool to understand how media work." As to whether students might be harmed by yet more exposure to advertising, YNN counselled the worried not to underestimate the cynicism of youth, adding that "we believe that teens should be given more credit for being able to recognize commercials for what they are." Not that all the commercial time would be corporate, of course—YNN promised that an unspecified share of the nearly nine hours of commercials plugged-in students would view annually would be of the public service variety, emphasizing healthy lifestyles and staying in school. Apparently, cynicism is selective. To those who wondered how advertising might shape news content, YNN's president was dismissive. "Suggestions that the corporate sponsors will influence the editorial content of the program are absurd." In response to concern that twelve minutes a day totals six full school days per year, YNN proposed "reducing the time allotted for students' travel between classes and using that accumulated time for YNN." In other words, walk faster, talk less.[27]

The appeal of this proposal, of course, to ministries, trustees and teachers was the promise of free hardware, even though the proposed contract specified that some of the equipment would be kept under lock and key, dedicated to YNN use only. But something is always better than nothing, particularly where technology is concerned. As YNN put it, "Schools do not have the money to pay for the hardware that media education requires.... We can't keep looking to the taxpayers for more and more resources in schools." No risk is involved, YNN assured teachers, as "by nine years of age, children are sceptical and by eleven they are often cynical." To those who might worry that exposure to YNN's programming might escalate this effect, the prospectus promised, "Perhaps YNN will have its greatest impact in the moral and religious education and in the personal and social education programs. No other medium other than television can best illustrate social issues such as human rights, religious freedoms, social injustice and justice, sex education, and interpersonal relationships."

YNN's success in selling its proposal has not been nearly what it had hoped; it purchased a newspaper ad accusing trustees, teachers' unions and grass-roots parents' organizations of applying the pressure of "special interest groups" and of displaying attitudes that were "not progressive."[28] The backwardness of Canadians in this regard must have come as a surprise to YNN's backers, who no doubt believed their enterprise would be as successful as Channel One, the U.S. original from which it was cloned (and which is described in the next chapter). American school boards continue to sign up for Channel One, despite dubious results: one study found knowledge of current events increased by only 3.3% among students participating.[29] However, educating students was never the point, so if YNN is before its time, what patience won't remedy, "restructuring" may.

MASSAGING THE MESSAGE

The school-related efforts of corporations operating in "sensitive" areas of public policy are particularly noteworthy. Today's students are tomorrow's public-opinion makers as well as today's and tomorrow's consumers. In order to get to them, however, companies must first get to teachers. Teacher and environmentalist David White attended the much-hyped—and government- and industry-sponsored—environmental education conference Eco-Ed, only to find himself surrounded by "promotions from all the bad boys of the world of industrial pollution and toxicity. Hydro-Québec was there with its 'polished' environmental ethic, there were two really slick booths from the nuclear industry and Alcan's display made it appear that it was a recycling company. Who would have guessed that we could learn so much about environmental education from the forest industry?"

Exposure to the selective truths of those corporations heavily invested in swaying public opinion is likely to redouble committed and informed teachers' efforts to prepare students to identify and withstand manipulation. Less well-informed teachers, however, particularly those strapped for time as well as cash, may be prepared to trade a little corporate exposure for an attractively prepackaged lesson plan. In a 1991 article for *Canadian Consumer*, Michelle Hibler lists Esso, Kellogg's, the Canadian Sugar Institute, Abitibi-Price, the Coal Association of Canada, Shell Oil, the meat and dairy marketing associations, Pizza Hut, McDonald's Restaurants, Procter & Gamble, Imperial Oil, MacMillan Bloedel, the Canadian Meat Council, NutraSweet, the Canadian Forestry Association and the Canadian Soft Drink Association as among the commercial voices in our classrooms.[30] It doesn't take much imagination to recreate how the soft-drink manufacturers promote good nutrition. Might the Egg Marketing Board's abundant materials happen to forget to mention cholesterol?

The pedagogical price is low, after all, for a prepackaged unit such as "A Season of Harmony," an elementary-school music program sponsored by McDonald's Restaurants. The fact that timeliness may have to be sacrificed to advertising deadlines is a minor inconvenience. Surely children won't mind writing a Christmas song before October 20 for a chance to be featured in a McDonald's commercial! What's wrong with getting them in touch with the true meaning of Christmas as early as possible?

Faced with the reward-and-gratification track already imprinted on most students, and given their disinclination to read, teachers may see Pizza Hut's rewards for reading three books a month to be great motivation for their reluctant readers. (In one family, the program motivated reading of only the shortest and simplest books throughout the entire year. Recreational reading became a race to get to the last page. After all, three books are three books. No one said you had to enjoy them.) Hibler quotes an enthusiastic incentive grants co-ordinator for the Ottawa Board — surely a new-paradigm job description—as calling the Pizza Hut program "one of our success stories." After all, it did win an American award for promoting literacy.

Whether Pizza Hut is more interested in promoting literacy or sales is open to speculation. Companies marketing to children already produce more than 85% of children's television programming. Do corporations in schools have more altruistic motives than toy manufacturers? Is Mattel in TV production to promote media literacy?

But business is not prepared to stop at providing classroom materials and cultivating brand loyalty. Some want to shape the basic assumptions that drive the curriculum, and at the curriculum itself. In British Columbia, business leaders are acting as reviewers for seven curriculum-development committees, including Dance, Music, Visual Arts and Drama.[31] According to Robert Syme, head of the Curriculum Development Branch of the B.C. Ministry of Education, members of the corporate sector are providing "a perspective of what's going on in the real world." The Business Council of British Columbia, the provincial clone of the BCNI, is providing the ministry with names of "volunteer business leaders who are willing to serve as curriculum developers or reviewers." Syme notes that such "experts" frequently ask sophisticated questions such as "What is the subject area?" and "What is the rationale for this subject?" Restructuring, after all, means starting from square one.

It means rethinking the possibilities. Perhaps children's appetites and school cafeteria deficits are an undiscovered business opportunity. McDonald's thinks so; so does Pizza Hut. In Boulder, Colorado, turning over the cafeteria to McDonald's necessitated a few sacrifices, including lunch-program subsidies to low-income students, but business found a way. "McDonald's came up with the kind of response Oliver Twist might have appreciated: Target those students—along with teen parents and the disabled—to staff the McCafeteria. (You want lunch? Work for it!)"[32]

In tough times, what's one more small corporate intrusion into public education? If classrooms can give "free" exposure to corporations, what's wrong with some cash benefit? Such reasoning, surely, explains the decision of the Toronto Board of Education to enter into a million-dollar deal with Pepsi.

GENERATING THE PEPSI GENERATION

This three-year agreement gives Pepsi exclusive control over all soft-drink and juice-vending machines in Toronto schools. "In return, the soft-drink giant will give the school board one million dollars over three years and supply schools with student-of-the-month plaques, prizes, Pepsi T-shirts and hats." Pepsi also negotiated the distribution of its own videos on substance abuse and the importance of staying in school, favourite themes of corporations trying to earn goodwill and brand loyalty simultaneously.

But the board has standards—a bid from Pepsi to declare itself "the official drink of the Toronto board" did not become part of the deal.[33] Condemned, but not unanimously, by teachers' and students' groups, the deal went ahead for budget reasons, according to trustee Pam McConnell, who called the agreement "one little tiny baby step" in efforts to reduce the budget by $30 million. Education minister Dave Cooke apparently "likes most aspects of the idea," according to the *Ottawa Citizen*, although he says, "We would not want as part of the deal the ability for Pepsi or any other private-sector company to have an influence on curriculum, to have their materials or videos that have advertisements.... There can't be any influence on curriculum or teaching."[34] Perhaps Cooke has been badly briefed. The videos and other education materials produced by the Canadian Nuclear Association, Ontario Hydro and Inco Ltd. used in Ontario classrooms can hardly be said to have nothing to do with curriculum or teaching.

Trustees outside Toronto seemed enthusiastic about the possibilities opened up by the Pepsi precedent. Ottawa trustee Lynda Woods doesn't like the means, but she is prepared to bend if it means revenue: "I'm afraid my principles would have to go out the window a little bit," she admits.[35] It is this kind of thinking that outraged Allan Fotheringham:

> The Toronto Board of Education has signed a contract with the devil, the devil going by the name of the Pepsi-Cola gurglers, makers of things that make your teeth rot.... The people who run the Toronto education system have decided that their students are marketable qualities.... Corporations, who have lots of bucks, will pay lots of bucks if compliant and naive school trustees will lie down with their legs open.[36]

Ron McEachern, president and CEO of Pepsi-Cola Canada, claimed that few people share Fotheringham's negative views. Restructuring requires the public to understand that everyone is just here to help: In a letter to *Maclean's*, where Fotheringham's comments appeared, McEachern said,

> An initiative like this demonstrates the fruitfulness of enterprising, innovative partnerships between the public and private sectors. Regarding Canadian education, we are proud to be part of the solution.[37]

Perhaps it depends on what you consider to be the problem.

RENOVATING THE STUDENT

The survival of the children of the fittest.
JONATHAN KOZOL

IN A WORLD OF DISAPPEARING BORDERS, WHAT IS HAPPENING TO Canadian education cannot be examined in isolation from world trends. The assault on public education is global.

A child in China's Hubei province waits hours in line to sell his blood, in order to pay his school fees. In Brazil, a country suffering 65% unemployment, thousands of street children play a daily game of cat-and-mouse with death squads mandated by local merchants to clear them from the streets. School is the last thing from their—or their government's—minds. Mexican public school teachers sell food, pencils and supplies to their students, as their government wages are no longer sufficient to support them. There are 900 million people in the world today who cannot read and write, two-thirds of them women. An estimated 400 million school-age children will never have an education.

The substantial progress to educate the planet's billions—an effort of the 1950s, 1960s and the first half of the 1970s—is in retreat. During those decades, universal education was a goal of most governments, backed up by government and international aid money. Spending on education for children and adults rose steadily. In 1970, education was the first priority of publicly financed social programs in eight OECD countries, second in another seven.

Women were singled out for special attention in many countries, for higher education for women meant healthier—and smaller—families, and more productive communities. Universal public education was seen as the key to development; the United Nations and other international agencies singled out education, along with public health, as the most important goal of society.

Now, however, governments are eyeing education funds for other uses. They are cutting teachers' salaries, increasing class sizes, severely cutting back public funding and closing schools. Many no longer provide school supplies, thereby burdening poor families; in many parts of the world, parents are taking their children out of the classroom and putting them in factories or brothels. Although 90% of children in developing countries start primary school, up to half complete less than four years.

There are numerous factors to consider in the world-wide decline of education. Deep cuts to funding for global birth planning during the Reagan and Bush years and the rise in religious fundamentalism around the world are serious setbacks to women and population planning. Ethnic wars and famine ravage many areas of the world and force all but subsistence concerns from government agendas. And governments everywhere are no longer able to harness the profits from business towards social ends. However, it would be a mistake to think that this reversal is merely the conjunction of random happenings. The same economic ideology that is driving the global economy is pushing the goal of universal education to the bottom of the political agenda.

A special edition of the *New Internationalist* was devoted to the state of global education. It found that education reform is linked almost everywhere to a right-wing assertion of a market model for education:

> As soon as education becomes a market then it becomes something available only to those who can afford it—and puts society's most vulnerable groups at an even greater disadvantage. In these circumstances if you are poor, or black, if you have a disability or learning difficulty, if your country has been disrupted by war, if you are a girl rather than a boy, and particularly if you combine any of these elements, then your chances of not completing school are high indeed. Your chances are better if you live in the North rather than the South, but even then your education is more likely to be guaranteed if you are white and middle-class.[1]

Education trends are following global social and economic trends. Both governments and international organizations are giving up on the goal of equality and universality—some reluctantly, others with enthusiasm. Instead, they are acquiescing to a class system born of deep economic disparities. They have accepted, by and large, the corporate model of competitiveness and the "inevitability" of Social Darwinism. As a result, the shape of society, both within nation-states and globally, resembles a pear, or a pyramid: the top third is getting richer and increasing its power; the middle third is sliding slowly down to meet the bottom third, which is in increasingly desperate poverty.

All over the world, within countries and between countries, the disparity between rich and poor is growing dramatically. In Canada, the disparity in the level of incomes between the top 20% and the bottom 20% is 7:1 and growing. In the United States, it is 9:1 and growing. World-wide, it is 150:1 and has doubled in the last thirty years. But it will take far less than thirty years to double again, says Dr. Mahbub ul Haq, development adviser to the United Nations. The chasm is widening very fast.[2]

Goals and policy design for education in a world that accepts this economic model are different than goals and policy design for education in a world seeking equality. Governments are restructuring education in order to ensure that those at the top of the pyramid have access to the best education possible; however, under the rubric of deficit fighting, they are diverting funds once used for the public, universal education of those near the bottom to the private sector. Thus education mirrors society's design to serve a world dominated by transnational business and its needs.

DEVELOPED COUNTRIES

Public education is still said to be a key priority in most developed countries, but there has been a steady decline in the growth of public education spending in all the OECD countries since 1975; in the United States and Great Britain, education spending declined between 1975 and 1980.

The share of public expenditures on education decreased in several countries, quite dramatically. In Canada, it fell from 24.4% in 1970 to 17.7% in 1980; in Japan, from 20.2% in 1970 to 17.7% in 1980. As a percentage of the GDP, public education expenditure dropped from 10.2% in Canada in 1970 to 6.7% in 1991; from 6.2% in Great Britain in 1970 to 4.8% in 1988; from 6.0% in the United States in 1970 to 4.8% in 1988. Capital expenditures on education declined in most OECD countries throughout the 1980s, leading to the deterioration of facilities and equipment.

Although both the GDP and spending on other public programs slowed in OECD countries in the last half of the 1970s, the decline was much smaller than that of education spending. And when the GDP and public spending picked up in the 1980s, education spending did not keep pace. Governments justified the continued underfunding of education by pointing to declining enrolment rates, but the fall in education spending was almost everywhere greater than the drop in enrolment. Governments have simply pushed education down the public-policy agenda, with, according to the OECD, "undesirable effects on both the quality and character of education outputs."[3]

It is commonly believed that Japan places great emphasis on education, and that we would do well to emulate its results-oriented system. However, as a percentage of GDP, public education spending in Japan in 1970 was only 5.0%, very low by the standards of developed countries. By 1991, it had dropped to 3.7%. Students attend after-class, privately run "cram schools" (often taught by public school teachers to top up their incomes), to prepare for the all-important university entrance exams. The *Globe and Mail*'s Edith Terry says, "In Japan, undergraduate education is widely regarded as a four-year holiday. Serious education, even in technical fields, begins only when the new graduate joins a company."[4] The priority in Japan is preparation for business, and public education takes a back seat.

The European Community may be headed in the same direction. Although it has placed education and training high among key priorities—along with agriculture, transport and competition policy—education is increasingly geared to global competitiveness. In its Green Paper on Schools, the EC's Commission on Human Resource Development has directed that all 300,000 schools, 4 million teachers, and 67 million pupils in the European Community be placed in "partnerships" with transnational corporations within the decade.[5] Reacting to record unemployment, particularly among youth, governments are increasingly turning to the private sector for aid to education, while attacking expenditures for public education.

Perhaps the most startling example of a developed nation

changing course suddenly is New Zealand, whose experiment in massive privatization of its public sector is used as a model by the business community and right-wing governments everywhere, including Alberta. The introduction of "consumer preference," as school choice is referred to by New Zealanders, combined with dramatic cuts to the public system, has created a tiered system of education in just several years. A survey of per-capita spending in schools by the Anglican Church of New Zealand found wide differentials in student funding, leading to "inequities arising from growing trends to 'user pays' in education." The church reports the creation of an underclass in the country and warns of great future unrest as a result of these decisions. Meanwhile, to save money, the government recently permitted corporate sponsorship of most school materials. New Zealand teachers report that students are distracted by the advertising on matriculation exams.

THE REST

Nowhere is the gap between global rich and poor more apparent than in educational expenditures. In 1988, the developed countries, with roughly one-quarter of the world's population and a smaller proportion of its school-age children, spent more than seven times on education than that of the developing countries, where the commitment to universal education has been eroded by debt and externally imposed economic and social restructuring.[6]

Unable to meet debt payments to the World Bank and the International Monetary Fund, developing countries are given debt relief in return for undergoing economic transformation on a free-market model. They must privatize large areas of government services; deregulate transportation, telecommunications and utilities; lower minimum wage standards; favour transnational companies over domestic industry; convert subsistence farmland to corporate agribusiness; and cut back on public spending on education and health.

Essentially, countries are forced to export their way out of debt, even if that means less food and poorer opportunities for their citizens. CUSO says that more than seventy Third World countries have now gone through this economic and social shock treatment and in almost every case, they have emerged poorer than they were before they began the process. The United Nations estimates that at least 500,000 Third World children have died as a direct result of structural adjustment. UNICEF reports that the poorest have paid their countries' debt with their health.[7]

Spending on education in the poorest thirty-seven countries declined by 25% in the last decade; primary student numbers declined by 20%. The assault affects people remarkably similarly throughout the developing world. The countries of sub-Saharan Africa, for instance, cut their education expenditures by 30% in the early 1980s. In absolute terms, spending decreased by $4000 million, a decline for each pupil from $33 to $16, now the world's lowest rate. Most countries in sub-Saharan Africa and Latin America increased education spending at annual rates of 5% or more from 1970 to 1980; two-thirds of them now allocate well under 5%: Africa, at 3.4%; Latin America, at 4.0%.

Drop-out rates throughout Africa have increased sharply. Governments lay off teachers in massive numbers and are recruiting unqualified replacements. In many countries, teachers have not been paid for many months. Schools go without materials altogether; in Sierra Leone, the cost of a textbook for students can be equivalent to six years of a graduate teacher's salary. Governments have replaced the policy of free education with cost-recovery programs whereby parents and communities are asked to pay for facilities and teachers. Some are encouraging missions, churches and private agencies to take over their schools.[8]

Costa Rica has the highest literacy rate in its region, thanks to a concerted public education drive between 1950 and 1980. But in

1981, the government was given an IMF loan on condition that education expenditures be cut. By 1986 education expenditure had fallen to 4.3% of GDP from a high of 6%. The Costa Rican Ministry of Education reports an alarming decline in the condition of schools and equipment and high drop-out rates as a result.

In Brazil, support for public education has deteriorated so far that it is almost impossible to pass university entrance-level exams as a graduate of the public system. Schooling at all levels consists of shifts of no more than four-hour days—except for private schools, of course. The wages of teachers are so meagre that they must all work multiple shifts and supplement their income with other work. And one of the major growth industries in education in Brazil (and many other Latin American countries) is private schools set up specifically to prepare public school students for the university entrance exams.[9]

Even the emerging nations of Eastern and Central Europe are operating under the direction of the IMF and the World Bank. With a foreign debt of $20 billion, Hungary has the highest level of per capita indebtedness in the region. The IMF and World Bank put Hungary on a monetary diet, with strict instructions to cut expenditures in the public sector, especially education. By 1989, the government was openly discussing state disinvestment in pre-school teaching, handing schools over to the churches and making local authorities responsible for the entire educational system.

In a June 1991 letter to the Hungarian Teachers' Union, the minister of education admitted what many had long suspected— that the World Bank was sending teams of "advisers" to "restructure" education. It soon became clear that the World Bank was behind government plans to reduce the period of training for primary school teachers and to transfer their training from higher- to secondary-level education; thus, primary-school teachers would require only high school graduation. The bank had also criticized the state's financial participation in supervised instruction and objected to what it called overstaffing in the Hungarian public education sector.[10]

In Mexico, the abolition of illiteracy and the creation of a system of universal education were central to the revolution of 1910. The government boasts that the rate of illiteracy dropped from 66% to 6% between 1921 and 1990, and the percentage of Mexicans attending school increased from 22% to 98%. While this may be an exaggeration, there is no doubt that great progress was made. Institutions of higher learning have increased from 31 in 1960 to 763 in 1991, and they became steadily more democratic in their access to Mexicans of all economic backgrounds. The system of education in Mexico had become, as a result, over-whelmingly public at all levels; it has also been, until recently, the responsibility of the federal government. Delivery and standards were highly centralized in order to ensure that education contin-ued to receive national priority and to safeguard equality of access for all students.[11]

Concurrently, one of the strongest teachers' union on the hemi-sphere emerged in Mexico, and it wielded great influence on educa-tion policy. Most teachers were of peasant origin, deeply committed to the land-reform movement, and many became leaders in the attempt to democratize Mexican politics. However, universal educa-tion is threatened by education "reform" brought in a decade ago. With the support of the World Bank, the IMF—Mexico was the first country to implement structural adjustment in return for debt relief—and the big corporations, the Mexican government initiated massive cuts to education. Teachers' salaries have declined by more than 50% during the last decade. Mexico is dismantling its national system of education, leaving impoverished states to do what they can, and is allowing full private sector participation in the revision of curriculum and in school boards. As well, industry-school part-nerships are safeguarded by a government-business agreement intent on transforming education to the needs of industry.

Private education services are rapidly attracting wealthier

families who do not want their children attending impoverished public schools, and poorer families are left to foot many of the bills for their children's public education. Not surprisingly, the teachers say, decentralization of education will break their union— and with it will go the last strong voice for national commitment to public education.

TWO WORLDS MEET IN AMERICA

East St. Louis Senior High School in Missouri sends its students home every time the two local pumping stations fail, as the halls and kitchen area are flooded with raw sewage emitting gaseous fumes. Five Haitian youngsters in a high school in Brooklyn's Crown Heights take classes in a washroom. At Sand Hill Elementary School in Greene County, Mississippi, children must bring their own toilet paper to school. At neighbouring Humphreys County High School, the temperature often reaches 100°F. The only air conditioning is a hole in the roof.

Every few months, someone starts a fire with a kerosene-filled beer bottle at Pyne Point Junior High in Camden, New Jersey; the school fire-alarm system has not functioned properly for twenty years. Nearby Camden High can't afford a lunchroom, so the students leave the school at noon; many do not return. Paterson, New Jersey, is so short of classroom space that four elementary schools have taken over abandoned factories: they even hold classes in the boiler room and bathroom. In low-income Irvington, one school is short eleven classrooms. The kids study in the auditorium—one class in each corner, in a coat room, a storage room, a closet and a coal bin. In Anacostia, a suburb of Washington, schools are next door to crack houses. In one school, dead rats are regularly found in the cafeteria.

The drop-out rate of students at Chicago's inner-city schools is at least 50%. At some schools, the drop-out rate is 85%. By the time spring comes to the city, substitute teachers are so scarce, due to lack of funds, that 18,000 students attend classes with no teachers. Twenty-seven per cent of high school graduates read at eighth-grade level or below. Nearly half the kindergarten children in Chicago's public schools will leave school virtually illiterate. Many of the city's schools have no library or physical education facility, no art or music classes, no playgrounds or science labs. Hundreds of children share one or two stinking bathroom facilities, often with no toilet paper, usually without soap or paper towels, in schools all over America.

As many as three of four blacks and four of five Hispanics in New York City fail to complete high school within the traditional four years. Of the 1400 students at Woodrow Wilson High School in Camden, New Jersey, only sixty take college-entrance exams. A principal in a public school in New York says he is forced to take any teacher that is "still breathing." "I take anything that walks in," says a Chicago principal, referring to both students and teachers. "Nobody in his right mind would send his kids to [an inner-city Chicago] public school," says a Chicago alderman.

And, of course, there's the violence. Firearms have outstripped traffic accidents as the leading cause of injury-related death among young American adults—a 14% increase in the past three years.[12] Nearly one in four students and one in ten teachers have been victims of violence on or near school property.[13] The Atlanta Center for Disease Control reported in 1992 that one in four U.S. high school students carried a weapon to school at least once during the month before they were surveyed. Nearly 35% of the 100 largest school districts now use metal detectors at school entrances.

New York City employs 3000 school security guards; more than 2600 assault incidents in or near New York schools and 2500 incidents of weapons possessions were reported there in 1992. The city's Office of School Safety distributed 2300 pairs of handcuffs to its schools. Ninety per cent of the male inmates of the city's prisons are drop-outs from the city's public schools.

However, not all public schools are created equal.

Ninety per cent of the students at New Trier High School in the wealthy Chicago suburb of Winnetka go on to four-year colleges, including Harvard, Princeton, Berkeley, Brown and Yale. Situated on a twenty-seven-acre site, New Trier boasts a physical education centre that includes three gyms, a fencing room, a wrestling room, studios for dance instruction and an Olympic-size pool.

New Trier offers seven foreign languages, drama, art and music, elective courses in the literature of Nobel winners, aeronautics, criminal justice and computer languages. In senior literature classes students are reading Nietzsche, Darwin, Plato, Freud and Goethe. The school operates a television station with a federal broadcast licence; it broadcasts on four channels to three countries. New Jersey's wealthy Cherry Hill High offers fourteen physical science courses and eighteen biology electives and houses a greenhouse for the study of horticulture. Nearby Princeton High has seven well-appointed "music suites," and computer-equipped subject-related study halls, staffed at all times by "faculty."

The average class size at New Trier is twenty-four children — it's forty in inner-city schools—and every freshman is assigned a faculty adviser with whom the student remains until graduation. Each adviser, who is given a reduced teaching load in order to free up time for counselling, advises about twenty-four children. There is one counsellor per 420 children at Chicago's inner-city schools; in Paterson, New Jersey, one counsellor serves 3600 elementary children.

The United States of America houses the best and some of the worst schools in the world. The disparity is greater in 1994 than it was in the 1960s, when the effort to eliminate racial and class inequality began.[14] And the economic and social chasm is growing in America. Labor secretary Robert Reich says that if current trends continue, by the year 2020, the richest 20% of Americans will earn more than 60% of total American income; the share of the poorest 20% may drop to 2%.[15]

Education professor emeritus Arthur G. Wirth of Washington University predicts, "Well-educated élites will withdraw further into their secure enclaves, living a life with excellent health care, challenging work, effective schools, global travel, and international electronic linkages. The urban and rural poor will live largely out of sight in their decaying communities. The despair and hopelessness of their children will be facts of life."[16]

The startling difference in the quality of education offered to Americans of different ethnic and economic backgrounds mirrors class divisions. Public schools depend on local property taxes as their primary source of funding. The United States is the only major industrial nation to promote the radically inequitable school-financing system based on this tax structure.

Not only do wealthier areas have a larger tax base, but they do not have to stretch their dollars as far as poorer, inner-city areas, which must provide increased police and fire protection, public housing and health care to low-income people. Moreover, property tax is income-tax deductible; therefore, wealthy home-owners get back a substantial portion of the funds they pay for their children's school. Local funds are supplemented by state and federal money, but the federal portion is very small, and decreasing—down to about 6% of total school expenditures from 7.4% a decade ago.

In a word, wealthy communities have wealthy public schools; poor communities have poor public schools. Each year, a high school class in Chicago receives approximately $90,000 less than a comparable class at New Trier. New York City spends less than $6000 annually on a child in Harlem, and more than $11,000 on a child in Manhasset. Total yearly spending on public education in Illinois ranges from $2100 on a child in the poorest district to $10,000 in the richest. Teachers' salaries, of course, reflect these disparities: those who teach in wealthy schools can make twice as much as those who teach in poor schools. Guess which schools get the pick of the best teachers?

The high drop-out rate for poorer children means the accumulated total investment in their education is even lower. Even if you accept this perverse view of economics, children of the poor have no choice. Unless parents have the wealth to send them to private schools, children are required by law to attend their local school. Jonathan Kozol, educator and writer, sums up the dynamic: "Thus the state, by requiring attendance but refusing to require equity, effectively requires inequality. Compulsory inequity, perpetuated by state law, too frequently condemns our children to unequal lives."

The business community and some media argue that society must be "realistic" and offer low-income children limited career objectives suited to their lives. Investment strategies, they maintain, should be matched to each student's potential economic value. Future service workers and plumbers need different schooling—and even different schools—than future scientists and lawyers. As Kozol puts it, "First we circumscribe their destinies and then we look at the diminished product and we say, 'Let's be pragmatic and do with them what we can.'"

This view of education as a preparation of the young to serve the economic system is not new. Calvert and Kuehn show that a major part of the vision of the creators of the "common schools" in the 1800s was to serve the economic and workplace needs of industrialists: 20% were needed to be the leaders and professionals and run the institutions; 30% were needed as middle managers and white-collar workers; 30% were needed as factory workers; and the remaining 20% were not needed at all.

As American industry increasingly became centralized into large corporations, schools were built to mirror their structure and form, complete with a bureaucratic hierarchy of professional administrators and a top-down system of management. Children were being well-trained to take their respective places in industry; conformity of attitude towards the free market was strongly encouraged.

The myth that America's schools were founded on equality was just that—a myth. Systems of testing, streaming and tracking —the forerunners of the current obsession with national testing — largely reproduced existing class structures. Blacks were never assimilated into the great "melting pot"; rather, they were deliberately kept apart to be educated as a source of cheap labour: legal racial educational segregation of the past has been replaced by legal economic educational segregation. Opportunities for the children of the ghetto are not much brighter than they were for their grandparents.

To be sure, there continue to be passionate, progressive voices calling for genuine universal education in America. Thomas Jefferson dreamed of a free, democratically controlled common school for all citizens. Many writers and activists argued powerfully for the need to teach critical thinking, social awareness and democratic values. The great John Dewey reacted to the impact of early industrialization with a warning: "Democracy has to be born anew in each generation, and education is its midwife."

The influence of Dewey and like-minded leaders of later decades could be felt in the 1960s and 1970s, in the growing confidence of Americans that their public education system could, with time, promote both excellence and equity. There are also progressive education champions in America today giving public voice to reform alternatives. Their ideas are disseminated by social activists such as Jesse Jackson and Ralph Nader and they have their supporters in Congress and state legislatures.

However, by the 1980s, the political climate in the United States had changed. The state came to be viewed as the cause of rather than the solution to the nation's troubles. Ronald Reagan ran and governed on a platform of removing the state from the business of the nation and allowed the free market to set the rules for the social and economic lives of his citizens.

George Bush followed suit, even giving his vice-president,

Dan Quayle, a mandate to head up a roving task force to slash regulations and standards wherever he encountered them in the name of boosting competitiveness. Nothing was safe from Quayle's zeal —not food-safety standards, not food stamps, not spotted owl protection. For these presidents, government's only purpose is to broker the system for private business. Public service and public rights were assaulted at the highest level.

Many Americans thought that they had elected a president with a different view when Bill Clinton took power and, indeed, in some ways this is so. His health-reform proposals indicate a desire to bring some equity to health services in his country, but they are still based on a for-profit model. Moreover, his enthusiasm for health care has not matched the aggressive support he gave to NAFTA, which locks in a private, deregulated model of future government and economic policy against unions, environmentalists and human rights workers—the very sectors who rejoiced when he was elected.

As well, President Clinton's foreign policy, like Jean Chrétien's, puts diplomacy and human rights second to commercial interests. The *Toronto Star*'s David Crane says, "The Clinton administration is embarked on an 'America First' campaign in the world economy and is willing to resort to almost any device— from Japan-bashing to diplomatic strong-arming—to push U.S. economic interests." American embassies are much more aggressively promoting domestic industry, and their diplomats are undergoing intensive training to prepare them for their new function as marketers of American business.

The Clinton administration has launched the toughest campaign to cut welfare payments to single mothers. Millions of young mothers and their babies—mostly black and uneducated—have been affected. It appears that Bill Clinton is following in the ideological footsteps of his predecessors; to the relief of corporate America, it is "business as usual."

THE BUSINESS OF AMERICAN EDUCATION

It is in this political climate that the state's right to run the education system has been challenged by conservative leaders in industry and government. The failure of governments to address deep social inequities in schools has muted support for public education from many traditional liberals. The business lobby has had the field largely to itself.

As a result, commitment to public education has been seriously eroded. Among the top nineteen industrial nations, the United States now ranks seventeenth in public spending on education and dead last in compensation to its teachers.[17] Subcontracting to the private sector for the provision of public services to schools has risen dramatically in the last decade. Transportation, food services, custodial and maintenance work are all affected. In one study, the Illinois Education Association found that 46% of its schools had subcontracted all or part of these services in 1993.

The number of private schools has increased by more than 25% since 1986. The school board of Minneapolis has turned over the running of the city's public schools, and their annual budget of $350 million, to a private firm. In Illinois, a recent ballot measure that would have "proclaimed education a fundamental right and given the state the primary responsibility for funding public schools" was defeated; it was not supported by the state's governor. In Louisiana, a constitutional amendment was passed that made it easier to "use dedicated elementary and secondary education funds to meet [other] budget emergencies."[18]

Court-ordered school equalization spending does not prove to be the answer: in 1977, the California Supreme Court, responding to a challenge of racial inequity in the funding of its schools, ordered the state to fund across community lines in a more equitable way. White voters revolted, lobbied for property tax cuts and gutted school budgets statewide. By the late 1980s, California ranked eighth in the nation in per-capita income, but thirtieth in school spending. As a result, white and affluent communities are turning to private schools, even if they support the idea of public schooling. The state, instead of seeing this as a failure, has declared that it wants private schools to capture 40% of student enrolment within a decade—up from the current 10%.

In Dade County, Florida, the American Bankers Insurance Group has built its own K–2 learning centre for the children of its employees. The building belongs to the company; the books, teachers and furniture are supplied by the taxpayers of Dade County. Honeywell Corporation operates a similar school in Clearwater, Florida. The state is so keen on these schools that it has passed a law giving property-tax exemption for the corporate buildings that house them.

In New York City, American Express sponsors Academies of Travel and Tourism in four city high schools. New Milford Savings Bank operates a full-service bank at the New Milford High School in Connecticut; its student "employees" get credits but no pay for their work.

Burger King academies—fully accredited quasi-private high schools—are now operating in fourteen U.S. cities. At a high school in Boulder, Colorado, McDonald's supplies not only the food, but also the curriculum. Students study McDonald's inventory, payroll and ordering procedure in math; McDonald's menu plans in home economics; and its marketing practices in business class. These companies are vying with Dunkin' Donuts, Pizza Hut, Dairy Queen and Taco Bell (Pepsico) for the $5-billion market of the National School Lunch and Breakfast Programs. Pizza Hut engineered an exemption for its meat-topped pies from meat-inspection regulations that apply to all federally funded school lunches.[19]

By far the biggest and most controversial corporate contenders on the scene are two for-profit companies in head-to-head competition for the spoils of public education. The Edison Project plans a chain of hundreds of private schools across America in the next decade; it is now in the business of managing public schools.

In its bid to run the Milwaukee public schools, the company has proposed bringing in its own, non-certified teachers (and to pay them as little as $10,000 a year). Led by the controversial and charismatic entrepreneur Chris Whittle, a man with important corporate connections and ties to the Bush White House, and former Yale University president, Benno Schmidt, Edison is the offspring of Whittle's Channel One. In exchange for supplying equipment, more than 12,000 junior and high schools allow Channel One to televise daily commercial news and advertising—"infotainment"— to 40% of the nation's students.

Whittle Communications charges $195,455 for each thirty-second commercial spot; advertisers are willing to pay for a captive audience. The contracts state that 90% of the children in a school must watch the program 90% of the time; each program must be watched in its entirety—a show cannot be interrupted— and the teacher does not have the right to turn it off. The company earns well over $100 million a year on the backs of the most disadvantaged students in America. A University of Massachusetts study found that poor schools are six times as likely as wealthy ones to say yes to Channel One, and the company targets low-income communities of colour.[20]

A Texas parent says, "Over half of the kids in Texas are too poor to buy their own school lunch. In light of this, it is egregious that students are forced to watch commercials at school and be reminded daily of the products they cannot afford to buy." Whittle defends his two companies. "Is there an inherent conflict between profits and education? No way. The biggest contribution business can make to education is to make education a business."

The other big contender in the for-profit market is Education Alternatives Inc. (EAI), a company that claims it can run public schools for the same amount of money as the government, improve achievement and make a profit. It has contracts with a number of public boards to operate their schools. The Pinckney, Michigan, board recently handed over its entire school district to

EAI for five years. But everywhere the company goes, it is dogged by angry protest.

EAI makes a profit the old-fashioned way—by cutting staff, wages and services. In Baltimore, where it operates nine city schools, EAI replaced ninety paraprofessionals—the majority of whom are African-American unionized workers earning $10 an hour and receiving benefits—with teaching interns—the majority of whom are white, non-unionized, earn $7 an hour and receive no benefits.

The company fires or shifts custodial, maintenance, secretarial, management and food-service employees among schools and sub-contracts these functions to non-union, hourly workers at lower pay and with no benefits. It cut art, music, reading, special ed and libraries. It is also receiving about $1500 more per student per year from public financing than comparable Baltimore schools, which has landed EAI in court against the Baltimore Teachers' Union.

Among the big companies allied with EAI to provide services in its schools is Computer Communications Corp., owned by Simon and Schuster, the largest educational publishing company in the world. Simon and Schuster is owned by Paramount, the firm that bought Canadian educational publishing companies Prentice-Hall and Ginn. Paramount is owned by Viacom, the biggest publishing-telecommunications company in the world.

Corporate money is all over education. In 1991, IBM and Exxon contributed $24 million each. Ford spent $22 million; General Electric, $17 million. A poll of the top Fortune 500 service and industrial companies found that at least one-quarter had donated more than $1 million to education. Research by Ralph Nader's organization found that free curriculum materials are provided to schools by nearly two-thirds of the largest American corporations.

This is not largesse; these contributions are tax-deductible. Moreover, many corporations have received local and state tax abatement in return for keeping jobs in the community. General Motors led a corporate tax revolt in Michigan and received a waiver on property taxes in Tennessee until 1995 in return for a new Saturn factory. Such abatements reduce local property taxes, which, of course, are the main funding source for nearly all public school budgets. The corporate component of property taxes fell from 45% in 1957 to about 16% in 1990.[21]

Cuts in the corporate tax base lead to dramatic decreases in public revenues, forcing public schools to scramble for private contributions. School administrators and teachers are spending enormous amounts of time and energy seeking private funding, often for their own jobs; some are hiring professional fund raisers. Dependence on private funding may result in school governance going to the highest bidder: the result—company schools.

Thus, corporate America looks like a knight in shining armour for its financial support of impoverished schools, while being handed an incomparable opportunity to influence how and what children are taught. Apple Computer has developed a sophisticated education/business partnership project that offers schools "bundles" of computer hardware, software and curriculum materials, teacher training and special Apple "community volunteers" to explain the system to children in the classroom. Apple describes one set of its bundles:

> In the kindergarten class, we introduce our youngest students
> to the computer and its basic operation with Kid Pix and The
> Playroom.... By the first grade, most children are comfortable
> using the mouse for drawing, so they use the story writer
> component of KidsTime or Storybook Theatre for the initial writing
> steps.... Later, we introduce our second and third graders to
> Number Munchers.... We round out our curriculum with The
> Factory, which introduces students to logical thinking and spacial
> orientation.

How will this benefit Apple? With the opportunity to "expand employee training through use of the (school) facility... Reduce

the need for on-the-job training... Influence curriculum....
Enhance their public image."

Cash-strapped schools are jumping on board. Thomas
Shannon, executive director of the National School Boards Association, wrote an enthusiastic introduction to the Apple Computer
supplement: "For this one brief, shining moment, education has
the full attention of the nation."[22] That attention brings together
an odd marriage of people and interests that might not have much
in common: far-right Christians, union bashers, sophisticated international business leaders and the U.S. military.

The United States army has plans to substantially increase its
Junior Reserve Officers Training Corps by doubling the number of
high schools offering their program from the current 1500 to 3000
by the year 1997. As well, the military is to be put in control of
"target schools," where students enrolled in ROTC will also take
all academic and vocational classes from military personnel. The
Pentagon is convinced that public schools are not teaching the right
values and discipline to young people. Junior ROTC's purpose is
"to instill military values and culture into the minds of youth."

Texts at one of the ROTC pilot schools in San Francisco not
surprisingly reflect those "military values and culture." The texts
clearly portray a convergence of U.S. military and economic concerns and suggest that military power is properly used to uphold
American investment interests at home and abroad. "Fortunately
for the Army, the government policy of pushing the Indians farther
west, then wiping them out was carried out successfully.... Settling
labour disputes was an honourable Nineteenth Century occu-
pation of the Army.... One of the most well-known instances
was when the Army put an end to the railroad strike of 1894."[23]
Military-industrial companies who have felt the pinch of the Cold
War may well see economic salvation in the running of schools.

Above all, however, the strongest attack on America's public
schools is coming from the powerful corporate interests that
stand to gain from their demise. The board of the New American

Schools Development Corporation, established by former president Bush to funnel corporate money into a new system of private schools, and kept alive by President Clinton to the surprise and consternation of many educators, reads like a Who's Who of the Fortune 500—Boeing, RJR Nabisco, Eastman Kodak, AT&T, Martin Marietta, Honeywell, IBM, Xerox, B.F. Goodrich, the American Stock Exchange and Exxon. Says David Kearns, former CEO of Xerox, former deputy education secretary and current head of the influential right-wing Business Higher Education Forum, "It is time for business to take ownership of the schools."

It is essential that parents and the public feel part of this transformation; hence, the heavy emphasis on school "choice" in the language of school reform.

RETOOLING THE POLITICS OF CHOICE

Destiny is not a matter of change, it is a matter of choice.
NEWSLETTER OF ALBERTANS FOR QUALITY EDUCATION

IN NEO-CONSERVATIVE RHETORIC, THE RESTRICTION OF CHOICE IS demonized as the root of all evil; the right to more choice in more areas is touted as the solution to our moral, economic and political conundrums. Governments are viewed as the agencies that limit choice, and the marketplace the venue in which choice triumphs.

Choice is being used skilfully as the enticement into the most important education-policy debate of this decade. The word is being recreated as conveying such innocent, inherent integrity that it cannot be opposed. As Harvard professor Gary Orfield points out, "Choice is a term that is difficult to disagree with in principle, but which has no clear meaning until many blanks are filled in. In other words, it is an almost perfect political concept."[1]

Choice has, of course, an honourable place in political and educational philosophy. The fundamental act of democratic politics is voting, the consummate act of choice. But universal suffrage ensures that the right to choose is equally available to all, and citizens are encouraged, at least intermittently, to think beyond personal gain in exercising this choice. Within modern civilizations, the right to choose has been tempered by the obligation to consider the effects of that choice on others. Freedom to choose must be constrained by its consequences to others and thus monitored in the public interest.

The educational philosopher John Dewey saw the role of choice in education as the exercise of our collective responsibility to choose from among competing possibilities what is best for all children. No doubt Dewey would be appalled to see choice appropriated by the conservative alliance to uncouple the fortunes of some children from the fortunes of others, claiming that everyone will be better off.

Parent activist Arnold Fege asks, "How did we come to define the national purposes of education not on what is best for the collective will or community, but on what is best for 'me' or 'my child' ... even if that action may be exclusionary, discriminatory, or even uninformed?"[2] Fege's question is well put, yet the more important query may be why, not how. Whose interests are best served when public education, committed to public purposes, is dismantled? Why is this goal worthy of such vigorous pursuit that coalitions of politicians, businesses and religious organizations fund it so handsomely and pursue it with such ferocity? What are schools of choice, and what opportunities do they offer to those who want them so badly?

Schools of choice come in many incarnations, but all share several explicit characteristics. They are as disengaged as possible from any central authority and vested with as much decision making as possible at the school level, with parent-run boards wielding more authority than most public school boards. Their pupils are selected from among those who have put themselves forward as candidates. They compete openly with other schools for enrolment, and their funding is tied to the number of students they can attract. At least some of the regulations regarding program, staffing, budget, etc., ordinarily under centralized authority, are put into the hands of individual schools.

Schools of choice also share a number of implicit characteristics. First, they must be financially successful, therefore schools must obey and profit from the rules of the marketplace. In the culture of the marketplace, maintaining and increasing market share is evidence of success. Thus, for some schools to succeed, others must fail; for some students to succeed, others must fail. These are the rules of the Social Darwinist model of education.

Second, schools of choice set out to be homogeneous. Whether its clientele is sorted by socio-economic level, religious values or academic proficiency, each school builds a filtering device into its purposes. As John Chubb, one of the most vocal American proponents of school choice explains, the problem with public schools is diversity—"they must take whoever walks in the door."[3]

Third, proponents of schools of choice view teachers as the agents of educational folly, at best, and destroyers of children, at worst. Teachers, they believe, have been either hoodwinked by the philosophy of feel-good education or beaten into submission by their unions. In this scenario, "good" teachers are forced to belong to associations that intimidate the public into paying them exorbitant salaries. They will be freed of this burden by schools of choice; they will be freed even of the obligation to undergo professional training and certification; for, if teachers—and their leaders and bureaucrats—are the problem, the solution is controlling them by parents who rule by moral conviction rather than regulation.

From these explicit and implicit foundations has grown a wide array of schools of choice, which, although they may vary in degree, vary little in kind. Each model begins with false premises about the failure of schools, supports the entitlement of parents to own education as well as their children, and condemns the evils of regulation. Each believes in competition, the necessity of failure to create success, the safety in similarity, and the need to control teachers. Fundamental to this philosophy is a sense of entitlement and a conviction that the elect, from an economic, intellectual or religious standpoint, have the right to disengage the future of their children from the future of other people's children.

It is the mechanism of competition that absolves the elect from personal responsibility for the consequences of their collective choices. It will be the impersonal, inexorable wisdom of the marketplace that will determine outcomes. The Word has its prophets. *Reinventing Government: How the Entrepreneurial Spirit Is Transforming the Public Sector*, by David Osborne and Ted Gaebler, is the best-selling bible of restructuring. No doubt book sales were substantially enhanced by a cover endorsement from Bill Clinton, who praises their work as providing "the blueprint" for the future. The authors spell out America's new vision of a restructured public education system:

> Under the concept of parental choice, schools will be held
> accountable for their students' performance.... Schools failing to
> meet the needs of their students would not be able to compete,
> and in effect would go out of business.... You need a system that
> holds schools accountable not from the top down, but through the
> competitive process.... Only competition for customers creates real
> consequences and real pressure for change when schools fail.[4]

Such promise! But how could these principles be realized? John Chubb is among those eager to promote his model of school choice, which he calls voucher schools. The product he has to sell will liberate the students he describes as the captives of democracy. Chubb and his business partners, including Chris Whittle, envision a chain of private schools ready to compete head to head with public schools. He sees a market for "a constellation" of "different schools serving different kinds of students differently," schools that would "target their appeals" to "chosen segments" of the population. His chosen segment, of course, would be the high end, children of parents who are "informed," "supportive" and "encourage education." There will be large numbers of "specialized schools," he explains, "for the other kind" of student, although he will not be investing in them.[5] On one level, this sounds not much different from the pitch of an élite private school. The catch is that these schools of choice would be part of a profit-making thousand-school chain, funded with public dollars. Some may call this privatizing the benefits and socializing the costs, but not, of course, Mr. Chubb.

VOUCHER SCHOOLS

> Lower-income kids should not be left stranded in the public system
> if they can't win scholarships. Vouchers would go part of the way
> to liberating them; cheaper private schools would do the rest.
> Editorial in the *Globe and Mail*, May 28, 1992

Voucher schools passionately embrace the premises of the marketplace. They were first proposed forty years ago by Milton Friedman, right-wing American economist and adviser to the dictator of Chile, Augusto Pinochet.[6] Not surprisingly, the model has political and economic roots rather than educational ones, for it is a model of opportunism rather than opportunity. At the time Friedman advanced his ideas, there was little public receptivity, but times have changed.

All proposed and existing versions of voucher schools work on a simple, perhaps alluring principle. Parents receive, out of tax revenues, a voucher for each child, equivalent in value to the average amount spent per student by the district in which the student lives. Parents are then free to spend this voucher as they choose, either as a down payment on private-school tuition, which parents would top off as necessary, or to enrol their children in a public school. Parents who live in wealthier districts that spend more on education would receive a much larger voucher than those who live in poorer districts containing badly funded schools.

Voucher schools have new cachet but a long, dishonourable history. The first choice program in the United States was legislated to allow white students in Virginia to apply public funds to private school tuition, thereby avoiding the indignity of attending schools with black children.[7] Milton Friedman acknowledged the potential conflict between choice and equity inherent in his model, but came down firmly for choice as the pre-eminent value that should be sustained even if equity was a casualty of its realization. This willingness to sacrifice equity to choice is critical to an understanding of the intentions and consequences of voucher schools.

In the United States, voucher-school proponents have used a variety of strategies to realize their goals; however, according to the National Education Association (NEA), the largest teachers' union in the United States, skirmishes fought through referenda, lobbying and lawsuits launched "in the public interest" have so far had limited success. Only Wisconsin and Puerto Rico have approved voucher schools, but the NEA, which is leading and funding the anti-voucher forces, admits that it expects "substantial voucher efforts in twenty states in 1994."[8]

The NEA strategically claims the voucher movement is on its last legs, but privately it realizes that the movement is not about to disappear. Although it is billed as a grass-roots, populist movement, the pro-voucher lobby, Americans for School Choice, is headed by former Republican education secretaries Bill Bennett and Lamar Alexander and four state governors.[9] Nor is the United States the only battlefield. In Europe, the same strategies have resulted in two-thirds of Dutch children being educated in voucher schools. The Grant-Maintained Schools of England and Wales and the privatized schools of New Zealand remind us that what may be unthinkable today may be likely tomorrow.

The state of California is in the midst of one of the hardest-fought battles over voucher schools. Warren Furitani, a member of the Los Angeles City Board of Education and an anti-voucher activist, believes it is a battle that is as much moral as political, one that is about the élites maintaining power rather than sharing it. "When we talk about choice in California, we are talking about a mortal battle for the fundamental soul of public education in a democratic society. That is what the fight is about."[10] A school-choice referendum question appeared on the ballot in November 1993. The vigorous petition-signing effort undertaken by the conservative alliance gleaned 900,000 names (perhaps encouraged by the $1.50 per signature canvassers were paid) although some names were collected after the deadline. The referendum question, Proposition 174, was defeated, but received support from 30% of the electorate.

At the forefront of the California voucher crusade has been the religious Right, but the dollars have come from business. Robert Simonds, head of the ultra-conservative and increasingly influential lobby National Association for Christian Educators and Citizens for Excellence in Education (CEE) boasts that it had "no trouble getting help from EXCEL [a coalition of CEOs and corporations] and other corporate-funded groups" in its efforts to promote voucher schools in California.[11]

Leading the opposition to vouchers has been the National Education Association. In the heat of the California battle, *Forbes* magazine published an article that opens with a two-page bar graph attempting to correlate the rise of teacher unionism with declining student SAT scores.[12] Referring to the NEA as the "National Extortion Association," *Forbes* writers Peter Brimelow and Leslie Spencer claim that "the NEA fights all voucher and choice proposals that might allow students to 'escape' to a private school. They are needed as hostages." The NEA, they claim, is a formidable foe: "Its political organizers, like the Red Army, are unmatched and undefeated." Its objects are "socialism, in the form of government monopoly schooling." School choice initiatives are a boon to those campaigning to defeat school-funding bills. The National Taxpayers Union says it gets less opposition from the NEA when its attentions are divided. "We like to see a school choice initiative started. It distracts them."[13]

The opponents of this California plan object to it on four compelling grounds of inequity. First, because voucher schools in the private sector would be allowed to accept or reject students on whatever basis they choose, they could freely discriminate on the basis of income, gender, disability, sexual orientation, academic ability, IQ, religious beliefs or political philosophies. No for-profit school would have to brook learning difficulties or disobedience: each voucher school would be permitted to dismiss any student "deriving no substantial academic benefit," as well as any student deemed to be displaying "habitual misconduct." Second, although public schools would continue to be subject to all existing state and federal regulations regarding curriculum and the employment of qualified teachers, private schools would not be subject to any restrictions regarding program or staffing.

The third argument is fiscal. A voucher would be worth $2600 to a for-profit school; however, because of the particulars of granting formulae, each student lost to the public system would translate into $10,400—four times that amount—in lost revenue. In addition, should each of the half million students already enrolled in private schools in California receive $2600 from the state's education budget, funding for public schools would be reduced by $1.5 billion in the first year of the plan.[14]

The fourth argument is that private schools would milk the public system for its brightest students, best role models, and most able teachers as well as its funding. Starved of resources and leadership, public schools would deteriorate, encouraging yet more parents to seek private schools, which would further erode revenue and the quality of public school education.

The success of voucher school plans, however, rests on a

network of realities not exclusive to California, not the least of which is the manifest inability of the public school system to hold things together when it is surrounded by cultural chaos.

In some quarters, chaos is no excuse for poor grades. The failure of one San Francisco school to transcend the nature of its community resulted in sixty-four staff members losing their jobs. Teachers protested that the decision was made without the board or superintendent visiting the school. They said that they had done their best in the face of the "numbing apathy," poverty and despair of the children. Nonsense, replied school board officials. "They [the children] are not the problem. Everyone is capable of learning, even if they are living in crack houses, even if there's bullets flying around."[15]

Parents may be prepared to see other people's children try to transcend chaos, but they are not about to volunteer their own. As American professor Gary Clabaugh points out, it is "increasingly obvious that it is terribly difficult to make any school work if the community it serves is being destroyed."[16] Difficult becomes impossible when funds dry up, and affluent parents move their children to private schools, thereby ending their interest in the conditions of public schools. With voter turnout several times higher than that of poor Californians, the middle class is the group that has the power to decide whether the underfunding of public education, for which California is renowned, will be permanent. The voucher school proposal tempts voters to solve both the public school problem and the community problem by abandoning both.

It is the view of many that voucher schools are inevitable. Lamar Alexander, U.S. Secretary of Education from 1991 to 1993 and voucher school evangelist, says:

I have this prediction: by the time our fifth-graders, the class of 2000 are seniors, school choice will not be an issue. About the only people discussing it will be a few Ph.D. candidates who will have chosen to investigate that strange era when local government monopolies had

control of the most valuable and important enterprises in America—
our schools —and fought furiously to keep the doors to many of
the best schools closed to middle- and low-income children....
The public at large will have remembered that consumer power is
a tried and true American way to encourage innovation and
improvement.[17]

Alexander tugs at the familiar American heartstrings of private
enterprise, but he also introduces the argument that the true bene-
ficiaries of voucher schools will be the poor and disadvantaged; if
there is any greed and selfishness involved, it motivates those who
oppose school choice, not its proponents. This particular bit of
marketing hype was used in Minnesota: "Those who can afford it
already have choice. So you want to deny the extension of it to the
poor, is that right?"[18]

Yet the success of the proposal to set up voucher schools in
Minnesota required more than the odd specious argument. At the
forefront of the pro-voucher lobby was the Minnesota Business
Partnership, comprising the eighty largest corporations operating
in the state. According to *Reinventing Government* authors
Osborne and Gaebler, the state governor was lobbied for voucher
support by representatives of his entire corporate political base.
Not surprisingly, the governor came onside because he "instinc-
tively saw truth"—not to mention his political future.[19]

The promise of social justice through school choice has been
used to deflect criticism from liberals and also to attract a few
high-profile minority leaders to the cause. But those who look at
the track record of voucher champions are not fooled. As Columbia professor Linda Darling-Hammond puts it, the pious appeal to
public support for the promise of "equity through school choice"
comes most loudly from the very interests that have opposed
granting schools adequate and equal resources.[20]

The fatal flaw in the equity argument, of course, is that in
voucher plans such as California's, choice is not evenly distributed.

Not only are private schools free to take the cream of the crop from the public schools, and in so doing, boost both their profits and their test scores, but also private school choice is available only to those who are financially able as well as acceptable to private schools. While a few hundred able middle-class minority students might gain access, hundreds of thousands would be stuck in schools within walking distance and the financial means of their families. These schools for the rest would struggle on with even less funding and virtually no political base, abandoned by the middle classes in the name of choice.

California congresswoman Maxine Waters, known across the United States as the voice of the inner city, says, "'Choice' is not a reform—it is an abandonment of American children and teachers who rely on our public system for education and job opportunities. Contrary to claims, the school choice proposal will be devastating for urban, minority and poor students who desperately need quality education."[21]

Voucher schools are not about redistributing choice, they are about protecting privilege, and they are about fear. Los Angeles school trustee Furitani notes that it is no coincidence that the voucher plan is emerging just as its school districts become more populated by children of colour. Non-white students make up more than half of all those enrolled in California schools, and there are 1.8 million more children enrolled every year. Each year, fewer of these students would be deemed acceptable to the private schools of the suburbs. Nonetheless, not only must poor and marginalized parents be able to understand the choices theoretically available to them, they must feel both entitlement and hope. Jonathan Kozol says:

> They can only choose the things they have a right to, and the things they think they have some reason to believe they will receive.... Placing the burden on the individual to break down doors in finding better education for a child is attractive to conservatives, because it

reaffirms their faith in individual ambition and autonomy. But to ask an individual to break down doors that we have chained and bolted is unfair.[22]

Inside those doors, school is a very serious business, for the competitive imperative of voucher schools must carry over to the classroom. Because of the disproportionate emphasis on standardized test results as the yardstick of school success (and each school's chief marketing tool), voucher schools promise a more intense version of the kind of education that has consistently failed to serve or adequately engage at-risk students. It would become financially necessary to encourage students whose marks bring down the class average to drop out or transfer. Which school would enrol a student two years behind in reading skills, or one likely to require an "unfair" share of staff time because of blindness? When school survival depends on results, those teachers who don't produce may find themselves out of a job, but kids who can't produce may find themselves out on the street.

The competition for easy-to-teach, bright and appealing students will be fierce. Their photographs will look nice on the school's promotional brochure, and their SAT scores will be impressive. Average kids, with average intelligence, will be accepted reluctantly, for while their enrolment will produce revenue, as products they won't attract new customers. But who will want the ones at risk, the ones expelled for not doing their homework, the ones in wheelchairs, the ones whose parents don't come home at night? John Chubb suggests that "large numbers of specialized schools would soon emerge" which would specialize in these kinds of "problems."[23] We used to have these schools —segregated schools, reform schools and schools for the retarded.

Who will teach these children who lack marketable qualities? Surely desirable teachers will escape while they can, reinforcing the current practice of allocating teachers with the least experience and training to the most troubled inner-city schools. Neither poor teachers nor poor students will disappear, they will simply be said to be victims of their own choices. Voucher schools will entrench the responsibility for the welfare of the most vulnerable citizens to parents and schools: children will be warehoused in inner-city schools as the middle class tsk-tsks at the "poor choices these people make."

Ironically, some voucher plans may have lost supporters because they have begun to buy their own twisted arguments. An ardent California private school spokesperson was quoted in the *Wall Street Journal* as warning that "public money for private schools will inevitably end private schools as we know them.... [In] return for government funds, they will be 'blackmailed' into accepting and promoting affirmative action, euphemistically labelled 'civil rights' legislation, and political correctness in the misleading guise of 'diversity'." The *New Republic* worries that this equity thing might get out of hand: "Would 'school choice' zealots favour a 'park choice' system, whereby the government would pay for poor people to 'opt out' of the public parks and join country clubs?"[24]

Nowhere is this thought more frightening than in California, where the chasm between the haves and the have nots is vast. One in every four children in California lives below the poverty line. Most students in California are members of minority groups, and more than half do not speak English at home.[25] The voucher school movement appropriates the fears and the selfishness of the white middle-class minority, trying to garrison themselves from the "others," in a mistaken belief that their futures are not intertwined.

The voucher movement may be propelled by fear, but it is backed by greed. Waiting to profit from the choices of the fearful middle class are the privateers who are ready to move into the market niche. For although conventional American private schools may be sedately ivy-covered, or austere offerings to a God with very strict rules for his chosen, the new private schools will have, shall we say, a flavour all their own. The "corporate academies" of Burger King and a dozen other corporations have more than duty towards children on their minds as they watch the voucher school wars. They can afford to be patient.

CHARTER SCHOOLS

> Given that the continent's educational élites seem wedded to models
> of schooling that are either progressive, bland, or ineffective (and
> often all three together), governments must enact legislation that
> gives schools the power to break free of school board restraints
> and bureaucracy.
>
> Andrew Nikiforuk[26]

On February 14, 1994, the *Globe and Mail* reported that question period in the Alberta legislature had turned into a "rowdy exchange." Liberal leader Laurence Decore had asked Premier Klein to clarify his government's vague reference to piloting charter schools in the speech from the throne. Klein responded that he was not sure what a charter school was. The ensuing uproar caused the Speaker to adjourn the House.

Klein is not the only Albertan to be a little fuzzy about the precise nature of charter schools, although as premier he might be less blithe about his ignorance. As the first province to give public consideration and then endorsement to charter schools, Alberta has become the standard bearer of the hopes of school choice advocates across Canada. While the majority of the public and, indeed, many teachers had not heard of them, "charter schools" had been on the lips (and in the prayers) of many behind the scenes. To move the political agenda along, shortly after announcing a decision to "pilot" charter schools, Alberta Education released "Charter Schools: Provision for Choice in Public Schools."[27] The draft document reviews charter school models in several countries and American states, setting out the similarities and differences among the various models in operation.

In the matter of charter schools, Alberta is hardly starting from scratch. The ministry's discussion paper borrows extensively from an article by Priscilla Wohlstetter and Lesley Anderson,[28] the latter an adviser to architects of Britain's Grant-Maintained Schools. Margaret Thatcher's 1988 Education Reform Act authorized Britain's version of charter schools, along with a national curriculum, national testing, open attendance areas and school-based management. Each of these appears in a provincialized form in Alberta Education's Business Plan.

The discussion paper points out that charter schools are assuming an important place as schools of choice. Although charter school advocates take great pains to distinguish their model from voucher schools, they have more in common than not. As Wohlstetter and Anderson explain, "Charter schools are grounded in a philosophy of the education marketplace. Schools must compete for students, and those that cannot attract a sufficient number of students (and tuition dollars) may have to close." This is the same principle that underpins voucher schools.

All charter schools share certain characteristics that complement their market-driven premises. The charter upon which each school is based is a written agreement between a non-profit group seeking to establish its own school, and a granting authority. (In the United States, this granting authority is usually a school board; in Britain it is the national Department of Education.) The charter spells out the goals, objectives and responsibilities of the parties to the agreement, although control of nearly all functions other than taxation is typically given to the school. Each charter school operates under the direction of its own board, usually drawn from parents, teachers and perhaps community representatives, which wields extensive powers over staffing, budget, programs and instructional decisions. Boards of some charter schools are effectively decoupled from any policy decisions that would bind non-charter schools, such as the decisions of elected school boards or the requirement to engage only certified teachers. As autonomous units, charter school boards control their own budgets, which are determined by the number of students enrolled in the school.

In theory, the dollars available to charter schools should not exceed those available to public schools, as most charter school models prohibit tuition fees. However, in the first six years of implementation of Britain's charter schools, the national alloca-tion of money for capital expenditures to chartered schools exceeded capital grants to non-chartered schools by a ratio of 2:1. In addition, in 1993–94, the British government approved $1.35 million (US) to fund consultants to advise the 693 charter schools. Such persuasion helps to move all schools towards charter school status, a transformation that is expected to be complete by 1995.[29]

Britain's experience provides politicians with some guidance for "successfully" realizing a charter school system. School-based management is a key step towards charter autonomy, according to observers, and schools using this system "should be regarded not as two different types of institutions, but as institutions at different points on the same management continuum."[30]

School-based responsibility for all facets of budget and man-agement can become a burden, but many charter schools have created a new position at the assistant-principal level. This new member of the "senior management team" is usually chosen from outside the world of education, according to the discussion paper. The job description, in addition to personnel management and the supervision of contracts and leases, includes "capital development, marketing and fundraising." Other management roles are chang-ing, too. Principals are no longer to be principal teachers and instructional leaders but "money managers and marketers" of their schools. Management guru Stephen Murgatroyd advises that principals will find an MBA "more useful training than a degree in education."[31] Can it be entirely coincidental that the highly respected educational-administration program at the University of Alberta is rumoured to be moving to the Faculty of Business?

This may ensure that principals know no more about education than their boards, but what about some of the other "problems" charter schools inherit from public education? Alberta's discussion paper highlights a couple of ways to get around diversity. It notes that California's charter schools are permitted to set "admission requirements," but this entitlement to discriminate is allegedly offset by a requirement that each school's student population reflect the racial and ethnic character of the district in which it is located. Presumably, this superficially equity-friendly restriction means that white suburban schools must stay that way, as must black schools in inner-city black districts.

Minnesota's 1991 legislation allows the board of each charter school to determine the "ages, grade levels, and populations" to be served, as well as "the philosophical approach, the focus of the curriculum and the instructional methods" to be adopted. Although technically every charter school must "select any eligible student," powers granted to the school allow each board to filter its selections. For with the power to shape philosophy and curriculum comes the power to shape which families are likely to choose each school.

An Alberta charter schools advocate, John Mason, wants to set up a charter school, and he intends to be picky. "We're not interested in having academically challenged kids. And we're not going to have behavioral problems," he says. "We're taking the cream of the crop."[32] Mason may have to learn to be a bit more discreet, he can still have his way.

Say a charter school commits itself to provide a "rigorous academic program for able students committed to traditional Western values," which is entirely within its authority. Might the single parent of a struggling black student decide to choose another school? A school that promises students success because each parent will volunteer to be in the classroom ten hours per week will not have many applicants from families without a stay-at-home parent. A school might describe itself as "committed to character development through student participation in two hours of competitive sports daily." It is unlikely that many children with physical disabilities will seek entry to this school. But these students and their parents can always choose another school where soon, everyone will look the same, thus solving the problem of diversity.

A second problem left over from public education is what to do with teachers. Minnesota's plan allows charter school boards to hire and fire staff, California's 1992 legislation permits "individual charter school boards to decide whether their teachers had to be licensed by the state or remain part of the district's collective bargaining process," Alberta Education's document notes. But Alberta highlights the Colorado model, which declares that charter schools may waive all district and state regulations, "including union contracts with pay scales and hiring procedures, and the requirement that all teachers be certified."

And what about elected school boards? Might they be unenthusiastic about their restructured demise? Colorado's plan for charter schools, according to Alberta Education, "is seen as a way to break the exclusive franchise school boards have had in Colorado." Exclusive franchise? This turn of phrase takes the democracy-as-monopoly argument to new heights. Given that they are elected by citizens, most tend to view the authority of school boards as a mandate rather than as an exclusive franchise. The solution is to bypass boards entirely. The Colorado plan states that if elected boards are perversely "un-cooperative" about granting charters, the State Board of Education can step in as the granting authority.

At present, it is unclear which of these models, if any, is favoured by Ralph Klein's government but as the next chapter explains, all the groundwork is in place—from truncating the powers of school boards to mandating school-based management to "reviewing" teacher certification. Alberta Education admits there is no evidence that charter schools are more effective than regular schools, but this drawback to a business plan committed to outcomes does not appear to faze its supporters. For even if charter schools fail the test of educational effectiveness, they pass political expediency with flying colours.

Charter schools, they claim, will "generate innovation and improvements through competition," "attract entrepreneurs" and "reduce conflict." Notably, they do not claim to reaffirm equity nor improve student achievement. Perhaps modesty prevailed, for they also forgot to mention the almost limitless opportunities to cut costs and reap political benefit. By eliminating centralized planning and support and school boards, and by pocketing the profits from pillaging teachers' collective agreements, the government's deficit-reduction goals might come within reach.

Yet even Stephen Murgatroyd admits that the charter school model he advocates for Alberta "has not gone entirely smoothly" in Britain. It seems that citizens are reluctant to let go of their schools. As *Western Report* puts it, "One key hurdle is weaning the public away from its dependence on state education managers and selling them instead on a free market system where students are 'customers' of schools."[33] John Ballheim, chairman of the education committee of the Alberta Chamber of Commerce, is way ahead of the British public. He says he's "100%" behind the plan, even if the transition to charter schools will cause "a tremendous amount of pain."[34]

Few of those who attended a May 1993 conference sponsored by Albertans for Quality Education would disagree, provided the pain was inflicted on other people's children. This like-minded group of "concerned parents" got together to "focus critically on standards and curriculum, discipline, sex education and the creeping influence of new age philosophy in the schools," according to *Western Report*. The real energy of participants is said to have been focused on "parental control and choice":

Keynote speaker William Gairdner, author of *The War Against the Family*, argued that a small but influential element within western culture which is bent on destruction of the family has infiltrated the modern educational system.... Public education is incompatible with a free society in that it separates the child from the family and the parental responsibility for education. The only way to offset the threat to the family is to allow parents to choose the kind of school they will attend.[35]

Participants were urged "to speak with one voice in demanding a system in which provincial funding follows the child" and to demand independent parent-run schools. AQE spokesman Dan Levson was cheered by the large turnout and predicted that the quality education movement will "focus on voucher systems and charter schools as a means to introduce choice and control."

To the surprise of few, the most popular workshop at the "parent mobilization" conference was given by Dr. Joseph Freedman. A radiologist with a passion to break public education, Freedman became well-known in certain circles for producing and distributing a video called *Failing Grades*.[36] Less well-known are his financial backers, said to include the Royal Bank, the Bank of Nova Scotia, Syncrude, Kodak, and four provincial education ministries.[37] *Failing Grades* is devoted to criticizing the performance of Canada's schools, using the now-familiar (albeit discredited) conclusions of the Economic Council of Canada and the Conference Board (discussed in the chapter, "Our Schools Have Failed Us ... and Our Kids").

Freedman's seemingly askew attack on schools for their attention to affective goals at the price of academic excellence makes a great deal more sense when viewed in the context of the concerns of the religious Right. The evils of whole-language instruction, to which Freedman continually refers, appear genuinely threatening to those who believe it involves devil worship. His attack on child-centred education is warmly received by those who believe, in the words of one AQE member, that "another disturbing trend ... is the prevailing belief in education that children must be treated as individual and unique human beings": an approach that presumably smacks of humanism.[38] It is not difficult for those who see heaven as an entitlement of the righteous to conclude they should also be entitled to their own schools. The possibility of being morally contaminated by the collectivism of the educational establishment is much more dangerous if it is the very souls of children that are at stake.

None of this, of course, flows directly from the words of Dr. Freedman. His alliance with the Quality Education Networks may be no more than the coincidence of shared conclusions rather than a shared analysis. And although the bedfellows of right-wing education reform are not always comfortable together, they are prepared to sleep together when expedient. When Joe Freedman mailed copies of his charter schools proposal to every school board in Canada (courtesy of a "donor of national stature"),[39] he also ensured that every national business lobby group and think tank, such as the C.D. Howe Institute and the Fraser Institute, received a copy, as did the Quality Education Networks.

Under the auspices of his Society for Advancing Educational Research, Dr. Freedman proposes a "safe, low-risk experimental private-school model within the Canadian Public School System." Such an experiment is needed, the proposal explains, because of "an increasing perception that academic outcomes are slipping" when compared with our global competition. This slippage is due to "family breakdown, social disadvantage, immigration and an unmanageable agenda" and to teachers who "have been preoccupied with a number of child-centered strategies to improve the outcomes and graduation rates of at-risk and disadvantaged students." In other words, the problem is mediocrity, the culprit is diversity, and the folly is seeking equity. Such words, of course, would never be spoken; instead there is much verbal hand-wringing over the "relentless pressure" placed on the system, for which Dr. Freedman takes no responsibility. "Even worse, the whole concept of public education is itself being questioned as the spectre of the educational voucher is discussed ever more frequently." This has led to demoralized teachers, for whom he professes sympathy, and to "large segments of the Canadian public ready for alternatives to their local zoned school."

Freedman proposes that public boards establish a free education zone for his charter school experiment, a kind of educational Maquiladora, "free from control by the local school board and teachers' union and, as well, extreme parental self-interest." (How this last feature will be ensured is not explained.) The chief advantage of these schools would be homogeneity—disguised as harmony, of course. Because everyone would bond around a common philosophy and methodology, the board would be of one mind. "It may instantly achieve a strong consensus among parents on traditional values, behaviour, discipline, appearance, homework and academic expectations" and "among teaching staff on teaching methods, academic expectations and assessment, as well as a core of traditional values."

"The school would have the ability to defend itself" by "invoking its sanction" (a.k.a. expulsion) in the event that a student fails to live up to the "deportment, appearance and homework policies" to which the student's parents—plural—had agreed. This sanction, according to the document, would be invoked against the parents, not the child, although the child, not the parents, is dismissed from the school. The vacancy resulting from this act of self-defence would be filled so as to maintain "the same socio-economic blend of students."

School governance would be in the hands of a community board of governors struck—by an unnamed source—and charged with selecting a principal or headmaster. Together, they would select a staff—never referred to as teachers—with "a willingness to drive for results" but not necessarily holding a teaching certificate. Parents agreeing to abide by the terms of the school would then apply for their children to be accepted. Student applications would be selected by lottery, and the school would be "given its head to achieve results."

The proposal suggests that research be conducted in every community in which such charter schools are established. The additional expenses this would entail, along with transporting students to the charter school of their choice, could add up. Is this prospect dismaying? Certainly not. It is an opportunity for "national business organizations" and "individual firms of size"— and, presumably, deep pockets—to participate in helping charter schools get off the ground. One of the more creative aspects of this pitch to school boards is that time is of the essence: if they hurry, they may be able to snag one of these partners; if they wait, they may have to do it alone.

Like other school choice proponents, Freedman promises "stronger student outcomes from all students, but especially the disadvantaged." He predicts that the combination of direct— as opposed to child-centred—instruction, a structured environment, and codes of deportment will succeed where progressive education has failed. The only cost is "for parents and teachers to give up some of their freedom," although there is no claim that the losses of the two groups would be commensurate. Should the research "prove" the superiority of the charter model, Freedman asserts, we will finally have to concede "that it is the public system itself that is part of education's problem." With the "ever-increasing spectre of the educational voucher on the horizon," Dr. Freedman implores, we would be wise to choose this "fair and workable attempt at middle ground in reforming the public system."

To those unfamiliar with the ideological underpinnings of schools of choice, and to those not motivated to read between the lines, this carefully crafted proposal can seem persuasive. Certainly, a parent could sign up for such a school without any particularly unfriendly intent towards other children, their communities or public education.

How can the collective choices of loving parents undermine our common well-being? The answer to this question requires a careful deconstruction of the underlying ideology of charter schools and all schools of choice.

First and foremost, the battle over school choice is not about educational methodologies and school improvement. It is about ideology, not education. Under the pretence of improving test scores or better serving the disadvantaged, big business and the religious Right are attempting to hijack public education. For some, public education of any kind is inconsistent with parents' rights; for others it is inconsistent with reaping the rewards of privilege; for a few it is inconsistent with the unbridled right to profit from children. No parental anxiety is left unmined by school choice advocates: drugs, demons, diversity and deportment are equally susceptible to resolution for the chosen. Nor is any public anxiety left unexploited: the deficit, the power of unions, and global uncompetitiveness will all disappear if we "let go" of public education.

There will be two categories of victims if public schools are dismantled in favour of choice: some of us and all of us. The some will be those who already have the least cultural capital, political clout and recourse against those who would leave them behind. As Jonathan Kozol points out, the voices that are now championing choice as the salvation of the disadvantaged have been raised before in opposition to all measures fostering greater equity in education and fair taxation. He reminds those of us who might be swayed by the promise of extending choice beyond the wealthy that the rich have always had the choice of sending their children to school with poor children.[40]

That all of us will be victims may be less obvious, but no less true. For if the quality of education all children receive ceases to matter to each of us, we have acceded to the self-concern democracy attempts to restrain. If we believe in equity and justice, we will structure our schools one way. If we believe that our children are entitled to succeed on the backs of others, we will structure them differently. This is the choice before us.

One or two charter schools—in Alberta or any other province—will not bring public education to its knees. What it will do, however, is divert dollars and attention from improving all schools to enhancing a few. And because of the apparent injustice of only a few children "benefiting" from choice, the public may well conclude that all public schools should be put in the hands of parents and partners. It will not be long before taxpayers who are not parents resist funding something over which they have no influence. Corporations will spend education dollars not on taxes for the support of the many, but on partnerships for the benefit of a few. As funds for all schools decline, some parents will demand the right to top off tax-funded tuitions, or to insist that some programs—perhaps for high-level math and science—are more crucial to the economy than others—perhaps for special education students—and thus deserve more public investment.

And while these problems cause dissonance in our still quasi-public school system, the chorus of harmonization will be heard in the background. Canadians will watch as American businesses underwrite "boutique" schools, for which the capital investment will be worth its weight in tax credits. The middle classes, frantic to leave crumbling public schools, will find the tuition to get into the best school. Those without ambition or hope or resources will simply choose what's left.

It will be said that the problem in Canada is that we didn't go far enough. Charter schools may have been a typically Canadian compromise, it will be argued, but their fundamental anarchy is too confusing and unwieldy. The solution will be the utter deregulation of public education, an acquiescence to the imperatives of the marketplace. Although getting used to Burger King academies may require a little cultural accommodation, this is something with which we Canadians have had considerable practice.

In our classrooms, the writing may still be on the blackboard, but it is also on the wall.

RETROFITTING ALBERTA

*We Albertans are embarked on a historic journey to show
the rest of Canada that there's indeed a better way.[1]*

RALPH KLEIN

PREMIER OF ALBERTA

*Alberta ... has set the national agenda of Canada.
That is an exceptional feat.[2]*

JEAN CHAREST

LEADER, PROGRESSIVE CONSERVATIVE PARTY OF CANADA

TRYING TO TEACH

By 1992, no Canadian educational jurisdiction had been reformed
as much as Alberta. Successive governments decreed such a range
of school reforms that, taken together, education policy looked
like a scrambled roadmap. Teachers were being told to take all
roads at the same time,

In late 1992, the Alberta Teachers' Association (ATA) called
for submissions from its members to a task force established to document teachers' experiences with education reform. After hearing
several hundred submissions, the ATA assembled and published
Trying to Teach, an account of the frustrations of "over-reformed"
classroom teachers.[3] Many teachers said that although they were
supportive of the philosophy behind various new policies, things

were coming apart: poorly conceived implementation plans, the extension of innovations to settings in which they were inappropriate, and the contradictions among reforms contributing to failure and chaos.

Sound ideas, such as the integration of students with special needs, were failing because the resources and support required for successful integration were denied. Repeatedly, teachers pointed out the obvious: their time and talents were all they had, and these were being spread too thin—not just among students, but also among a host of trend-responsive educational philosophies.

The Department of Education had just announced that its existing programs were to be reformulated into "results-based curricula" (also known as outcomes-based and competency-based education). This approach, which is gaining currency throughout North America, shifts the curriculum from what is taught to what is learned by each student, recognizing that individuals learn at different rates as well as by different means. In this system, evaluation focuses exclusively on outcomes that are observable and measurable. As students progress through levels of knowledge and skill in various subject areas, testing diagnoses what should be learned next. Alberta teachers responded in quite predictable ways to this proposal. In theory, results-based education made some sense. In practice, teachers would have to figure out what would it mean to have thirty students at different levels on every topic within the curriculum. Others reacted to the mechanistic mindset that would parse the experience of students into boxes labelled outputs and levels. One teacher warned, "The danger comes in assuming that the worth and depth of an individual can be measured.... Does this leave room for intuition, invention, creativity, love?" Another advised, "Result-based evaluation works out quite well in measuring the value of a mechanical process, like an assembly line. If we are wise, we will leave it there."

The focus on results had followed fast on the heels of the ministry's Program Continuity Policy, which appeared to require that each child's school experience would be individually designed, so that, in the ministry's words, "what a student is involved in learning is dependent on what he/she is personally ready to challenge rather than what the cohort group is ready for." Many teachers saw this as the epitome of a policy half-baked in the ovens of the ivory tower. One teacher summed it up: "The concept looks fine on paper, but they have not been in a classroom for over a decade. It is humanly impossible to do the job that the program demands." Its implausibility, however, did not seem to deter ministry enthusiasm for program continuity.

Another initiative, "continuous progress," added more confusion. Some teachers got lost in the jargon: "To me continuous progress is [the same as] program continuity. Am I missing something again?" One of the rules of continuous progress is age-appropriate placement, in other words, never allowing a child to fail a grade, at least at the elementary level. How did this fit with the pressure being placed on high schools to make examinations more rigorous? Students were never to be held back, but class-average test scores were to keep going up. "Make up your mind!" demanded one frustrated teacher. "You can't have it both ways!" The right of all students to attempt a course, whether or not they had the academic skills to be successful, increased the failure rate for some courses, which resulted in stern letters from the minister of education to a number of schools.

The move to a results-based curriculum was closely related to another mandated reform: more external testing, more often, in more subjects. Alberta had been the most vigorous proponent of national testing, and its ministry had assigned more resources to the National Indicators project than had any other. As in other jurisdictions, public criticism became fixated on test-score results. While Alberta teachers claimed to accept the principle of accountability, they saw the imposition of external testing—a diversion of time, energy and money—as driven not by an educational agenda, but as a political concession to critics alleging that teachers could not be trusted to evaluate student progress. The misuse and mis-representation of test results had provided more fodder for the media's attack on educational mediocrity. Teachers struggling just to keep kids from dropping out of inner-city schools opened the newspapers to find their schools labelled the worst because their test scores compared unfavourably to scores of schools in the affluent suburbs. The public debate centred on what was wrong with these schools, rather than how to improve the capacity to learn of poor and marginalized students. While the ministry's rhetoric encouraged both equity and excellence, the political pressure was on in one direction.

Just when more standardized tests were being added at more grade levels, Portfolio Assessment was mandated by the ministry. This approach to student evaluation necessitates the analysis of many representative pieces of student work, collected over time. It is generally seen as a more authentic means of assessing student growth, particularly in areas less easily captured in one-shot standardized tests. But portfolio assessment depends on sophisticated levels of teacher subjectivity and requires a great deal of time, expertise and even storage space. How was this new practice supposed to fit with the hard-nosed, number-obsessed accountability through external testing?

The confusion was not cleared up when the ministry released a new vision statement, which was high on expectations but low on ways and means. It was widely viewed by teachers as a political ploy, and cynicism was widespread. Some teachers felt that a public trust had been betrayed. "When we play with the education of youth and the very essence of future society, then it is inconceivable that schooling should be politicized," wrote one. "We have witnessed the demise of education," said another, "spurred on by political leaders seeking popularity."

This was not how some external critics read the situation, however. In the same month the ATA published *Trying to Teach*, *Western Report* claimed that the ministry's adoption of Program

Continuity had been yet another mindless concession to the folly of teachers' "progressive philosophy."

> At a time when the Canadian economy is going through what many describe as a massive restructuring and facing severe competition from international competitors, why is it that our elementary schools despise uniform standards ...? The answer lies in a philosophical movement among elementary educational theorists.[4]

The same article went on to praise the government for taking a "hard line" with teachers and for reversing its previous decree on the implementation of program continuity, which the magazine ridiculed as precisely the kind of child-centred nonsense that had led to poor international performance by Alberta students and had encouraged widespread illiteracy. Such behaviour by teachers, it said, explained the increasing public demand for schools of choice.

To be victimized by conflicting policies and then blamed for creating them was driving the profession to the edge. "If the current situation continues, public education is likely to destroy itself," wrote one group of teachers. Another group warned its association, "Teachers feel suffocated, frustrated, angry and stressed to the point of collapse."

Obviously, something had to change, and it did. When Albertans elected a Conservative government headed by Ralph Klein, one of its first acts was to cut $239 million from the education budget.

"OUR KIDS COME FIRST"

> Meeting the needs of Alberta students is the highest priority for this government — that's what Albertans told us during our consultation — to make Albertans' priorities government's priorities. Our kids come first.
>
> Press release from Halvar Jonson, Minister of Education, Alberta

Indeed they do. In fact, they were the first to feel the effects of the Alberta government's all-out assault on the deficit. In his three-year plan to eliminate Alberta's $2.4 billion deficit by 1997, Premier Klein put small children at the head of the line to feel the full force of his spending cuts.

If Klein has his way, a significant proportion of the 20% education budget cuts will be achieved by reducing services to some of the youngest Albertans. Education minister Jonson assured parents that "preparing children for formal learning can be attained with less time in the classroom"; he then cut funding to kindergarten by 50%. The minister graciously allowed individual schools to decide whether to halve the hours of kindergarten instruction, or to bill parents to make up the shortfall. How even paying five-year-olds will get to school is uncertain, however, as grants for their transportation will be eliminated. Recognizing that these same small children also need daycare, the budget cut subsidies for this program by 20%.[5] Most taxpayers had not been aware that Alberta had too many government-dependent five-year-olds who merely needed encouragement to stand on their own two tiny feet. While he stopped short of offering them the one-way out-of-province tickets that he offered welfare recipients, the message was clear: there's room on the bus.

Had the minister stopped with these cuts, his government would still have made history, as the first in Canada to permit public schools to charge a fee for service. While the minister justified his decision to introduce user-pay education on budgetary grounds, the kindergarten clawback would appear to be an ideological reform. As the *Edmonton Journal* put it:

> There is a blind assumption, untested by fact or reality, that government can do nothing well. Everything that was once in public hands, maintained as a public trust for the public interest, must be turned over to private hands.... Much of what the government proposes has nothing to do with finances and everything to do with ideology.[6]

This ideology is simple; get rid of government. In the new Alberta, there will be 60 school boards; there used to be 141. Some of the usual functions of school boards, including the setting of the mill rate, the appointment of superintendents and the determination of how tax revenue will be spent have been transferred to the provincial government; the rest will be delegated to individual schools and parent councils. The minister broadly hinted that communities may no longer need to bother electing trustees, as their only function will be to advise government.[7] The Ministry of Education will also be restructured to develop performance standards and measures, as well as "evaluating/auditing/ensuring compliance." Alberta Education will be a busy place with all these additional tasks, particularly when its staff is to be reduced by 170 positions, taking it to the size it was in 1970.

The province's unanticipated raid on school board authority was widely seen as perverse, given the prevailing rhetoric about local autonomy. But as the government had planned, the public reacted most sharply to the reduction of funding, not to the transfer of authority. The depth and severity of the cuts to education planned for Alberta are more shocking when they are compared to the level of cuts in other provinces. For example, recently proposed education-budget cuts in Quebec prompted predictions that "schools will suffer to an important degree."[8] Yet, on a per-student basis, the Alberta cuts are nearly five times as large as those proposed for Quebec, and Alberta was already the province spending the smallest proportion of its GDP on education.[9]

With the announcement that local funding of education was to go the way of local boards, the government ensured that it would have complete control of the educational purse-strings and the educational agenda. When the government promised that it would move towards a common mill rate, urban trustees were outraged. However, most boards in rural areas, from which the government had drawn its electoral support, were happy to profit from sharing revenue generated by the larger tax base of the cities.

These abrupt changes in the governance structure would by themselves have shaken up education in Alberta, but restructured governance and financing was just the beginning.

The "business plan" of Alberta Education outlines the most comprehensive changes ever introduced to a provincial education system.[10] It promises that the reforms will "substantially alter the character of the education system," ushering in an era in which "schools and business can work in partnership with parents and the community" to "ensure our competitiveness in a global economy."

All schools will be required to adopt school-based management models. The number of standardized achievement tests will be increased; reporting on these tests will be "increased and improved." Sixty-six community schools that provide outreach services for families of at-risk students will lose their funding for community programming. Teachers will be placed on a province-wide pay scale; their salaries will be cut by a minimum of 5%. Teacher certification will be reviewed. But the political centrepiece of the Klein reforms is found in two phrases. The first is: "Provide more choice and more parental involvement"; the second is "pilot charter schools."

While many of the province's proposals might be attributed to cost-saving (at any price), substantial parts of the business plan have nothing to do with the budget and even less to do with education. The reforms include plans to "involve business in the delivery of career and technology studies," "increase the use of technology to deliver education," provide "incentives to schools for student achievement," "privatize some services" of the ministry, "expand provincial testing" and introduce "joint (i.e., government-approved) selection of superintendents" with the few remaining school boards.

The basis of these reforms is neither pedagogical nor fiscal, but ideological and political, consistent with ultraconservative beliefs about the role of government (as small as possible), the role of the private sector (as large as possible) and a deregulated marketplace. The deficit provided the Klein government with the opportunity to couch its extremism in the language of fiscal responsibility. With a fresh mandate, who cares if the *Edmonton Journal* condemns the Klein government as one "that neither cares nor listens"?[11] The important thing is not to blink.

Klein knows he is not playing only to Albertans. His right-wing reforms are widely viewed as a kind of political petri dish by governments and opposition parties of all persuasions. His education reforms are seen as tough rather than ideological by those conditioned to see education as apolitical. Yet the proposals contained in the business plan lay the groundwork for a realignment of public education in the image and in the service of the marketplace.

KNOWING YOUR ENEMY

Nothing in Klein's election campaign had pointed to such a fundamental restructuring or such deep cuts. Education minister Halvar Jonson was a teacher and even a former president of the Alberta Teachers' Association; surely he was an unlikely executioner of the system he had been part of for so long.

It was soon clear, however, that despite growing public protest, the government had no intention of backing down, and the premier was furious that the opposition was getting organized. The nature of his attacks on those who disagreed with the government led the *Edmonton Journal* to write that those the government characterized as the enemies of choice, the monopolists and bureaucrats have been dismissed "with the worst expletive this ideology knows — they're a 'special interest group' so they must be ignored." Critics of the government from the public sector were treated with particular contempt, as the government saw public employees as the "inferior, even evil" enemy of the private sector.[12]

Being both public employees and a special-interest group, the Alberta Teachers' Association drew more than its share of the government hostility. Twenty-eight thousand teachers could marshall considerable resistance, although public credibility of their opposition to the education reforms was strategically undermined by including teacher pay cuts in the reform package. This made it easier for the government to claim that the ATA was driven by selfish motives. The political positioning of the government's initiative as tough medicine in a time of deficit crisis had worked before. The sheer number of the reforms, and the complexity of their intertwined educational effects, left the opposition wondering which issues to fight, and how. The public was unlikely to have the patience to trace how the reforms could combine to transform not just how schools operated, but the very purpose of public education. Other organizations and unions might be sympathetic, but they were using their energies to oppose severe cuts to their own service areas. As for school boards, they were reeling at the prospect of their own demise.

Yet within days of the announcement of the broad outlines of Klein's plan, the ATA launched a half-million-dollar public information campaign. They chose to challenge the government's contention that the quality of education in Alberta was low and to convince the public that the budget cuts were so deep that they could not be absorbed without affecting the classroom. The ATA took out ads in Alberta newspapers, on television and radio to remind Albertans that they were already spending a smaller proportion of GDP on education than any other province, that educational investment paid off in jobs, and that Alberta's students were doing very well on national tests. The ATA commissioned an Angus Reid poll, and made some political mileage with the findings. Seventy-two per cent of the public reported that they thought the government had been spending the right amount or too little on education; half preferred to see taxes increased rather than $239 million cut from education spending.[13]

This attempt to move public opinion was not popular with the government. Suddenly there were rumblings that the ATA had become too militant and too powerful. Private members' bills attempted to split the organization into a professional body and a union body. Another sought to dismantle the union by withdrawing its entitlement to automatic membership and union dues. If the ATA really cared about education, the premier taunted, why didn't it volunteer pay cuts of 5% to help out? The ATA pointed out that teacher settlements had been behind private sector wage increases for the last decade, and that there was no logic in the profession funding education out of their own pocketbooks when the government was committed not to extract an additional cent from the public. Nevertheless, on February 15, 1994, ATA president Bauni Mackay offered the premier 5% of teachers' salaries in exchange for guarantees on class size and a 300-day delay of legislation to allow for public discussion of education reform. The ATA also asked Premier Klein for a commitment to maintain publicly funded schools open to all children, to prohibit tuition fees in public schools, and to ensure that all teachers in publicly funded schools would be certified professionals. The premier refused.[14]

Public opinion may not have been with the government, but it was not the public whom the Conservative party was trying to please. The *Calgary Herald* tracked down the government's ideological mentors, but only after the political course had been set.[15] Some sources believed the true architect of the education reforms was Jim Dinning, a former (and allegedly bitter) education minister and current provincial treasurer. Dinning was on record as saying that "the monopoly of public schools needs to be broken" and that he supported a free-enterprise school system. The *Herald*'s report also named Dr. Stephen Murgatroyd, Alberta advocate of total quality management and author of *Challenging the Culture of the Public Sector* as a key government adviser. His vision of reinventing government includes restructuring school governance. "I've been arguing we should abolish school boards completely and fire the superintendents and get rid of all that infrastructure," said Murgatroyd, "but they didn't go far enough."

John Ballheim, president-elect of the Alberta Chamber of Commerce, was modest about his influence on the government. However, the *Calgary Herald* reported:

> Like Murgatroyd, Ballheim sat on the secret committee to restructure advanced education, and also chaired a 12-member group set up to recommend how to increase partnerships between labour, education, business and government.

After twenty-five years as a teacher and administrator in the United States, Ballheim brought with him some ideas until recently foreign to Canadian education, including his belief that post-secondary institutions should "set tuition at market rates." Other sources suggest that the government's political template is not primarily American, but the deficit-or-die approach of former New Zealand finance minister Roger Douglas.[16] Having presided over the restructuring of New Zealand's sweeping economic and social reforms, Douglas advises Alberta's political architects on a regular basis. His specialty is not only content but style. Douglas's principles include abandoning incrementalism in favour of quantum leaps of restructuring; otherwise, he warns, the "interest groups will have time to mobilize and drag you down." Speed and momentum are of the essence and, above all, advises Douglas, "Don't blink." He believes that sick economies cannot be regulated back to health. Therefore deregulation of every public enterprise is the only cure. Douglas also advocates student enrolment based on individual choice, and having public money follow the student, a consumer of services in an open private/public educational marketplace. While there is little doubt that the Klein government is taking cues from the likes of Douglas, there are sources closer to home with at least as much influence, and with a political agenda even more frightening.

ALBERTANS FOR QUALITY EDUCATION

In Alberta, as in other provinces, organizations presenting themselves as grass-roots citizens' groups have mobilized effectively to advance populist right-wing educational reform.

"Parents, businessmen and educators" founded Albertans for Quality Education in 1993 because they had found a common concern, according to AQE promotional materials: their common concern was that "the quality of education in Alberta has declined to unacceptably low levels."[17] This new partnership is based on models developed by reformers in other provinces and American states. Every issue of AQE's newsletter provides an interesting cross-section of the issues of their greatest concern. Volume 1, number 1 includes a critique of multi-age classes (split grades), continuous learning, child-centred education, and the insufficient time devoted to pure science in the elementary grades. However, the greatest amount of print is devoted to the problems of school violence, drug and alcohol use and the values children are learning at school. A feature article warns parents that Planned Parenthood and Calgary Health Services are among the agencies sponsoring a video on AIDS being shown to high school students. Abstinence is not always getting top billing in discussions of safe sex, readers are warned. Prostitution and even homosexuality had allegedly been discussed during sex education classes! Two books by William Gairdner, (*The War Against the Family* and *Public Schools and the War Against the Family*) are favourably reviewed and recommended to AQE members. Nearly every article concludes with the same message: parents must reclaim their ownership of schools; choice will restore consumer power to its rightful place.

For a while, it must have seemed that AQE members were speaking only to one another; but the Education Roundtables sponsored by the Government of Alberta prior to announcing its education reforms provided AQE with a forum for its policy proposals. These policies bear such resemblance to the Klein doctrine that the AQE brief might have been the background paper to Alberta Education's business plan.[18]

AQE's brief affirms the need for quality education, but argues that as education spending has no effect on education quality, the education budget could be used to achieve deficit reduction. The specific cost-saving measures AQE recommends include reducing the number of teachers and administrators (and their salaries), and reducing funding for non-core programs and subjects. Which of these measures should be implemented must be the decision of each school, AQE contends. Only through school-by-school decision making can "the education priorities for the populist" emerge. Language arts, mathematics and science make the list of more essential courses and programs and thus deserve to be funded. So does Guidance Counselling, so long as it is "career-related" and supportive of "family values." English as a Second Language (ESL) appears last on the essentials list, and only if it is "funded by Federal Departments responsible for Immigration or [by] local immigrant communities."

But this still leaves many programs to cut. On the AQE's less essential list are the second half of kindergarten, second languages at the junior high and elementary level, and before- and after-school care programs. At the bottom of the list of the less essentials is hot lunch programs. AQE suggests that lunches might still be provided to the children of parents on social assistance, if costs were billed to Social Services. This ministry would then "deduct a portion or all of the expense from the social assistance payments made to the parents."

AQE's brief commends what members had seen of the government's intentions for education reform, but it takes great exception to what it describes as the omission of "an important ingredient essential to the long-term strength of Alberta's economy." It seems there had not been enough emphasis on the business sector in discussions of the curriculum. "Students should understand the role that innovation plays in spawning new entrepreneurial businesses as well as intrapreneurial efforts within the larger corporations and institutions that generate wealth and/or provide products and services to Albertans." Food for thought in lieu of a hot lunch.

AQE's brief then turns its attention to educational equity, which is really three issues: perceived inequities between special needs and other students; perceived inequities between school jurisdictions; and perceived inequities between public, private and home schoolers.

The first inequity turns out to be the unfair advantage of students with special needs: they get an unfairly large share of resources and attention, which can be dangerous. "Our commitment to be a compassionate society can degenerate into a coercive society where more and more of those best able to articulate their special needs gain access to a greater than average share of educational resources." Look at what might happen if you take equity too far:

> Parents of a learning-disabled student may feel that for their children to have an "equal opportunity" for an education, their children should receive two or three times as much funding as students who are not learning-disabled. Parents of other children may feel that their children have fewer resources because they are subsidizing learning-disabled children and this is inequitable. They might feel that the parents of learning-disabled children should fund the incremental costs above the average per student cost or raise the funds through charitable donations. The same perceived inequities could apply to the teaching of French, ESL, behaviorally handicapped children, children from broken homes, native children, and other groups.

The solution, according to AQE, is for the government to put limits on how much can be spent on any one student. "Funding requirements in excess of these limits would then be obtained from user fees, charitable donations or other fund-raising methods." Begging, the quintessential entrepreneurial activity, is never out of place.

The second great inequity, according to AQE, is the ability of some jurisdictions to raise more funds because they have a larger industrial/property tax base. This can be easily solved by moving towards equalized funding, a change that would require the province to take over the collection and distribution of taxation.

The third inequity is the unfairness inherent in giving preferential treatment to public education:

> Currently, those parents seeking alternative options to the public schools are paying taxes to support the public system and then paying significant additional fees and/or sacrifices of their personal time to obtain a quality education for their children.

The AQE solution is for the government to adopt a "market-based approach" to education. This would begin with a "careful review ... of the public schools' commitment to satisfy their customers as a precondition to the continuance of their virtual monopoly over education." The AQE also recommends "that any deliverer of education, whether private, public, or homeschooling, if proven to meet acceptable standards, should be properly funded by Alberta Education."

Other AQE recommendations include funding based on the number of instructional hours, which would mean that field trips and professional development days would reduce a school's budget. Increasing pupil-teacher ratios would both cut costs and encourage direct instruction. Implementing user fees for kindergarten would help, too; some of these measures get to the core of the problem: teacher salaries.

AQE sees two problems with teacher salaries. First, they are too high, especially as "there is an abundant supply of teachers" and "salary reductions might better reflect market conditions." Second, teachers are paid according to a district-wide pay scale. A merit pay system should be implemented: salaries of those teachers "producing only average results" would be cut, and the savings used as "quality enhancement incentives." Particularly deserving teachers, as selected by their principals, would receive "performance pay."

Ah, but how would excellence be assessed? By expanding the use and school-by-school reporting of standardized tests. These quality-control measures would guide parents as consumers and remind schools just why they are in business.

The bottom line of AQE's brief is that education can improve only through competition, and schools can compete only when parents have the right to choose with their tax-paid dollars. No other reform and no other alternative comes close to fulfilling this dream of schools of choice.

Albertans for Quality Education did not get everything they asked for in the first round of education reform; but nothing the government has announced runs counter to AQE's recommendations — and even a government committed to quantum leaps may wish to save some of its more radical propositions for a pre-election announcement. In addition to cutting teacher salaries and increasing standardized testing, AQE got its heart's desire: increased parent control, school by school, and the first charter schools in Canada.

The government's political friends were more than grateful. Noting that independent (private) schools have "received more provincial money under the Klein government" than from any prior regime, Gary Duthler, head of the Association of Independent Schools and Colleges, is frankly thrilled. But it isn't just the new money: "In terms of the political situation we're miles ahead. . . . Now I feel like I'm on a surfboard, on this huge wave, and it's a lot more fun."

GETTING CLOSE TO THE CUSTOMER

The Alberta government is banking on parents to create a school system that can accommodate the new realities, and to get this message across to children as soon as possible. As one parent activist put it to *Maclean's*, "Our children will have to compete nationally and internationally after they graduate. Why not start them now?"[19]

Getting them started requires leadership, but it also requires power. In the net of accountability, tangled though it might be, school board trustees, elected by their communities, are charged with governing schools in their jurisdictions. The difficulties boards face in carrying out this function have been discussed in the Introduction. Yet these difficulties do not nullify the principle that boards' legitimate claim to make meaningful decisions about how schools should function and to whom administrative responsibilities should be delegated. By moving to the provincial level most core-board functions, including taxation, teacher bargaining, curriculum priorities and the appointment of superintendents, Alberta boards of education have been made redundant. The *Calgary Herald* wonders how this decision could have flowed from the government's public consultations on education organized under the theme of greater local autonomy.[20] "The powerful school board of today will become merely the caretaker, bus driver and middle manager of tomorrow," writes columnist Don Martin. "By giving itself the divine right to appoint friends and philosophical allies as school superintendents, the province ensured it will have the power that comes with money, and direct influence on how it will be spent."

The government's response to such criticism has been to explain that the principle of local autonomy will be upheld by newly empowered parent councils. However, existing school-level councils have been frustrated because they have insufficient authority over board-controlled matters such as staffing and curriculum, and over teacher-determined matters such as methods of instruction. Just how much control parent councils will have over the selection and assignment of teachers and teaching methods isn't yet clear, but education minister Jonson says school councils will have a role in curriculum. Parent councils will determine which courses are not part of the province's definition of basic education that each school will offer.[21]

The apparent ideological contradiction between moving towards greater centralization and greater decentralization has led some to conclude that they are witnessing a strategy of political incrementalism. For if the government's plan is eventually to hand over unprecedented powers to individual parent councils, the government must first control the power it wants to give away. Stephen Murgatroyd, author of *Total Quality Management and the School*, is encouraged by his province's first steps. He believes that school governance in Alberta will soon go the way of New Zealand and Great Britain. "Neither country bit the whole piece at once," he says.[22]

A first step in this direction turns up in the business plan as a commitment to implement school-based management. In practice, decisions usually made by school boards and their officials regarding programming, staffing, teaching assignments, budget, supplies, maintenance, and so forth are delegated to individual schools — the Edmonton Public System has been in the school-based mode for fifteen years. How much power will each school have? Minister Jonson says extending this system across Alberta will mean that schools will receive a lump sum from their boards, and they can decide how to spend the money. As schools are buildings, however, the minister rather begs the question of precisely who will decide, and who will be accountable for the decisions made.

The promise of school-based management, according to its advocates, is greater autonomy, greater accountability, and close-to-the-customer responsiveness. It's hard to find an article praising this management model that doesn't resort to the phrases "teacher empowerment," "total quality," "mission" and "vision," often in the same sentence. The pitch to teachers is that their wisdom is being recognized and utilized; the pitch to school boards is that they are innovative cost-cutters; the pitch to the public is that entire levels of inept and expensive bureaucracy will disappear. What could be better?

The reality, however, is quite different. Is the work of school management to be taken on by teachers, who are already exhausted and spread too thin? If so, they must acquire budgeting and interviewing skills and find the time to become knowledge-able about all facets of school organization. On what does the music teacher form an opinion as to whether the science lab needs a wave generator? Is the advice of the math teacher on refinishing the gymnasium floor particularly valuable? Most teachers do not want a say in matters peripheral to their own work or incidental to their students' education. The ATA's report, after all, was called *Trying to Teach*.

The most common way of coping with school-based manage-ment is dumping decisions on the principal. This approach may be encouraged by an administrator sympathetic to teachers or by one eager to build a modest empire. In other schools, the staff defers to vociferous opinion leaders who are prepared to take sides on every question, whether or not they are well-informed. Teachers uncom-fortable with endless debates on priorities may seek transfers to a school less caught up in staff politics. Others retreat to their class-rooms rather than compete, making do with whatever they get. The opportunities for making schools effective through school-based management cannot be realized unless leadership, time and patience are extended along with authority. Nothing in the Klein reforms suggest that these elements have any place in "just-in-time" education.

PARENT POWER!

School-based decision making already promises to become even more disruptive and frustrating with the implementation of "empowered" parent councils. In theory, everyone wants parents involved. In practice, there are many problems to be worked out. Is each school expected to negotiate its own balance of power between parents and staff? What new possibilities for school-based chaos are presented by encouraging the inexperienced to struggle over the undefined? Without a coherent plan, empowering parents is not just a downloading of decision making, it is the downloading of the tensions created by a system in which expectations exceed resources, and in which pedagogical and political directives are in conflict.

Yet parent control is the rallying cry of restructure-from-the-right advocates, and the doctrine of groups such as AQE. It fits into an ideology of populism, of reduced government interference, the panacea of deregulation and "accountabilism"—however, only if the control is substantive, not superficial. "Parents have the ultimate authority over education ... but we have surrendered that to government," says influential Alberta education critic Joseph Freedman.[23] But it is not just populists who see potential in breaking the hold of the system. According to *Maclean's*, parent- and teacher-run schools are models of co-operation that are "finding enthusiastic support from one sector with a particularly sharp eye on public school—the business community. 'We don't have the luxury of solitudes any more, or the luxury of enemies,' says Gordon Cressy, president of The Learning Partnership, an organization devoted to creating closer ties between schools and the private sector."[24]

The question of the appropriate role of parents is not the exclusive concern of the far Right or business lobbies. Reaching out to parents is a philosophy preached (if only intermittently practised) by schools everywhere. When parent involvement is low, the school is usually blamed for being unfriendly, condescending or secretive. *Maclean's* suggests that parent activism is a response to the incompetency of schools:

> Employing a vocabulary of so-called "edubabble" about "child-centred learning" and "the primacy of self-esteem," parents feel

that the educational establishment has closed ranks, excluding
outsiders from the debate. In the process, they say, educators
have camouflaged their own failure to ensure that children learn
the basics.[25]

There appears to be enough blame to spread around. Parents are
sometimes scapegoated as uninterested, but just as many are disinclined to become involved with the school, perhaps because of negative memories of their own school days, often because contact
with the school usually means discouraging news about the
achievement or behaviour of their children. Some believe that
what happens at school is the school's business; but more seem to
be unable to find the time or energy to be active in the life of the
school. Statistics Canada reports that the average two-job, two-
parent family with children puts in a seventy-five-hour workweek.
Fixing school lunches at midnight is an immediate necessity; dropping in on class during the school day is a luxury. Whatever the
appropriate role of parents under ideal circumstances, day-to-day
realities shape the parent-school relationship more than does the
philosophy of the school.

Every school that takes parent participation seriously knows
that its most active parents are not necessarily representative of
the parent body. This is clear even when parents play a small role
in school decisions; it becomes a major equity issue when individual
schools control program, staffing and budget decisions. There is a
significant danger of disenfranchising those families who feel that
the school is not responding to their needs. It is reasonable to
assume that parent councils will attract the most confident, vocal
and persuasive — read middle-class — parents whose life experiences
and priorities may not be the same as those of the less-privileged
members of the school community. What's the likelihood of an
immigrant single parent becoming spokesperson of the parent
council of a typical suburban school? The opportunities for a
narrow group sharing a particular religious, political or pedagogical

persuasion to seize control are abundant. It has been said that 80% of successful life is determined by just showing up. Just showing up may be all that is required to take control of a volunteer council, no matter how important its work may be.

Adding inter-school competition to this situation can only make things worse, even for a parent council that is functioning well. With schools vying for students, decisions to benefit the most students currently in the school must be tempered by whether these decisions will attract more students next year: the quality of each decision will be measured by its marketing potential. If the choice before the decision makers is between hiring a social worker or upgrading the computer system, the decision is not on educational merit, but how it will be perceived by potential customers. Schools facing the incentive of competition may find it especially difficult to choose to meet the needs of the few. How can the cost of building a wheelchair-friendly play structure compete with a proposal to update the physics lab?

These choices are currently determined outside the individual school, by school boards and ministries obliged to make decisions in favour of balance and equity. In the past, it has not been considered wise to leave choices such as whether to set up a sheltered classroom for emotionally disturbed children to the whims of school or parent politics. Many systems have created specialized schools, particularly at the high school level, because school boards can ensure the overall balance in the system: schools emphasizing the fine arts can be a complement to schools specializing in science and technology. However, if no one is obliged to consider system balance, passionate parents will consider only their own interests, as they do when opposing the closure of a low-enrolment neighbourhood school.

The promise of greater parent control at the school level will create greater confusion and conflict unless premises and principles common to all schools are established. This is what regulation means. The problem is not that parents are likely to be mean-spirited or incompetent, but that even the most able can find their good intentions thwarted by factors beyond their control. Even without the immediate extension of parent power to the selection of teachers, curriculum and instruction, there is greater likelihood of bitterness and disappointment than of co-operation.

The subtext of the debate on parent involvement is how various groups answer the question, whom do schools serve? All decisions about governance, taxation, accountability and direction in education flow from how this question is answered. Until now, public education has answered this question with the principle that in a democracy, education serves and protects society by balancing the particular needs of the individual with the need for common experience, knowledge and collective values. Schools have had no clients or customers of special merit; the elderly and the young, parents and non-parents have an equally vested interest in the success of education for all. Sharing the funding of public education through general taxation reinforces this principle. Decision making by elected bodies removed from the intensity of self-interest ensures that the public interest is the basis for decision making.

Only when parents "own" their children can they claim to "own" education. Many argue that the consequence of the privatization of children has been the breakdown of community. If it is none of anyone's business how other people's children are educated, the public can hardly be obliged to provide decent child-care options or pediatric health services. If you own your children, then you own their problems, too. If child education is the exclusive property of parents, so too is child poverty.

From the principle of the privatization of children flows the privatization of education; from the privatization of education flows the privatization of responsibility and compassion. This is the true direction of the Alberta experiment.

CONCLUSION: DEAR FRIENDS OF PUBLIC EDUCATION

A BOOK ABOUT EDUCATION IS EXPECTED TO BE REPLETE WITH RECIPES for reform, lists of inspired innovations, calls for immediate action. However, if the improvement of education required only another few hundred pages of recommendations, this book would not have been necessary. The problem is not one of technique, but of commitment; education is not short of advice, but of common purpose. Our intent has been to challenge the premises of current education reform and the consequences of continuing to cede to selfish and political interests.

We have too much respect for the complexities of educational change to pretend that the alternative can be usefully described in a single chapter. We are not about to set out yet another restating of the goals of education or desirable student outcomes. What already exists in many other sources is more than adequate for these purposes. Implicitly, what we have asked within this book is why the actions and words of Canadians are so far apart, and what interests interfere with improving our schools. In general, the answer is that those determining the ideological agenda of our country are not interested in keeping or improving the schools we have, but in restructuring them in ways that serve neither children nor the public. Until we deal with this issue, there is little point in tinkering with the wording of goals and objectives.

Having said this, it is still true that schools are more susceptible to the assault from the Right because of their vulnerabilities, and because of the vulnerabilities of the gatekeepers responsible for the effectiveness of the system. To strengthen our ability to protect and renew schools, each sector must look to its own obligations and its own integrity. To this end, we do offer some suggestions.

DEAR TEACHER,

Yes, your lot is hard, and the world is not fair. But you didn't enter the profession to take things easy or keep things exactly as they are.

Many of you have been forced to act against your best judgement by following policies that make no sense and by implementing experiments set up to fail. You've been frustrated by an administration that is often political rather than educational: you have been made bitter by criticism that is unwarranted. Yet you have also been known to take the path of least resistance, and enjoyed the relative privacy of what goes on in the classroom. Sometimes you have been silenced, but other times you have silenced yourself.

You need to push the edges of your competency, and test your political power in the interests of your students. Many of you are close to retirement. Live a little! Take some risks on behalf of your students and in the name of your profession. It is, indeed, relatively hard to get fired from this job; use your security to speak out for what you believe, because your grudging acquiescence to bad education is tantamount to support.

You have a powerful influence on the curriculum. Teach children that they are entitled to a good education, to respect, and to protection from exploitation. Teach them their obligations to one another: political literacy does not undermine these objectives, and it will take students much farther than one more unit on self-esteem.

And, please, you are pivotal to the success of current "reform." It cannot happen without you. If you believe, as we do, that public education is at risk, you must take a stand, however and wherever you can. This will be hard for you because you are a professional who has not regarded politics as germane to your work. But the long-term interests of your students are at stake, and they need you now. Given a chance, they will supply you with motivation.

DEAR TEACHER ORGANIZATION,

We described you as being between a rock and a hard place, and you will stay stuck so long as you continue to be reactive, bowing to special interests within your membership. Your members wonder where the good leaders are; some of the best teachers in the profession want nothing to do with their organizations, and see them as lacking integrity and democracy. This is either their problem, or your own. Renewal starts at home.

You need direction, not more policies. You need to nurture the capacity of teachers to become impassioned about the future of education, and to see that their organizations become the vehicles of realizing the future. We know you've been trying, but there is more to do.

Of all the gatekeepers, you are in the best position to name and confront the ideological issues we have raised in this book. This will require that you work with your own members as well as with the public and other gatekeepers; teachers may well be frustrated with the direction of school reform, but this is no guarantee that they will automatically accept your analysis of the problem. Both they and the public have to be shown alternatives to losing control of our schools.

Work with your natural allies. Within the education sector, old enemies might well become new friends. If the goal is to save and renew public education, trustees and parents are there to be brought on side. As well, your individualism, which some have perceived as snobbishness, has kept some of you at a distance from other public sector unions, from volunteer-based child-advocacy groups and from overtly political movements; it has kept you isolated. You need friends, and you need them badly.

Now is the time not only to defend the rights of your members, but to advocate for the needs of the broader community. In order to protect teachers, you must protect the quality of teaching; for, ultimately, communities will judge teacher unions primarily on whether you promote quality education for their children. Your interests are bound up with your communities, other working people, other public services, the poor and the unemployed.

Your organization was built on a long tradition of choosing principle over advantage. Nourish this tradition of integrity, and live by it. Take the lead now.

DEAR ADMINISTRATOR,

The matters you deal with every day have such urgency that it is hard to get to the fundamentals of enhancing the teaching and learning that takes place in your school. Nonetheless, you know that all the research says that what you do—or don't do—can make or break your school. It's a huge responsibility.

As a leader, there is something for you in each of these letters, because you are the one who can encourage, or discourage, the participation of others in your school. On matters such as partnerships, your task will be much easier if there is a policy filter that will restrict the access of profiteers to your students. You deserve the assistance of regulations made in the public interest; as a group, administrators can advocate effectively for much of what we have proposed. Until these rules are in place, however, apply your own. Make sure that the true partnership that is nourished is between teachers, students, their families and communities.

Your average age tells us that you have been in this profession for a long time: you are closer to retirement than to your first teaching job. For many, your current position will be your last. It is never too late to leave your mark.

DEAR MINISTER OF EDUCATION,

It might not be the portfolio you asked for, but it's the one you got. You have our sympathy, and if you do it right, you can also have the support of the other gatekeepers.

This is more likely to happen if you start to think education, not just politics. Your primary responsibility is not to the premier or treasury board, or even to your constituents; it is to the children in schools. Often, however, it is hard to believe that their welfare is what you have in mind when you announce your policies.

We know that the other gatekeepers could help you out by being less self-interested, but you have responsibility, too. Don't surround yourself with people who know nothing about the system they are trying to reform. Recognize that each change you make will have as many unintended consequences as intended ones; that sustained change takes time; and that the first stage of real change is confusion and slippage. The benefits take a while. We realize that politics is about the short term, but education is about the long term. It is your obligation to choose substance over show.

Become as informed as possible about the issues associated

with schools of choice, for this will be the education-policy issue of the next decade, ready or not. You will be lobbied furiously, and you need to prepare, now, to stand up for the universality of high-quality education. Establish strict guidelines for the partnerships springing up all over your province. Business should not be allowed to sit down one-on-one with schools to set the direction of education. Take leadership to prevent the commercialization of the classroom.

Talk more to teachers, informally and formally. Without their support, your reforms will be sabotaged. That's how it works. This doesn't mean doing only what they like, but you might try convincing teachers rather than commanding them. And please be honest. Things cannot stay exactly the same and change at the same time. Promising the public that schools by themselves can do the work of families and communities only makes everyone more cynical.

Finally, stop using the language of the boardroom to describe what goes on in schools. Schools aren't companies; school boards aren't corporations; principals aren't CEOs. Stop confusing children with outputs, and quality with quantity. Drop by a few schools.

DEAR LEGISLATOR,

You ran for office because you care about your country. Once elected, you discovered reality. Every day you are confronted with tough choices and diminishing public resources. You often feel helpless to make any real change.

Well, this is your chance! Please don't buy into the argument that an impoverished public sector is inevitable, or that the corporate vision of the global economy is predestined. There are jobs and resources for everyone, if we build economic and social policy to this end. If we accept the inevitability of a pear-shaped society underpinned by a contingent workforce, we will permit the reform of our schools to serve this model.

It is your job to make sure that control of public schools remains in public hands. Pass legislation to ban corporate logos and sponsorships in our schools, on educational or curriculum materials, and in academic programs or contests. Get the commercial presence out of our schools. Donated curriculum materials should be vetted before a board-curriculum committee to ensure they conform to public guidelines and are not industry public relations for commercial profit.

Establish guidelines for school-business partnerships. At present, they are operating as a parallel structure, competing for control with elected school boards. The partnership that works for children is that between the school and the community; business involvement must support this model. Set up a publicly operated foundation to funnel corporate donations to education so that they are distributed fairly to all schools. Consult front-line teachers on school reform. They are not a special interest group but the backbone of the system, and they know what they're talking about.

Please, please, show leadership. The more democracy is threatened by global economic forces, the more we need you to take a stand. If our public programs are to survive, the wealthy and big companies will have to pay their share of taxes. They won't like that, but you didn't go into politics to subvert the democratic process that elected you.

This is not a time for the faint of heart.

DEAR TRUSTEE,

We do not envy you your job. To do it right, you need wisdom, strength and passion. Without doubt, this job is harder than you ever expected it to be.

But please, try to see the big picture beyond your board documentation: there is a world of educational thought beyond the rationales provided by your administrators. It is easy to get caught up in debating the smallest item in the budget, especially when some of your fellow trustees are as enraging as you find them to be. However, when you act like children in board meetings, when you use the press to castigate the schools for which you are responsible or to belittle teachers, you are helping to dig the grave of public education.

We urge you to be particularly alert to propositions described as partnerships. You are a trustee—your trust is the partnership between schools and their communities, which are to be strengthened; all other parties claiming to want to help education must be tested against this criterion. Be suspicious; there are many ready to take advantage of your frustration. Resist the temptation to download this frustration through the mechanisms of school choice. Think universality, diversity and quality.

Finally, if you are angry with schools, please do not seek a trusteeship as a form of therapy. Your anger may well be justified, but we need hope and leadership, not revenge.

DEAR BUSINESS LEADER,

We have been hard on you in this book; your record makes it difficult to do otherwise. And we have lumped you all together, which is probably unfair.

In fact, the big players have changed the rules of the game so much to their (and your) advantage, that the ethical among you are operating at a disadvantage. You need to work with other sectors of society to establish rules—a kind of moral level playing field. Start investing again in Canada. If you wish to have real influence on young people, help us create full employment and give us a future. Stop blaming the unemployed for being the victims of the economy you are creating. Use your global influence to wage war on joblessness. Develop and observe an international corporate code of conduct. Build strong environmental, social and human rights standards into trade agreements.

Start paying your fair share of taxes. Teachers and other government workers have had to accept tough wage restrictions. You could wipe out the entire federal deficit if you just paid the taxes you have deferred. Don't try to break up unions. A decently paid workforce is the backbone of the economy and your best security. And while we're on the subject of salaries, please cut the obscene amount you pay yourselves. You can hardly ask the rest of us to tighten our belts when we see how you skim the system.

As for your concern about schools: you would be a lot more effective if you stopped bashing teachers and undermining public education. Yes, it can do better; but you could make an important contribution by gathering real data on skills needs instead of fictionalizing numbers in order to scare everyone half to death. Teachers would welcome the information.

Don't try to buy your way into schools. Please stop advertising to children. If you want to support education financially, set up a foundation that works with government and other social partners to distribute the money equally so that all children benefit. You are one partner in our nation's social compact. Don't use your money to elbow out the others.

The legacy of the new economy is spiritual and cultural impoverishment. Help us nurture the minds and souls of the children. They are your future, too.

DEAR MEMBERS OF THE PRESS,

This is probably not the assignment you wanted. Education reporting can be dull; it has a limited readership; the issues are complex and just because you master them doesn't mean more people will read you.

But education is emerging, along with health care, as the key public-policy issue of the decade. Where education was once of interest to a small group of insiders, now it's everyone's affair.

Please help your readers understand the political and ideological issues surrounding education reform. When governments say cuts, do they mean reformation? What is school choice? What has been the experience of other countries that have gone through this process? Is the deficit crisis one of overspending on public programs or of lack of revenue because there are sources of money we're not tapping?

Speak to more teachers for your analyses, and not just for stories of violence in the classroom. They have their own ideas about the future of education.

Oh, and could you see if you can get your newspaper to publish the odd education supplement that isn't paid for by ads for corporations and private schools?

DEAR PARENT,

You have a lot of power when it comes to our education system, whether or not you are aware of it. When you use this power—as a volunteer, a critic or an advocate—things do change. It's sometimes hard to see the results, and hard to believe it's worth the effort, but your involvement is key to a healthy and responsive system.

You are pressed for time. You are pressed for optimism about your children's future. We urge you to waste neither your time nor your optimism on "magic bullets" of school reform. Schools cannot go backwards any more than can your family. Please contribute to renewing public schools; it's the only guarantee of a system that will work for all children.

Teach your children to be responsibly rebellious. If they learn that it is best to tolerate injustice by silence, it is a lesson they will never forget. But if they learn from you that taking responsibility for change is more worthwhile than blaming others, they will take this lesson with them all their lives.

If you are unhappy about your child's life at school, please speak up, and speak up where and when it can make a difference. You are needed as an advocate for other people's children as well as for your own. If you are satisfied, please don't be silent. Good schools, like good families, need nurturing.

DEAR STUDENT,

You are part of the best-educated generation of one of the best-educated countries in the world. More of you will go on to post-secondary education than ever before. Your generation looks to formal education to guarantee you a future, but this is a time without guarantees, and a time of many false promises.

One of these false promises is that your education can be a ticket to a good job. It can't. Elementary and secondary schools were never intended to be employment training centres. The education you are receiving is supposed to be in the tradition of a liberal education, which means schools are to help you acquire the skills and knowledge to live "in liberty" alongside your fellow citizens. Your education should be about how to make a life, not how to make a living.

Yes, making a life includes paid work. But it also includes making choices, developing relationships and finding a purpose. Getting a job may be a goal, but it is not in itself a purpose for living.

Some of you are harshly critical of your schools' ability to help you to make a life. You see other people's convenience put ahead of your own needs, and when your opinion is sought, it is often as an afterthought, with adults already prepared to explain why things can't work the way you want them to.

In part, your being left out of the debate is due to your very quiet voices. You seem to be invisible unless one of your numbers deals drugs or carries a weapon. But no one reads your great essay, sees your line drawing, admires your chemistry mark. We are a society greatly frightened by you and your friends, even when we know none of you personally. But our real fear is a fear of the future, and since you represent this future, we are afraid of you. We talk a lot about controlling you, when what we really want is to control the future.

So we talk too much about making sure you can cope with the future and give you little hope that the future is yours to create.

You can, of course, adapt to this state of affairs. Most reasonably able students whose lives aren't too chaotic can master the rules of success at school. This will certainly improve the credentials you leave with, but these won't necessarily attest to a good education. Too often, this system trains you to play the game, put up with injustice and bide your time until your "real life" starts.

Well, this is your real life. Some schools will treat you about as badly as you let them, or as well as you demand. As individuals—and as a group—you have power that you have never tested, not just to oppose what offends you, but to support new ways, programs and people who respect what you want to accomplish. And please remember, it is not just you alone who will build the future. You will live there with every one of your classmates, and with those who drop out, and with the rest of the planet.

One of the lessons of liberty is that we are all in this together.

DEAR PUBLIC FIGURE,

You are a featured keynote speaker at conferences and conventions. You get asked by the press for your opinion. Groups are always after you to be a patron for this or that good cause or to grace their letterhead. You represent something steady and substantive in turbulent times. You are a Prominent Canadian.

Canada's public services are in deep trouble. In one decade, we are dismantling what took others many to create. Whatever your field of expertise, these changes will affect it. Please speak out on education. Please be counted as a friend of public schools. Read as much as you can and never let an opportunity go by without going to bat for Canada's public programs.

If you don't become involved, you may wake up soon to a harmonized continent in which it's nothing special—or different—to be a Canadian, prominent or otherwise.

DEAR CITIZEN,

You are a caring Canadian, a decent person generally uncomfortable with ideological conflict. The overt patriotism of Americans embarrasses you. You pay your taxes, raise your kids and quietly give back to your community in a hundred ways.

But you are uneasy. Things are changing very fast. You are worried about your job. You don't understand why, if we are coming out of the recession, we are having to take additional hits to social programs. You see a pretty grim future for your kids.

Please don't buy the theory that there is no alternative, that the global economy is a scientific, immutable fact about which mere humans can do nothing. To sell this message, politicians and business leaders need the silent majority to go along. If it is true that there is no alternative, why do we bother to vote?

Public schools are community organizations. That's where you come in. This is not the time for reactive measures. We need to launch a pro-active campaign *for* public schools. We could call it *Public Schools Serve Canada*. Talk to your family, your co-workers, your neighbours. Challenge your business friends to co-operate in confronting unemployment, inequality, violence. Remind them that while they must primarily be concerned with profit, schools must concentrate on children. Ask them to be better partners in Canada's economic life.

Don't be afraid to become politically engaged. We're changing the definition of politics anyway. It no longer belongs only to elected representatives. Remember that public education is fundamental to democracy; no other institution can fulfil this role.

One last thought: look in a mirror. Leadership sometimes shows up in unexpected places. We now need leaders, not necessarily elected or highly educated or experienced in public speaking, but committed leaders who will come forward. Absolutely nothing is more effective.

DEAR SENIOR,

As above with one addition. You lived through times like these in the 1930s and you saw suffering. You also lived through world wars. You have a great deal to teach us about not losing sight of our values and sense of responsibility to one another when the going gets tough. We need your direction and example. You are probably the only group who can honestly say you get involved for others.

Remind us what it was like when not all kids could go to school, or when families lost their homes to pay for medical treatment. We've forgotten. Be our teachers.

FIRST CALL FOR CHILDREN

If, as we passionately hope, Canadians reject the model of education reform described in these pages, there is no shortage of other work to be done. We suggest as a start, the principle of "first call."

Canada helped create and is a signatory to the United Nations Convention on the Rights of the Child. Under this convention, all signatories are obligated to adhere to this principle: whether nations' resources are great or limited, children have a prior right—a first call—on what is available. This is not only a statement of economic principle or of political priority, it is a moral imperative. Yet as a society, we would be hard-pressed to demonstrate that we live by the creed of first call. So would some families. So would some classrooms.

Putting children first—especially the youngest among them — is not only the right thing to do, it is the smart thing to do. If there is one subject around which 'expert' opinion agrees, it is that prevention and early intervention when children are at risk is the most effective strategy available to us. Not only do we know that children's cognitive powers are greatest in the first years of their lives, we also know that their patterns of emotional and physical health are established at that time. Once established, negative patterns are difficult to reverse; but nurtured, strong minds and bodies have great resilience. If we follow the best advice available to us, we will direct our resources to the well-being of our youngest citizens and our youngest students.

We have strange priorities. It costs taxpayers nearly $70,000 to keep one young offender in secure custody for one year—and this figure does not include treatment or rehabilitation. There are few young offenders whose lives would not have been put on a different course if a fraction of this money had been invested in prevention; yet the public outcry is centred not on early intervention, but on tougher measures for young offenders. We champion harsher criminal-code amendments for those who abuse children, but in many jurisdictions, young children can wait more than two years before they are professionally assessed—let alone treated—for emotional problems.

In some school jurisdictions, it is forbidden to identify children as being in need of special help during their first three years in school, because this might stigmatize them. We are told that acquiring full fluency in the language of instruction by newly arrived students takes an average of seven years of special support, but many jurisdictions offer six months of assistance, and some none at all. The ratio of guidance counsellors to students at the high-school level is estimated at more than 300:1; at the elementary level, most students have no counsellor at all. We can predict with frightening accuracy which ten-year-olds will drop out of school, but we focus our stay-in-school resources at fifteen-year-olds. We revise Canada's food guide and send it home with hundreds of thousands of students who depend on food banks. We pay child-care workers less than animal-care workers and allow thousands of children to languish in unregulated and sometimes haphazard daycare. We set up a Children's Bureau to guide federal policy on children, and it spends more than half its budget on public opinion polling rather than programs.

In Canada, we have designed and implemented some of the most creative and effective programs for children anywhere in the world—but most children at risk either have no access to them, or access too late. Without timely availability, effective prevention and intervention programs intended to improve the quality of children's lives are only false promises. We have turned to our one universal system for children—education—to make up for the lack of universality of food, care and ordered lives.

If this is what we are asking of schools—to nurture capacity to learn—then they must be properly resourced. The resources schools need, however, are not only financial; what schools most require is the commitment of the public to their success in the interests of all children. If we buy into different types of schools for different types of children, we renege on this commitment.

It would be simpler, certainly, to conclude that schools were never designed to nurture capacity to learn, but only to transmit information, and that it is to this task that they must return if they are to succeed. However, this makes sense only if we can deny the true nature of education and the characteristics of our students and their world. We would do better to remember that schools are our own invention, created to respond to the needs of children and society. They have been—and can be again—recreated to respond to these needs, but only if these needs are recognized for what they are, not manufactured to serve another agenda. The principle of first call can answer many questions about how we should proceed in creating school reform.

In business seminars, leadership gurus are fond of saying that if you get the vision right, everything else will fall into place. They are rarely considered naïve. Surely it is no more naive to claim that our education system should also be subject to the power of one over-arching idea against which our reforms and our progress are to be measured. Giving our children first call may not make things fall into place, but it will make sustained, meaningful school reform possible. This is the first item on the agenda if we are to avoid class warfare, a conflict in which all our children, whatever their background, would be the casualties.

NOTES

INTRODUCTION

1. A. J. C. King and M. J. Peart, *Teachers in Canada: Their Work and Quality of Life* (Ottawa: Canadian Teachers' Federation, 1992), p. 4.
2. Neil Postman and Charles Weingartner, *Teaching as a Subversive Activity* (New York: Delacorte Press, 1969).
3. Statistics Canada, *Education in Canada*, Cat. no. 81–229, 1991–92 edition, (Ottawa: Minister of Supply and Services, 1993), Table 55, p. 223.
4. Paul Viera, "Food for thought could run out for lack of cash," *Globe and Mail*, December 6, 1993.
5. Elizabeth Payne, "Hard part begins for commission," *Ottawa Citizen*, December 15, 1993.
6. *Saturday Night* magazine, December 1993.
7. Bertrand Marcotte, "Canada's schools failing the grade: business leaders," *Montreal Gazette*, May 5, 1993.
8. Richard Pinet and Jim Sands, "What Facts, Whose Arguments?" A paper prepared for the British Columbia Teachers' Federation, March 1993.
9. Canadian Teachers' Federation, *Education and Teachers in the Canadian Economy* (Ottawa, 1993).
10. Information provided by the Canadian Teachers' Federation, based on published and unpublished figures from Statistics Canada, January 1994.
11. Scott Feschuk, "Klein will save, Albertans will pay," *Globe and Mail*, January 19, 1994.

12. Child Poverty Action Group, "Campaign 2000: Child Poverty in Canada. Report Card 1993." Canadian Council on Social Development.
13. Tom R. Williams and Holly Millinoff, "Canada's Schools: Report Card for the 1990s." A CEA Opinion Poll. Canadian Education Association, September 1990.
14. Council of Ministers of Education, Canada, "Education in Canada: Report to the 43rd Session International Conference on Education, Geneva," 1992.
15. Marcotte, "Canada's schools failing the grade."
16. Conference Board of Canada, "Matching Education to the Needs of Society. A Vision Statement Working Paper," April 1993.
17. John R. Gardner, "Dilemmas in Education: A Speech to the Rotary Club of Toronto," April 16, 1993.
18. Mark Holmes, "A Blueprint for Educational Policy in Canada." *Journal of Education Administration and Foundations.* 7/2 (1992).
19. Marcotte, "Canada's schools failing the grade."
20. Ontario Secondary School Teachers' Federation, *Public Education: Retracing Our Path: A Brief to the Royal Commission on Learning* (Toronto, December 1993).

OUR SCHOOLS HAVE FAILED US ... AND OUR KIDS

1. John R. Gardner, "Dilemmas in Education." A speech to the Rotary Club of Toronto, April 16, 1993.
2. "Back to the Future: Tests, Competition, Performance," *Western Report,* January 25, 1993, p. 30.
3. Economic Council of Canada, "A Lot to Learn: Education and Training in Canada." A Statement by the Economic Council of Canada, 1992.
4. Statistics Canada, *Survey of Literacy Skills Used in Daily Activities* (Ottawa: Minister of Supply and Services 1990).
5. Saskatchewan Teachers' Federation, "The Need for Critical Thinking: The Case of Education, the Economic Council of Canada and the Media." *Professional Perspectives* 3/2 (April 1993).
6. Brian Harrison, "I can't speak English or French," *Canadian Social Trends,* Winter 1993.
7. Denise Avard, *"Meet Canada's Student Population." Different Visions of the Future of Education.* Conference report (Ottawa: Canadian Teachers' Federation, 1994).
8. Economic Council of Canada, "A Lot to Learn."
9. Conference Board of Canada, "Matching Education to the Needs of Society: A Vision Statement." Working Paper of the National Council on Education, n.d., 1993.
10. Meeting of H. Robertson, G. Gilliss and H. Weiner (CTF) with Mary Anne McLaughlin and Florence Campbell (Conference Board), June 2, 1993.

11. *Ottawa Citizen*, November 6, 1993.
12. Statistics Canada, Education, Culture and Tourism Division, *High School Non-Completion Rates: A Map of Current Measures* (Ottawa: Minister of Supply and Services, May 11, 1993).
13. Tom Fennell, "A Measure of Hope," *Maclean's*, June 14, 1993.
14. Jennifer Lewington and Graham Orpwood, *Overdue Assignment: Taking Responsibility for Canada's Schools* (Toronto: John Wiley and Sons, 1993).
15. Fennell, "A Measure of Hope," p. 49.
16. J. Paul Grayson and Michael H. Hall, "The Hall-Grayson Report: Survey Defines Characteristics of Dropouts," *Education Today*, March/April 1993.
17. Government of Canada, Minister of State for Youth, *Equation: The Newsletter of the Stay-in-School Initiative*, September 1991.
18. Walter G. Pitman, "My Turn," *Education Forum*, Winter 1989.
19. Caroline Mullin, "Education not cost efficient, Wilson argues," *Toronto Star*, May 14, 1993.
20. Organization for Economic Co-operation and Development, Centre for Educational Research and Innovation, *Education-at-a-Glance: OECD Indicators* (Paris, 1992).
21. The Liberal Party of Canada, *The Red Book* (1993).
22. Michael J. Barrett, "The Case for More School Days," *Atlantic Monthly*, November 1990.
23. Geraldine Gilliss, "Length of Japanese School Year Exaggerated," *LINK*, December '91/January '92.
24. Diane Francis, "Canada's Education System Needs Some Discipline," *Financial Post*, May 6, 1993.
25. Tom R. Williams and Holly Millinoff, "Canada's Schools: Report Card for the 1990s." A CEA Opinion Poll. Canadian Education Association, September 1990.
26. Gardner, "Dilemmas in Education."
27. Economic Council of Canada, "A Lot to Learn."
28. "What's Wrong at School." *Maclean's*, January 11, 1993.
29. Robert Fulford, "Business must lead school reform," *Financial Times*, April 27, 1992.
30. Conference Board of Canada, *Reaching for Success: Business and Education Working Together* (1990).
31. David F. Robitaille, "Canadian Participation in the Second International Mathematics Study," Working Paper 6. Economic Council of Canada, 1990.
32. Ibid.
33. Kazuo Ishizaka, "Japanese Education: The Myths and the Realities." Paper presented to the Canadian Teachers' Federation Conference, Visions of Education, Ottawa, May 1993.
34. Child Poverty Action Group, "Campaign 2000: Child Poverty in Canada. Report Card 1993." Canadian Council on Social Development. Ottawa, November 1993.
35. Alanna Mitchell, "Child's play becomes serious business," *Globe and Mail*, November 18, 1993.

36. Gallup Canada, *The Gallup Report*, February 1, 1993.
37. D. W. Livingstone, D. Hart and L. E. Davie, *Public Attitudes Towards Education in Ontario, 1992: Ninth OISE Survey* (Toronto: OISE Press, 1993).
38. "MTS Releases Public Opinion Poll on Education Issues." *The Manitoba Teacher* 72/2 (1993).
39. Stanley M. Elam, Lowell C. Rose and Alec M. Gallup, "The 25th Annual Phi Delta Kappa/Gallup Poll of the Public's Attitudes Toward the Public Schools," *Phi Delta Kappan*, October 1993.
40. Prosperity Secretariat, Government of Canada, *Learning Well . . . Living Well* (Ottawa: Queen's Printer, 1991).
41. The Angus Reid Group, "Education Issues Confronting Canada: A National Survey of the Public's Views and Attitudes." A Syndicated Study. Spring 1993 (Proposal).

OUR GRADUATES JUST DON'T HAVE THE SKILLS

1. Jock Finlayson, Presentation to the Conference Board of Canada Corporate Council on Education, Business Council on National Issues, June 1993.
2. Quoted in "The Skills Squeeze," *Globe and Mail Report on Business*, December 1993.
3. "Data show boom in higher education," *Ottawa Citizen*, May 12, 1993.
4. *UNESCO Yearbook, 1989.* Quoted in the *Canadian Federation for the Humanities Bulletin*, Autumn 1990.
5. Statistics Canada Quarterly Survey, quoted in "Job prospects improve," *Ottawa Citizen*, February 3, 1994.
6. "StatsCan report refutes skills shortage theory," *Canadian Human Rights Reporter* 5/6 (March 26, 1992).
7. James Turk, "Education for Work: A Narrow Focus We Cannot Afford," International Conference on Education and Work, Toronto, March 1993.
8. G. Silvestri and J. Lukasiewicz, "Occupational Employment Projections," *Monthly Labor Review*, U.S. Bureau of Statistics, November 1991.
9. John Akers, "Let's get to work on education," *Wall Street Journal*, March 20, 1991.
10. Secretary's Commission on Achieving Necessary Skills, *Learning a Living: A Blueprint for High Performance* (Washington, D.C.: Department of Labor, April 1992).
11. National Center on Education and the Economy, *America's Choice: High Skills or Low Wages!* (1990).
12. Economic Policy Institute, *Declining Wages for High School and College Graduates* (Washington, D.C., May 1993).
13. John Bishop, *Workforce Preparedness*. Working Paper No. 92–04 (Ithaca, N.Y.: Cornell University Press, 1992).

14. Robert J. Samuelson, "The Value of College," *Newsweek*, August 31, 1992.
15. "Black Hole Opens in Science Job Rolls," *Wall Street Journal*, April 14, 1993.
16. David C. Berliner, "Mythology and the American System of Education," *Phi Delta Kappan*, April 1993.
17. Daniel Tanner, "A Nation 'Truly' at Risk," *Phi Delta Kappan*, December 1993.
18. Jonathan Weisman, "Skills in the Schools, Now It's Business's Turn," *Phi Delta Kappan*, January 1993.
19. Quoted in "The Commercialized Classroom," by Holley Knaus, *Multinational Monitor*, March 1992.
20. Christine Finnan, Henry M. Levin and Russell Rumberger, *Escalating Skill Requirements or Different Skill Requirements* (Stanford, C.T.: Stanford University Press, 1990).
21. Stan Karp, "The President's Hidden Curriculum," *Z Magazine*, October 1991.

BIG BUSINESS IS CREATING HIGHLY SKILLED JOBS

1. *World Investment Report 1993: Transnational Corporations and Integrated International Production* (New York: United Nations Publications, 1993).
2. Richard Barnet and John Cavanagh, *Global Dreams, Imperial Corporations and the New World Order* (New York: Simon and Schuster, 1994).
3. Richard Barnet. "The End of Jobs," *Harper's*, September 1993.
4. Joseph Bower, "Back to Work, Survival of the Fittest," *World Link Journal*, Spring 1993.
5. Douglas Noble, "New American Schools and the New World Order." Paper presented to the American Educational Research Association, San Francisco, 1992.
6. "Jobs in Age of Insecurity," *Time*, November 22, 1993.
7. "The Junking of America," *Maclean's*, December 14, 1992.
8. "GM shifts parts work offshore," *Globe and Mail*, December 13, 1993.
9. Canadian Auto Workers, Northern Telecom, "An Economic Overview." Prepared for the International Conference on Northern Telecom, October 24–5, 1991.
10. Richard Rothstein, "As the Good Jobs go Rolling Away, Who Will Buy?" *CEO International Strategies*, January 1994.
11. Walter Russell Mead, "Bushism Found," *Harper's*, September 1992.
12. Samuel Bowles, David Gordon and Thomas Weisskopf, "An Economic Strategy for Progressives," *The Nation*, February 1992.
13. Larry Cohen, "An International Mobilization Strategy," Internal Research Paper, Communications Workers of America, 1991.
14. "Youth 'big losers' in recession, StatsCan job report finds," *Ottawa Citizen*, January 27, 1994.

15. S. Krajewski, "Intra-Firm Trade and the New North American Business Dynamic," Conference Board of Canada, September 1992.
16. Statistics Canada, reported in "Long-term job loss a record, agency says" by Shawn McCarthy, *Toronto Star*, September 2, 1993.
17. "Wages trail inflation, StatsCan study says," *Toronto Star*, March 1, 1994; Canadian Labour Congress, "The Economy, An Economic Review and Outlook," Fall 1993.
18. Canadian Labour Congress, "The Myth of the 'New Economy'—Positive Restructuring in Manufacturing," October 1993.
19. "Why the end of the recession is kept private," *Globe and Mail*, March 27, 1994.
20. Canadian Press, June 28, 1993.
21. Wood Gundy report, cited in *Ottawa Citizen*, September 9, 1993.
22. Reported in *Ottawa Citizen*, December 19, 1993.

WHAT DOES BUSINESS REALLY WANT?

1. Stewart Allen, "Corporations Woo Young Students," *Rethinking Schools*, Summer 1993.
2. Gord Ekelund, "Ethics and the Corporate Classroom," *Education Forum*, Winter 1993.
3. Conference Board of Canada, "Matching Education to the Needs of Society." Working Paper, April 1993.
4. Ellen Wartella, "The Changing Consumer Environment and the Commercialization of Youth: Whittle in Context." Comments for American Education Research Association Convention, New Orleans, April 5, 1994.
5. From research by Erica Shaker, for Ralph Nader's Consumer Organization, 1993.
6. Nuala Beck, "Education is an industry in itself," *Globe and Mail*, February 3, 1993.
7. Gerald W. Bracey, "What If Education Broke Out All Over?" *Education Week*, Spring 1994.
8. United Nurses of Alberta, "Total Quality Management Programs, More Work for Less Pay," June 1993.
9. "Telephone competition is a long-distance battle," *Globe and Mail*, January 13, 1994.
10. Mark Surman, "It's the future, and you're not invited," *Globe and Mail*, March 25, 1994.
11. Fred Bacher, "A controlled-access highway," *Toronto Star*, January 29, 1994.
12. Advertisement, *Globe and Mail*, January 27, 1994.
13. Futurescape, Advertising Supplement, *Globe and Mail*, January 26, 1994.

HIJACKING A CULTURE

1. Government of Canada, *The Canada-U.S. Free Trade Agreement* (Ottawa: Queen's Printer, 1988); *The North American Free Trade Agreement* (Ottawa: Queen's Printer, 1992).
2. John Calvert and Larry Kuehn, *Pandora's Box, Corporate Power, Free Trade and Canadian Education* (Toronto: Our Schools/Our Selves Education Foundation, 1993).
3. NAFTA, Articles 1201, 1202.
4. NAFTA, Article 1205.
5. NAFTA, Chapter Ten.
6. NAFTA, Article 1024.
7. NAFTA, Article 1206.
8. John Harris, "Universities for Sale," *This Magazine*, September 1991.
9. Corporate-Higher Education Forum, *Spending Smarter*. Update, Montreal, May 1986.
10. David Noble, "The Multinational Multiversity," *Z Magazine*, April 1989.
11. NAFTA, Annex 1210.
12. The School of Education, University of Southern California, "The Educational Impact of the North American Free Trade Agreement: A Proposal to Support a Conference Between Educators in the United States, Canada and Mexico." San Diego, March 1992.

THE RIGHT-WING ALLIANCE AND
THE POLITICS OF EDUCATION

1. Michael G. Fullan with Suzanne Stiegelbauer, *The New Meaning of Educational Change*, 2nd ed. (Toronto: OISE Press, 1991).
2. Larry Kuehn, "Schooling Under the NDP: The British Columbia Experience," *Our Schools/Our Selves*. October/November 1993.
3. Anita LoSasso, "Being Properly Resourced," *Teacher*. (British Columbia Teachers' Federation), January/February 1993.
4. Canadian Association of School Administrators, "Facing the Realities: An Agenda, Process and Leadership for Reinventing Schools and Communities" (1993).
5. David Clanfield, "The NDP and the Corporate Agenda in Ontario," *Our Schools/Our Selves*, October/November 1993.
6. Kathryn Chang Barker, "Accountabilism as an Educational Reform Strategy: The Case of the School Achievement Indicators Project." Unpublished paper, Department of Educational Administration, University of Alberta, Edmonton.

7. Ibid.
8. Ibid.
9. Tom R. Williams and Holly Millinoff, "Canada's Schools: Report Card for the 1990s." A CEA Opinion Poll. Canadian Education Association, September 1990.
10. Michael Apple, "The Politics of Curriculum," *Education and Urban Society*, May 1991.
11. "Smothered by Its Own Weight: Total Privatization May Be the Only Way to Fix the Crumbling School System," *Western Report*, July 5, 1993.
12. Heather-jane Robertson, *The Better Idea Book: A Resource Book on Gender, Culture, Science and Schools* (Ottawa: Canadian Teachers' Federation, 1992).
13. "More Than Just Numbers." Report of the Canadian Committee on Women and Engineering, University of New Brunswick, Faculty of Engineering, April 1992.
14. Robertson, *The Better Idea Book*.
15. Bruce Curtis, D.W. Livingstone and Harry Smaller, "Stacking the Deck: The Streaming of Working-Class Kids in Ontario Schools," *Our Schools/Our Selves*, June 1992.
16. Michael Valpy, "The 40% factor," *Globe and Mail*, October 2, 1993.
17. Quoted by Valpy, ibid.
18. Andrew Nikiforuk, "Commitment counts for more than social class in schooling," *Globe and Mail*, April 1, 1994.
19. Arnold Burron, "Traditionalist Christians and OBE: What's the Problem?" *Educational Leadership*, Association for Supervision and Curriculum Development, March 1994.
20. Kuehn, "Schooling Under the NDP."
21. Quoted by Robert J. Marzano, "When Two Worldviews Collide," *Educational Leadership* (Association for Supervision and Curriculum Development), December '93/January '94.
22. Ibid.
23. Robert L. Simonds, "A Plea for the Children," *Educational Leadership* (Association for Supervision and Curriculum Development), December '93/January '94.
24. Jonathan Freedland, "Florida board teaches Americans 'Superior'," *Ottawa Citizen*, May 17, 1994.

RESTRUCTURING FROM THE RIGHT

1. Penelope Gurney and Bernard W. Andrews, "Studying the Roots of Restructuring: Rethinking Education's Form and Function," *Education Leader*, November 26, 1993.
2. Ibid.
3. Jonathan Kozol, "Whittle and the Privateers," *The Nation*, September 21, 1992.

4. Randall Denley, in the *Ottawa Citizen*, February 26, 1994.
5. Jeff Adams, "Market players can now invest in education," *Saskatoon Star Phoenix*, February 1, 1994.
6. Jim Downey, in "Reaching for Success: Business and Education Working Together." A paper delivered at the First National Conference on Business-Education Partnerships, Conference Board of Canada, July 1990.
7. Ivor F. Goodson and J. Marshall Mangan, "Computer Literacy as Ideology." January 7, 1994.
8. Ibid.
9. Ibid.
10. Randall Denley, "Software hard sell at schools," *Ottawa Citizen*, March 4, 1994.
11. Jennifer Lewington and Graham Orpwood, *Overdue Assignment: Taking Responsibility for Canada's Schools* (Toronto: John Wiley and Sons Canada Ltd., 1993).
12. Neil Postman, *Technopoly: The Surrender of Culture to Technology* (New York: Alfred A. Knopf, 1992).
13. Burnaby School District 41, "An Introduction to Burnaby South Secondary School." (Kit, undated.)
14. Jennifer Gray-Grant, "A School of the Future That's Open Today," *Education Leader* (British Columbia School Trustees Association), May 14, 1993.
15. J. Blades, "Thinking ahead," *Chicago Tribune*, March 24, 1991.
16. "Multimedia Anytime, Anywhere." *Multimedia Solutions* (undated).
17. Neil Postman, "The Judgement of Thamus," in *Technopoly.*
18. Michael Apple, "Conservative Agendas and Progressive Possibilities," *Education and Urban Society*, 1991.
19. Tom R. Williams and Holly Millinoff, "Canada's Schools: Report Card for the 1990s." A CEA Opinion Poll. Canadian Education Association, September 1990.
20. Pat Bell, "Savings in the works, OBE says," *Ottawa Citizen*, March 4, 1994.
21. *Computer Learning: The Official Annual Publication of the Computer Learning Foundation*, 1993–94.
22. Michelle Hibler, "Classroom Commercials," *Canadian Consumer,* September/October 1991.
23. "Call for Entries: The Conference Board of Canada's National Awards for Excellence in Business-Education Partnerships," 1993–94.
24. Conference Board of Canada, *Reaching for Success: Business and Education Working Together.* (1990).
25. "STF Objects to Business Group's Pro-board Stand," *The Saskatchewan Bulletin*, Saskatchewan Teachers' Federation, January 19, 1994.
26. *Globe and Mail*, December 24, 1992. Quoted in "A Survival Guide to the Youth News Network's Project and Methods," Parents Against Commercial Television in Schools, December 1992.
27. Parents Against Commercial Television in Schools, ibid.

28. *Edmonton Journal*, November 19, 1992, p. 7.
29. Stephen Godfrey, "Ads in the classroom cause furor," *Globe and Mail*, December 29, 1992.
30. Hibler, "Classroom Commercials."
31. D'Arcy Richard, "Business Gets a Crack at School Curriculum," *Education Leader*, October 29, 1993.
32. Ira Emery Rodd, "McLunchrooms," *The Nation*, September 21, 1992.
33. Andrew Duffy, "Pepsi deal 'dangerous in schools,' students say," *Toronto Star*, January 19, 1994.
34. Wendy Warburton, "Corporate intrusion in the classroom," *Ottawa Citizen*, January 29, 1994.
35. Ibid.
36. Allan Fotheringham, "Pepsi Goes to the Head of the Class," *Maclean's*, February 7, 1994.
37. "Letters," *Maclean's*, February 21, 1994.

RENOVATING THE STUDENT

1. Nikki van der Gaag, "Back to the Drawing Board, The War on Education," *New Internationalist*, No. 248 (October 1993).
2. Dr. Mahbub ul Haq, "Rich and poor," *Globe and Mail*, March 1, 1994.
3. *Public Educational Expenditure, Costs and Financing: An Analysis of Trends, 1970–1988.* (Paris: OECD, Paris, 1992).
4. Edith Terry, "Japan discovers a class act at work," *Globe and Mail*, March 23, 1992.
5. *The Times* (London), International Report Education Supplement. "Shot in the Arm for Schools and Training," December 31, 1993.
6. "Teachers: Challenges of the 1990s, Second Joint Meeting on Conditions of Work of Teachers." International Labour Organisation, Geneva, 1991.
7. David Gairdner, *Here to Stay: A Resource Handbook Linking Sustainable Development and Debt* (CUSO, November 1990).
8. "Effects of Structural Adjustment Policies on Education in Africa," *Education International*, Autumn 1993.
9. Mike Farren, "International Health and Social Development Consultant." Unpublished paper, April 1994.
10. *Echo, Quarterly Publication of the World Confederation of Organizations in the Teaching Profession*, October 1991.
11. John Calvert and Larry Kuehn, *Pandora's Box*, Corporate Power, Free Trade and Canadian Education (Toronto: Our Schools/Our Selves Education Foundation, 1993).
12. "Guns top cause of young adult deaths in U.S.," *Toronto Star*, January 28, 1994.
13. "Violence moves next door," *Times* Education Supplement, December 31, 1993.

14. Jonathan Kozol, *Savage Inequalities: Children in America's Schools* (New York: HarperCollins, 1991).
15. Robert B. Reich, *The Work of Nations: Preparing Ourselves for 21st Century Capitalism* (New York: Alfred A. Knopf, 1991).
16. Arthur G. Wirth, "Education and Work: The Choices We Face," *Phi Delta Kappan*, January 1993.
17. Margaret Spillane and Bruce Shapiro, "A Small Circle of Friends," *The Nation*, September 1992.
18. Doris Lyon, Research Analyst, Washington Education Association, The Future of Public Education in North America Conference, Evergreen State College, January 29, 1993.
19. Ira Emery Rodd, "McLunchrooms!" *The Nation*, September 1992.
20. Michael Morgan, "Channel One in the Public Schools, Widening the Gap," Department of Communication, University of Massachusetts, Amherst, October 1993.
21. Nancy Folbre, "Business to the Rescue?" *The Nation*, September 1992.
22. "Becoming Partners." Special Section by Apple Computer Inc. in *The Executive Educator, Politics Descends on Your Schools*, January 1993.
23. "Education Infiltration: The Pentagon targets high schools," *The Progressive*, February 1994.

RETOOLING THE POLITICS OF CHOICE

1. Gary Orfield, "Playing Politics with Choice," *False Choices*. A special edition of *Rethinking Schools* (1992).
2. Arnold F. Fege, "Public Education: Can We Keep It?" *Educational Leadership*, November 1992.
3. Jonathan Kozol, "Whittle's Raid on Public Education." *False Choices*.
4. David Osborne and Ted Gaebler, *Reinventing Government: How the Entrepreneurial Spirit Is Transforming the Public Sector* (New York: Plume Books, 1993).
5. Kozol, "Whittle's Raid on Public Education."
6. Jonathan Kozol, "I Dislike the Idea of Choice, and I Want to Tell You Why," *Educational Leadership*, November 1992.
7. Robert Lowe, "The Hollow Promise of School Vouchers," *False Choices*.
8. Michael D. Simpson, "Voucher Backers Are in Courts of Last Resort," *NEA Today*, February 1994.
9. "A Battle for the Soul of America," *NEA Today*, March 1994.
10. Warren Furitani, "A Battle for the Soul of Public Education," *False Choices*.
11. Robert L. Simonds, "A Plea for the Children," *Educational Leadership*, December '93/January '94.
12. Peter Brimelow and Leslie Spencer, "The National Extortion Association," *Forbes*, June 7, 1993.

13. Ibid.
14. Deborah Smith, "Mandating Choice," *Thrust for Educational Leadership*, May/June 1992.
15. Timothy Appleby, "Teachers learn the hard way," *Globe and Mail*, March 10, 1994.
16. Gary Claybaugh, "School Choice: Easy Out, Poor Solution," *Educational Horizons*, Fall 1992.
17. Lamar Alexander, "School Choice in the Year 2000," *Phi Delta Kappan*, June 1993.
18. Osborne and Gaebler, *Reinventing Government*.
19. Ibid.
20. Linda Darling-Hammond, "Choice Is a Smokescreen," *False Choices*.
21. Maxine Waters, "'Choice' Will Devastate Our Urban Schools," *False Choices*.
22. Jonathan Kozol, "Chicago Public School Choice and Inequality," *False Choices*.
23. Kozol, "Whittle's Raid on Public Education."
24. "On Guard: What Now for the Voucher Movement?" *Rethinking Schools*, Winter 1993.
25. Paul D. Houston, "School Vouchers: The Latest California Joke," *Phi Delta Kappan*, September 1993.
26. Andrew Nikiforuk, *School's Out: The Catastrophe in Public Education and What We Can Do About It* (Toronto: Macfarlane Walter and Ross, 1993).
27. "Charter Schools: Provision for Choice in Public Schools." Policy and Planning Branch, Alberta Education, September 1993 (draft).
28. Priscilla Wohlstetter and Lesley Anderson, "What Can US Charter Schools Learn from England's Grant-Maintained Schools?" A discussion paper for the Consortium for Policy Research in Education. New Brunswick, New Jersey, 1992.
29. Ibid.
30. Ibid.
31. "The Shape of Things to Come?" *Western Report*, May 17, 1993.
32. Jennifer Lewington, "Pioneering parents push for more choice in schools," *Globe and Mail*, April 7, 1994.
33. Ibid.
34. Ibid.
35. "Take Back the Schools: A Calgary Conference Urges Parents to Seize Control," *Western Report*, May 17, 1993.
36. Joseph Freedman, *Failing Grades: Canadian Schooling in a Global Economy*. Society for Advancing Educational Research, 1993.
37. Andrew Nikiforuk, "Andrew Nikiforuk views a video that focuses on what works best in the classroom," *Globe and Mail*, March 12, 1994.

38. Colin Penman, "Alberta Education Invitational Forum on Violence and Student Conduct," *AQE News and Views*, January 1994.
39. Joseph Freedman, "Proposal for an Alternative Model School." Society for Advancing Educational Research, February 1994.
40. Larry Hayes, "An Interview with Jonathan Kozol: A Simple Matter of Humanity," *Phi Delta Kappan*, December 1992.

RETROFITTING ALBERTA

1. Neil Waugh, "Ralph may yet rise in Ottawa," *Calgary Sun*, April 11, 1994.
2. Joan Crockatt, "Klein setting national agenda, Charest says," *Edmonton Journal*, April 10, 1994.
3. Alberta Teachers' Association, *Trying to Teach* (January 1993).
4. "Jonson Blows the Whistle," *Western Report*, January 25, 1993.
5. "Education Is Hit Hard," *ATA News*, January 25, 1994.
6. "The Klein Agenda: A Government That Neither Cares Nor Listens." Editorial, *Edmonton Journal*, February 11, 1994.
7. "Who Will Control the Schools?" *Western Report*, February 14, 1994.
8. "Budget plans threaten schools," *Ottawa Citizen*, March 18, 1994.
9. Statistics Canada, cited by the Alberta Teachers' Association, "Know More," February 1993.
10. Alberta Education, *Meeting the Challenge: Three-year Business Plan.* Government of Alberta (Edmonton: 1994).
11. "The Klein Agenda."
12. Ibid.
13. Paul Marck, "Cuts will hurt kids in school, says poll," *Edmonton Journal*, February 11, 1994.
14. "Klein Says No," *ATA News*, February 23, 1994.
15. Lisa Dempster, "Inner circle re-draws classroom," *Calgary Herald*, February 11, 1994.
16. Alberta Teachers' Association, communiqué to teachers, February 2, 1994.
17. *AQE News and Views* 1/1 (September 1993).
18. Dan Levson, et al. "Presentation to Government of Alberta Education Round Table." Albertans for Quality Education, November 5, 1993.
19. Victor Dwyer, "Are We Cheating Our Kids?" *Maclean's*, March 14, 1994.
20. Don Martin, "Education revolution doesn't add up," *Calgary Herald*, January 19, 1994.
21. "Jonson Blows the Whistle."
22.
23. Joseph Freedman, "Proposal for an Alternative Model School." Society for Advancing Educational Research, February 1994.
24. Dwyer, "Are We Cheating Our Kids?"
25. Ibid.

INDEX